Just Walking
The Zen of the Appalachian Trail

James C. Purdy

upperfalls press
2010

Copyright 2010 by James C. Purdy

upperfalls press
Newton, Massachusetts
jcpurdy02464@gmail.com

Book Design:
Susanna Anthony

Photo credits:
Front cover: ©iStockphoto.com/Benjamin Tupper
Back cover: ©iStockphoto.com/Sebastien Cote
Page 28: ©www.trailjournals.com/Nate Olive
Page 46: USNPS webcam

ISBN 10   0-615-33727-9
ISBN 13   978-0-615-33727-2

Long conversations

beside blooming irises,

joys of life on the road.

-Basho

Table of Contents

Introduction	5
Prologue	6
1. A Crazy Dream	7
2. Going	13
∘ Over Springer Mountain	15
∘ On the Brown Trail	19
∘ An Encounter	25
∘ Leaving Georgia	28
∘ Trail Buddies	30
∘ Last Leg	37
3. Enjoying the Scenery	41
∘ The Smokies	44
∘ Southern Hospitality	53
∘ Gaps, Knobs, and Humps	56
4. Marathon	63
∘ Pastoral	65
∘ Introspection	76
∘ Imaginary View	90
∘ Sunshine	97
5. Flyin'	103
∘ Crossing State Lines	105
∘ Ridge Walking	109
∘ Pennsylvania Rocks	120
∘ In the Garden	125
∘ Reunion	130
∘ An Interlude	132
6. Homecoming	135
∘ A Wet Walk	138
∘ The Berkshires	146
∘ On and Off the Long Trail	152
7. Tasty Stuff	165
∘ Approaching the Whites	167
∘ Live Free but Don't Die	170
8. The Way Life Should Be	185
∘ The Hardest Mile	187
∘ Walking in Beauty	194
∘ Between the Acts	202
∘ The Hundred Miles	204
∘ Almost	212
∘ Finally	215
∘ Postscript	220
Epilogue	221
∘ What Does It All Mean?	223
∘ Walking	223
∘ Going Somewhere	223
∘ Connecting to Your Surroundings	224
∘ Where Am I?	225
∘ Physical Changes	227
∘ Mental Changes	227
∘ Fellowship	227
∘ Getting Away?	228
∘ It's Not About Winning	229
∘ The Spiritual Nature of the Hike	230
∘ Jewels	231
∘ Ecology, Mindfulness, and Time	232
Appendix A: My Email to Last Minute	235
Appendix B: Gear List	237
Appendix C: Itinerary	239
References	243
∘ Hiking	243
∘ Zen	243

Introduction

This book is composed of layers. At the bottom is a stack of 150 or so loose-leaf journal entries written in ballpoint pen at the end of each day while I hiked the Appalachian Trail. I transcribed them when I got home and later edited them with the aid of memory and photographs to add detail and correct the grammar. The idea was, and still is, to give people interested in thru-hiking a taste of the experience as it really was.

Before the hike, I knew a little bit about Eastern philosophy and Zen Buddhism, but only in an intellectual sense. I had never practiced Zen, although I had done some general purpose meditation from time to time. I knew there was something called walking meditation and while I was actually hiking, I did it from time to time.

But my perspective on my thru-hike changed in retrospect.

Some of this new perspective emerged in the little essays that I wrote soon after returning home to try to find the meaning I knew underlay my hike. When I was introduced to Zen practice at the Cambridge Zen Center I was struck by the similarity of Zen sitting and thru-hiking. (See my reply to Last Minute in Appendix A.) More similarities between long distance hiking and Zen occurred to me as time went on, and I added some of these ideas to the chapter commentaries. In the end, I believe that long distance hiking is not just like zazen (the practice of Zen), it *is* zazen if you do it with the right attitude.

Although Zen helped me to make sense of the whole experience, the book is not intended to be a religious tract, and I want to make it clear that I'm less than a novice when it comes to Zen practice. Rather, I hope this book describes the day to day reality of a six month hike and offers some explanations and suggestions for people who are more interested in hiking than in Zen.

Besides, sticking to a day-by-day description of the hike is more faithful to the

Journal Page

Just Walking

spirit of Zen than spinning out abstractions.

My thoughts and thanks go out to the many hikers and plain folks who offered small kindnesses along the way, be it a ride to the post office or a shared cheese sandwich sitting on the trail. And thanks to my family for putting up with my absence for six months.

Prologue

There have been many books written from personal experience on the Appalachian Trail, including Earl Shaffer's *North with the Spring*, which is to the rest of the AT books what Homer's *Iliad* is to Western literature. A story is supposed to have conflict to be interesting – man against man, man against nature – or personal growth and self-revelation. This story of a middle aged guy living a dream has some of that, but in a pretty subtle way.

There is a Zen quality to hiking, especially hiking long distances.[1] The climax in Zen narratives comes after years of practice, so don't look for one here. On the other hand, if you have some experience hiking, whatever the distance, you may find some interesting rhythms and progressions here.

Ordinarily, undertaking a six month journey, coming face to face with large animals that could tear you limb from limb, sleeping side by side with women you don't know, making friends with strangers, even hitchhiking in out-of-the way places, all have some drama to them. It's just that, on the AT, these events become embedded in a long, rhythmic dream.

---

[1] To quote and then paraphrase Robert M. Persig's *Zen and the Art of Motorcycle Maintenance*, "this account should in no way be associated with that great body of factual information relating to orthodox Zen Buddhist practice." And it's not very definitive on hiking either.

1
A Crazy Dream

A Crazy Dream

The first and last question is, "Why Do It?" But, of course, no one really gets to the bottom of that one. There are all sorts of reasons. You're unhappy in your job. You're bored. There's too much stress in your life. You want to prove something to yourself. And lots more like it, different for every person. But the ultimate "why?" is elusive.

The opening chapter of Moby Dick is instructive. It is an essay on why men are drawn to the sea and to water in general. According to Melville, there's an attraction to the sea that today we would call unconscious. A similar unconscious attraction draws some of us to the trail.

The Appalachian National Scenic Trail, the AT for short, goes over many mountain tops. You may think when you see a mountain, "I'd like to be up there." It's a natural enough urge, just because of the idea of the thing. This idea may be bolstered by the thought of panoramic views or it may be dampened by the fear of accidents or discomfort. And based

Getting from here to there: Presidential Ridge

on an internal calculus, you either go or decide not to go. And then perhaps you dream about it.

For me, there's a different paradigm. In this one I'm on a mountain already – maybe just a small one – and I see another mountain in the distance and feel an urge to walk over there. The idea is not of a point or pinnacle, but rather a line draped across the landscape. The wonder is that I could, in fact, traverse this line simply by putting one foot in front of the other and walking.

The AT is the most famous line there is, at least in the Eastern United States. (This is not to take away anything from the Pacific Crest Trail and other great trails in America and abroad.) The AT really is a line draped over the landscape, not an abstraction. The trail is one to three feet wide in most places and is a continuous route, marked at

Just Walking

intervals by standardized vertical white rectangles. It was 2,171.2 miles long in 2003 – the distance seems to grow a little every year as they relocate sections and add switchbacks. That's closer to an ideal geometric line than the one you can draw with a pencil on a piece of paper. And it's real.

I was 55 years old when I started my thru-hike. I live near Boston, so when I became interested in hiking ten years before, there were many occasions to cross the AT or walk a short section of it, say ten miles or so on a day hike in Massachusetts, Vermont, or New Hampshire. Every time I set foot on the AT or passed a trailhead in my car, the same idea came to mind: keep walking north and you'll eventually reach Mount Katahdin; walk south and you'll come to Springer Mountain in Georgia.

This is where the calculus of costs and benefits comes in:

- It could be uncomfortable to take a long-distance hike.
- I could become injured, more likely from chronic wear and tear than a catastrophic fall.
- I would be away from my wife and kids for a long time.
- And I wouldn't be able to keep my job, which I've been at for over 20 years.

On the positive side:

- It would be really cool to live this dream.
- I'd lose weight and dramatically lower my stress level.
- And I wouldn't be able to keep my job, which hadn't been much fun for the past few years.

I went on some nice hikes while dreaming about the AT: sections of the Long Trail in Vermont (which is the oldest long-distance trail in the U.S. and coincides with the AT for a third of the LT's length). A week in the San

On the AT in Maryland

A Crazy Dream

Juan mountains of Colorado with my friend Phil. Many day hikes in the White Mountains, bagging the summits of the 4000-footers. These experiences raised the temperature of my hiking fever.

I started dreaming more actively. I bought the *AT Data Book* and the *Appalachian Trail Thru-Hiker's Companion* (about which, more later) and several of the AT trail guides and maps (of which there are 11 sets in all). I started reading the thru-hiker journals (highly recommended) on *www.trailjournals.com*. I worked out a spreadsheet itinerary. I was convinced that with luck, and if my body didn't decay too fast, I might actually thru-hike the thing after retiring.

After Colorado I was fired up to do more great hiking, and I used my itinerary practice to plan a four-week end-to-end hike of the Long Trail in September 2002. It never happened, because one of my project assignments at work needed to be finished by the end of that month.

2003 was not a good year for the planning business. There were very few projects in the market and heavy competition for them. There were only enough billable hours to work part-time, and when February came, my project assignments were finished. The rest of my year was going to be spent beating the bushes for new projects and not getting paid until I found one. You see where this is going.

So, one day early in February 2003, I decided to seize the time. I had some of the maps and most of the gear. I had an itinerary. I consulted my sons, who were 16 and 19 at the time, and they told me to go for it. I asked my wife. She was not happy about this crazy idea, but finally she acquiesced. One of the truths about a thru-hike had emerged: you have to be a little selfish to see it through.

After a couple of years of feeling beaten down and exhausted by office politics, I suddenly found new energy. I ordered more maps and books. I fiddled with the itinerary. I planned my diet and what would go in the packages of food to be mailed to me at regular intervals; my wife was forgiving enough to agree to take them to the post office. Each piece of gear and clothing was weighed and the packing list was adjusted until I had a satisfactorily low pack weight. I did the income taxes. My partners at the office granted a leave of absence with a happy sigh of relief that there would be one less mouth to feed.

> **Mail Drops**
>
> *A basic problem of long distance hiking is re-supply: no one can carry enough food for a five- or six-month thru-hike, and managing weight is the key to success. So you have to acquire food at intervals. The more frequent the resupply, the lighter your load. You can buy groceries in convenience stores or the less frequent supermarkets, which may or may not be close to the places where the trail crosses roads, but most hikers resupply in part by having friends and family send them boxes full of dry foodstuffs and items like toilet paper, replacement gear, books, etc. These can be mailed to general delivery at post offices along the way for the hiker to pick up, or to outfitters and hostels that serve hikers.*

Just Walking

I played with start and finish dates and picked April 14, so the spring snow in the Great Smoky Mountains would probably be gone. I scheduled visits home from trail towns where you can catch a bus. As April 14 approached, the kitchen floor was covered with foodstuffs bought in bulk, and two days were spent packing it into ziplock bags and then boxes for mailing.

On Saturday, April 12, I went to the Berklee Performance Center in Boston with my 16-year old son Greg to hear Sonny Rollins, still a saxophone colossus at age 73.

On Sunday, April 13, I flew to Atlanta on a one-way ticket. There was still a lot of snow on the Smokies as the plane passed over them.

The Promised Land (Bigelow Range in Maine)

2 Going

Going

○ Over Springer Mountain

Amicalola to Stover Creek
[Mile 8.8 to Mile 2.8]

Sunday, April 13, 2003. I took the Metro from Hartsfield Airport to the downtown bus terminal in Atlanta, hung around waiting for a couple of hours, and finally boarded a bus to Gainesville, Georgia. Halfway there, the bus hit a high curb while pulling into one of the stops along the way and sprung open an access panel. It was judged no longer roadworthy, so the twenty or so passengers sat around in the pleasant late afternoon sun until a replacement bus showed up. In Gainesville I took a cab to an economy motel. The driver smelled a good fare and arranged to take me to the trail the next day for sixty dollars. I bought stove alcohol and lunch fixings at a convenience store – flour tortillas, cheese, and cookies. After some barely edible fried chicken at a Popeye's, I went to bed early and slept pretty well.

The gateway to the approach trail at Amicalola

The next morning the cab driver picked me up and waited outside the Gainesville post office while I retrieved a package of items I wasn't sure I could carry in my checked baggage – an alcohol stove and a Swiss Army Classic knife with a 2-inch blade.

We hit the road. The driver talked about fishing and then NASCAR, two subjects I don't know much about. "You really have to go to the track and see it up close – those cars going by at 200 miles per hour. Man, the hairs on my arm stand up just thinking about it." I told

Just Walking

him I'd try it if I had the chance, and some time I might.

He dropped me at Amicalola Falls State Park – the first in a long list of great place names. As in most travel, the place names along the way add a lot to the experience, and there are plenty of them on the AT. Every gap (a saddle point on a ridge) has a name, and you pass through one every few miles. Indian Grave Gap, Cheese Factory Gap, Licklog Gap, Swinging Lick Gap, Tesnatee Gap, Hogpen Gap, and on and on.

I signed the trail register at the visitor center and wrote "Mt. Katahdin" in the destination column. There were many of these thru-hiker entries, and the ranger was polite enough to wish me good luck. I went outside and filled my water reservoir at the faucet. I weighed my pack on the hanging spring scale: 22 pounds without food and water, 35 pounds fully loaded. I picked up my hiking sticks and stepped off through the stone archway.

[2] A mile of elevation gain (5280 feet) is a very respectable climb for one day's hike. Even a thousand feet is enough to require healthy exertion.

At mile 0.0 on Springer Mountain

You must realize that this was not actually the start of the AT, whose first blaze is at the summit of Springer Mountain, 8.8 miles and 2,082 vertical feet from the visitor center.[2] The warm sunny morning slowly turned into a hot, sunny day. There are all kinds of stories, many of them true, about novice hikers shedding gear, food, and clothing along the trail up to Springer. I was in decent hiking shape and was carrying a reasonable pack weight, but it was still a hot, steep climb with a lot of stops to suck air.

Going

It had been a typically cold April day in Boston when I left. Now it felt like mid-summer, probably 80 degrees. This creates a strange feeling similar to deja vu, in which you feel that you've suddenly jumped in time. New Englanders experience it when the weather becomes unseasonably warm during the January thaw, making it feel and smell like spring for a couple of days. Walking under the hot sun in Georgia while it was icy in Boston was a jump from spring to summer that was an even more convincing dislocation. It was a pleasant one, too.

The woods were still bare, except for a few tiny leaves just beginning to emerge on some of the bushes. The trees were mostly young oaks, and the ground was covered with a carpet of last year's leathery brown oak leaves. There was an occasional trillium in bloom. Juncos peeped and towhees called. I met a thru-hiker named Marcie, chatted with her for a minute, and walked on.

At a campsite next to the trail a number of people were standing around. The camper was blind and his companion had gone off to find water a couple of hours before and hadn't returned. Someone had already gone to talk to a ranger, and the situation appeared to be under control. I walked on. I began to run out of water and spent a while searching in vain for a spring whose location was marked on the trail map. I ate lunch and then walked some more.

I reached the summit of Springer Mountain in the early afternoon. The famous plaque marking the southern end of the trail was mounted on a chunk of grey pre-Cambrian rock. A string of Nepalese prayer flags flapped lightly in the breeze. From the starting point, one could see the gray countryside spread out below, a mass of bare trees. I was living the dream. My work-mates were back at the office, and I was here. I felt a palpable surge of joy.

The trail register was a spiral-bound notebook stowed in a metal box. After I signed it, a day hiker took the ceremonial photograph with my camera. I stepped off, touching the white blazes that mark the trail as I passed them. (A few hikers actually try to touch every blaze on the trail, of which there are approximately 40,000; I tried to acknowledge them by tapping the tree with my hiking stick or shooting with a pointed index finger – it keeps you mindful of the trail.) The trail was smooth earth bordered by the carpet of brown leaves. There were very few rocks. It went up and down over the hills.

Another 2.8 miles brought me to Stover Creek Shelter, the first on the trail proper. (Black Mountain Shelter is on the way up to Springer. This was where Lumberjack, a guy I met later, was stepped on by a bear that ran over his tent.)

AT shelters consist of a raised wooden floor, three walls, and a roof. Some have a loft to increase the sleeping space. They are generally big enough for six to twelve people to sleep side by side. Most have

Just Walking

open areas nearby for tenting. In front of the shelter there is usually a picnic table and a fire ring. A side trail leads to the water source, a spring or a brook. Another side trail leads in the opposite direction to a privy. Simple, logical, and all you need at the end of the day.

To save weight, instead of a tent I use a Golite tarp, the single best piece of gear I carried. I found a good place to pitch it between the shelter and Stover Creek. Since there is no floor to a tarp, a "good place" is one that is flat, not dished, and not likely to be on a drainage path if it rains hard. You really need to do the same thing with a tent, because their floors leak if you set them up in a puddle. The tarp is basically a rectangle of light, waterproof sil-nylon. It is bisected by a ridge line and has a line at each corner to stretch it out. It can be pitched with a hiking stick at each end of the ridge line or just stretched between two trees, which is what I prefer. It takes a little bit of walking around to find a site with the right characteristics, but doing so is the key to a good night's sleep.[3]

After stretching the tarp, I unrolled my Tyvek ground sheet, a half-inch RidgeRest pad, and my sleeping bag. I unpacked the spare clothes bag and changed out of my sweaty T-shirt, shorts, and boots into a dry T-shirt, light pants, and sandals.

The tarp pitched high at a campsite in the Grand Canyon

I filled a plastic spring water bottle (free with the water at your favorite convenience store!) at the creek and transferred the water to my soft drinking reservoir. It has an in-line filter to remove Giardia cysts and other possible pathogens. You just suck the water through the filter as you drink or squeeze the reservoir to force the water out into a cup. Most trail cooking involves boiling some water, so

---
[3] The full gear list is in Appendix B.

you can take your cooking pot right to the source and rely on boiling to make the water safe.

With my food bag, cooking kit, lighter, and knife I walked up to the shelter to make dinner. I squeezed some alcohol into my Brasslite stove, lit the priming cup, set up the aluminum foil windscreen, and put the pot on to boil. I added couscous mix and olive oil to the boiling water, stirred, took it off the stove, and after five minutes had the main dish, ready to eat with a Lexan spoon right from the pot. Besides being a source of healthy calories, olive oil has the advantage of leaving the pot in shape to be cleaned up with plain water, no detergent needed.

There were two other hikers at the shelter. We talked while I cooked and ate. One was a recently retired Army sergeant who told us all about his two divorces. The other was a guy in his twenties who was cooking over a wood fire with a Boy Scout mess kit. I didn't see either of them after that night. Nonetheless, we had a nice time talking around the fire. If you've read Bill Bryson's book about the AT[4] or any others, you know that this stage of a thru-hike is rife with anxiety about who will manage to finish, and this leads to all sorts of nonsensical talk, posturing, boasting, and the like. The three of us managed to steer clear of these topics.

I was tired, so when it started to grow dark I headed down to my tarp and tucked in for the night.

On the Brown Trail
Stover Creek to Whitley Gap:
[Mile 2.8 to Mile 36.9]

On Tuesday I hiked for a while and then pulled off on the side trail for a breakfast of granola at Long Creek Falls – a pretty spot, often photographed. I sat on a rocky outcrop leaning against the cliff as I ate. The day's sightings along the trail included a couple of black-and-white warblers and a common yellowthroat, several tiger swallowtail butterflies, some soaring turkey vultures, and pretty stands of rhododendrons and hemlocks. I had lunch on the trail on Justus Mountain and cooled my feet in Justus Creek. At Gooch Mountain Shelter there was a troop of Boy Scouts and another retired thru-hiker, a computer programming teacher from Detroit. We talked about gear as we cooked and ate. The shelter has a loft, accessible by a ladder. After we bedded down, someone upstairs would occasionally shift their sleeping pad, and grit would sprinkle down through the cracks between the boards. Mice scampered somewhere as I lay there, dropping off to sleep. I slept all right once the resident mice finished work for the night. I rose at 5:45 am on Wednesday. A gibbous moon was setting over the ridge as I stepped onto the trail, and the sun rose during the first mile.

The trail went up and down over several small mountains, the biggest one being

[4] Bill Bryson, *A Walk in the Woods*, Broadway, 1999

Just Walking

From Big Cedar Mountain

Big Cedar (3,737 feet). I took a rest there around 9 am. The woods were still very brown, and the weather was still hot and sunny. From the top of Big Cedar Mountain you can look back to Springer and down to the low country beside the ridge of which these small mountains were just the highest parts. There was a nice lookout with a rock to sit against and an overhanging branch to frame the view. A maple tree was bursting with red leaf buds. The bare trees in the distant lowlands were suffused with a faint green haze formed by millions of buds beginning to open. Here and there were little puffs of white: the crowns of serviceberry trees covered with blossoms.

One way to pass the time as you hike is to compose haiku poems in your head. Each poem has three lines of five, seven, and five syllables. You count them on your fingers until you can make the lines work out.

> On Big Cedar Mountain:
> Towhees and warblers
>   Sing in the bare spring hillside.
> Old vulture glides by.

In the afternoon I walked for a while with a guy named Don, a graphic designer from Atlanta who had thru-hiked in '94. He was cooling his feet in a stream when I met him. His blisters were giving him trouble. He told me half of those who start don't make it to Neels Gap, forty miles from Springer Mountain.

I was now in the Chattahoochee National Forest. One not altogether wonderful feature of this section of the trail is that there is a U.S. Army Rangers training course nearby, and at night you can hear the gunfire from training exercises. Even though I knew this, I wasn't prepared when I came around a bend and encountered a Ranger wearing green face paint and toting a green assault rifle. Perhaps as part of the training regimen, he acted as though I wasn't there.

An old gentleman who was day hiking happened by. He asked how I liked the area.

-"Beautiful", I said.

-"People from New England don't realize there are so many up-and-downs here," he said with a smile. I agreed.

In truth, it was a pretty easy trail if you were used to the jagged mountains of the Northeast.

The trail remains much the same for the first few days of the hike: smooth earth bordered by brown leaves and duff and a few rocks here and there. It crosses an

Brown trail in early spring

occasional creek on a little wooden deck bridge put there to keep your feet dry. The AT goes up and down the hills and through the gaps, high above the land on either side of the ridge. In many places the trail, imagined in cross-section, is a bench that has been carved into the ridge's steep side slope. These side-hill trails wind around the steep ravines (called "coves" in the South) where streams have carved their way back into the flank of the ridge. The trail makes an inflection point where it crosses the cove and then curves on around the next hill.

In some of the coves there is a flowing stream, maybe as much as five feet wide. In others there is only a trickle or no water at all. The trickles start at springs where the ground water breaks out and becomes surface flow. These springs are marvelous things, sources of naturally filtered, cold, delicious drinking water. There is no way to describe how good water like this can taste when you've been climbing hills. After refilling at a spring, you suck at your drinking tube and feel the water turn cold as the new supply displaces the old. Count this as one of the joys of hiking.

I stopped in one of these coves, where water trickled across the trail. The spring itself was a little above the trail in a crease in the hillside. Water was running out of the earth and over a rocky lip, but there was no pool deep enough to immerse my water bottle, not even a place to put the bottle in position to catch the flow. Someone had left a rhododendron leaf on the pillow of moss next to the spring. The leaf was still green, about five inches long and curved like a tiny chute. I put one end of the leaf on the lip of rock and a little stream of water poured off the other end, into the neck of my bottle.

Although the woods along the ridge were still mostly brown, there were some green places. The trail passes through groves of rhododendrons with broad glossy dark green leaves and clusters of small stems an inch or two in diameter. Their bark is smooth and tan in color. The rhodos are often dense enough to create a literal tunnel that the trail passes through.

The banks of the wet coves were covered with soft green mosses. Where the soils were right, wildflowers were beginning to show. There were white trillium blooming in damp spots and nine-petalled white bloodroot flowers. A black swallowtail butterfly perched on a twig, backlighted like a stained glass window. A rufous-sided towhee, black, white, and pink, perched where I could have a good look at him. Once I had identified their song, I heard towhees everywhere.

I stopped for the night at Woods Hole Shelter, 12 miles from Gooch Gap, which required a short back-track on a blue-blazed side trail which ran almost parallel to the AT. Its water source was a spring downhill from the shelter. Wearing sandals, I picked my way down, carrying the soft plastic reservoir in one hand and the plastic bottle in the other. After filling the reservoir I walked a few steps below the little pool and rinsed out my shirt, bandana, and socks one by one, wringing out each item away from the stream and piling it carefully on a rock. I used the bandanna to wipe the sweat from my face and torso and to scrub off the patches of dried mud that had formed on my calves. My feet were mostly OK after three days of hiking — just a little blister on one of my fourth toes and a fifth toe rubbing a bit on the inside of the boot.

The next morning, Thursday, was day four of the hike. I woke up at 6:30 am and was soon back on the trail, heading for Blood Mountain, a landmark. I

Woods Hole Shelter

walked through Slaughter Gap (named, like the mountain, for a battle between Native American tribes), and I started climbing the switchbacks to the 4,461-foot summit. It was quiet up there, and the cold-looking stone shelter was empty. At an overlook I could see the mountains to the north and east in a slate-blue atmospheric perspective. There was a tall one sticking its head up through a low cloud layer. This had to be Standing Indian Mountain, a 5,498-footer just over the border in North Carolina.[5]

I took a break at a pretty, exposed ledge covered with lichens and small succulent plants growing in little pockets of soil.

I saw the first bluets of the spring: sprays of lovely little four-petalled flowers which may be blue, white, or lavender. As I descended the switchbacks on the other side of the mountain, clouds began to cover the sky.

After a few more miles, the sound of cars became noticeable. I'd come to Neel's Gap. The trail angled down the steep slope to the road. Across it was the Walasi-Yi Outdoor Center, a fieldstone building where the AT goes under a roof and out the other side. I picked up my first mail drop, a cardboard box full of dried food, energy bars, sheets of toilet paper in a ziplock bag, and waterproofing goo for my boots. I bought a black stuffsack to hold my food, replacing the flimsy grocery store bags I'd started with. On the way out I

---

[5] If you're from Colorado, a mile-high mountain doesn't seem like much, but keep in mind that in the East, the trailhead is often less than 1000 feet above sea level.

Just Walking

Morning view from Blood Mountain

saw Marcie, stowing a carton of Camel Filters in her pack.

It started to sprinkle, then rain, the first precipitation of the hike. I'm a devotee of Ray Jardine's trail philosophy, which includes carrying an umbrella; mine is a nine-ounce red-and-black Golite. Don't make the mistake of thinking that raingear keeps you dry. Its real purpose is to keep you warm in a driving horizontal rainstorm, but you sweat inside it, Gor-Tex and pit zips notwithstanding. With the umbrella, you get only slightly damp and remain comfortable in vertical rain.

By 2 pm I came to Tesnatee Gap and the side trail to Whitley Gap Shelter. The shelter is a long 1.2 miles from the trail, but it was the right distance from the previous night's stay at Woods Hole. The side trail was a nice one, passing over several gentle knobs with open rocky tops. Walking on rock is common in New England but a novelty on the AT in Georgia.

I unpacked and stretched out in the shelter and relaxed. There were several other hikers there, including a guy named Michael from California. He carried a very light pack, and a lot of his gear was home-made, which takes talent. He later came to be called "Jug" because, in typical minimalist fashion, he carried his water supply in a plastic milk jug, which he held in one hand while walking.

It began to rain harder, and more wet hikers arrived. This was when I first learned that thru-hikers are a special bunch. A couple arrived, very wet. The shelter was nearly full of people, and dripping gear was hanging from clotheslines and hooks everywhere. There was nowhere for them to change into dry clothes. The man sat down on the edge of the sleeping platform and peeled off his pants and underwear without attracting much attention and slipped on dry pants. The woman looked around, looked out at the rain, and then stripped off her wet shirt and bra with her back to the rest of us. What was interesting

Walking through the fog

was that without being asked, everyone in the shelter just found other things to pay attention to, so as to offer her a little privacy.

○ An Encounter
Whitley Gap to Tray Mountain:
[Mile 36.9 to Mile 56.2]

Friday, April 18. There was a bit more rain at night, and in the morning the weather was cloudy and the trees were dripping. I left at 7:15 am, made it back to the AT by 8 am, and promptly slipped on some mud and fell on my butt. No harm done.

The trail mounted a short steep section which was reportedly hiked by John Muir once upon a time. The terrain was easy for the rest of the day. It was foggy early in the day which gave the trail an eerie feeling, and there were showers for a while after Low Gap. While I was taking a break there, sitting on a log next to the trail and eating a food bar, I met a thru hiker who had camped near the shelter a bit off the trail. He was wearing

Just Walking

a garbage bag for a raincoat[6] and trying to look cheerful, but I think he was feeling a bit low because of the wet conditions. There was a long gradual downhill run to Chattahoochie Gap, where I stopped for a break by a pretty spring, which was probably a headwater of the Chattahoochie River. The last stretch of trail before Blue Mountain shelter had the novelty of a little rock slide to cross, reminding me of my stomping grounds in the White Mountains of New Hampshire. The Georgia trails certainly have plenty of ups and downs, but for the most part, the footing is soft and relatively free of things to catch your toe or twist your ankle.

The weather improved a bit by the time I reached the shelter, where I stopped for the night. Christy, Kelly, and Curley Dan from Mississippi were at the shelter. I dried out the contents of my pack, which was a bit damp. Michael came by a bit later.

The previous two days had been wet and cool, although there was a pretty sunrise on Saturday morning. I walked through fog and under dripping trees. Ferns were beginning to punch up green fiddleheads through the layer of brown leaf litter. I passed a huge clump of Dutchman's britches, whose flowers look like miniature white pantaloons hanging on a clothesline.

I was impressed by the very large trees, both standing and fallen. In New England there is virtually no more old-growth forest, the land having been cleared for farming and the trees sawed up into lumber or burned in fireplaces and stoves. In Georgia it isn't unusual to see trees with trunks two or three feet in diameter, sometimes fallen across the trail with a huge chunk chain-sawed out to provide passage for hikers. I tried to count the rings on one of the cut ends and reached one hundred twenty before I lost track.

As I walked, I surveyed my body for aches and pains that might be incipient injuries. At the beginning of the hike, when my right boot flexed, the crease pushed down on my metatarsals (the bones your toes connect to), and it hurt. This pain was better now, either because my foot was getting used to it or because the boot crease was getting softer. The boots, which had been wet for three days, started squeaking with each step.

I'm a natural worrier, as will become clear in this narrative. My basic worry was that I'd become injured and forced to leave the trail. I was particularly concerned about my knees, because I had experienced pain in them after strenuous hikes in the past. But five days and sixty miles into the hike, they seemed to be holding up all right. When the trail descended steeply, I reminded myself to watch my step and avoid spraining an ankle.

---
[6] Suggestion: Invest in good rain gear!

Looking down at the footing on steep sections, I noticed things on the trail, for instance, millipedes. There are two common varieties of millipede in the south. One is slinky-shaped, about two inches long. It looks brown at a distance, but close up its thin ring-shaped segments alternate red and **gray**. The other millipede is flatter and flaunts a black, red, and yellow color scheme. This type of coloration is often the sign of a venomous creature, and this sporty millipede exudes a cyanide compound that has the pleasant smell of almonds but is toxic if eaten by a predator.

However, millipedes do **not** inject poison, and they are innocuous little animals that recycle decaying vegetation and help build the soil and complete the web of energy transfer in the forest ecosystem.

Four days into the hike, I was wondering about a trail name. Most thru-hikers either adopt or are given these sobriquets, which are part of trail culture. Before I left for the hike, my office-mates gave me a send-off party at which I was presented with a list of potential trail names, such as "Jim of the Jungle" and "Dances with Newts." I tried out the latter, but it didn't really seem to be a good fit, despite my affection for colorful critters that slink along the trail.

In principle, trail names are supposed to be given to you by other hikers, but many thru-hikers pick their own. I was worried that I hadn't acquired one yet, and with the noise my footwear was making, it was likely to be "Squeaky Boots". Not a great name. So I decided to adopt the name "Millipede." As I explained above, these humble little invertebrates make slow but steady progress and go about their recycling business without bothering anyone. (I guess this is an insight into my soul.) With a little stretch, "millipede" can also mean "a thousand steps," roughly the number needed to cover half a mile.

It was drier when I walked into Tray Mountain Shelter, a little less than a mile past the mountain's 4,430-foot summit. I met a doctor from Idaho named John, doing a short stretch with his thru-hiking brother, who is a land use planner like me. Michael arrived, as did Meredith and Chris and Vermonters Dale and Emily, all of whom had been at Whitley Gap two nights before.

Sitting around after dinner I noticed another hiker, a young guy with red hair and beard who looked somehow familiar. After trying to place him for a while I realized he looked like Nate Olive, a.k.a. "Tha Wookie," whose 2001 journal I had read on trailjournals.com.

Just Walking

Tha Wookie (Photo: Nate Olive)

If this was true it was surely a good omen. He walked over to the side of the campsite where I was sitting, and I started a conversation. I introduced myself as Millipede and asked if he had a trailname. When he said "Tha Wookie," I almost flipped. "You're Nate Olive?! Man, I'm a big fan of your on-line journal!" He looked a little startled to learn he had fans, especially a middle-aged guy like me. We chatted for a while.

He was getting ready to thru-hike the Pacific Crest Trail but had been delayed by a sprained ankle, and he was wearing a brace. We talked about the origin of my trail name, and other hiking business. After a while, he excused himself, having just hiked up for a visit, not to stay the night, and he wished me good luck.

Still inwardly grinning about this encounter, I set up my tarp on one edge of the clearing in front of the shelter. From this spot I could look down on the valley below and watch the turkey vultures soaring along the edge of the ridge. I pegged down the windward side of the tarp and slid into my sleeping bag. As I lay there on my side with my head propped on a pillow made from my folded fleece sweater, I heard a faint drumming sound. It was one of the shelter mice running along my Tyvek ground sheet. Before I fell asleep, the mouse tiptoed up to me and planted a little wet mouse kiss on my cheek. Good night.

○ Leaving Georgia

Tray Mountain to Muskrat Creek:
[Mile 56.2 to Mile 78.4]

> Third cold and wet day.
> Glasses fogged.
> The sound
> of droplets
> on hat brim.

Easter Sunday, April 20. The day after camping on Tray Mountain I walked over Kelly Knob to the highway that runs through Dicks Creek Gap near Hiawassee and hitchhiked to the Blueberry Patch hostel, a lovely place run by Gary Poteet and his wife Lennie, nice people who had thru-hiked in the 90's. Among the other hikers staying there were Leaf, a young man from Louisiana who had worked on oil rigs, and Todd, a tall guy from Washington state who was a massage therapist. The sun came out for a while, we had taken showers, and Gary had washed our stinky clothes (a service of the Blueberry Patch), so life was good as we sat out back by the creek. Around dinnertime another veteran thru-hiker named Ox dropped by to chat with Gary. He gave several of us a ride into Hiawassee for an all-you-can-eat buffet. AYCE is one of the pleasures of burning over 4,000 calories day after day.

The next morning, Gary presided over a long Grace before feeding us piles of pancakes studded with blueberries.

The Blueberry Patch

After breakfast, we loaded our gear onto a flatbed trailer and our bodies into Gary's van, and he hauled us back up the highway to the trail crossing.

As I started on the 11.6 miles to Muskrat Creek Shelter it began to rain again, and I put up my umbrella. One stretch of trail had been carved into the steep side of the ridge. It had begun to settle, giving it a pronounced cross-pitch, and other hikers had broken through the rain-softened trail margin in places. The rain stopped as I pushed on through Plumorchard Gap without detouring down the side trail to visit the shelter.

In the early afternoon, I crossed the 75-mile point and came to the hand-painted sign marking the North Carolina state line. I cheered and walked on. All thru-hikers are excited by crossing state lines, partly because it's another way of measuring progress (one down, thirteen more to go) and partly because of the awesome feeling of covering state sized chunks of territory, by just walking.

A couple of tenths of a mile later I came to Bly Gap, an open clearing with a famous gnarled oak in the middle. I took a picture and walked on, passing over two steep balds, as some of the mountains are called in this part of the world. Because I was in North Carolina now, the trail was being cared for by a different organization (almost all trail maintenance is done by volunteers) and although everyone uses the same 2 by 6-inch blaze, they were spaced closer together than in Georgia, giving the trail a slightly different feel.

It was about 4:30 pm, and I was tired from climbing Sharp Top and Courthouse Bald when I crossed a little wooden platform bridge across Muskrat Creek and pulled into the shelter. I pitched my tarp a short distance away, in a rhododendron thicket.

Todd and Leaf showed up soon after I did. Todd's knee was hurting, a result of having run along the trail in a fit of exuberance. A little while later a woman

Just Walking

in her 30s walked in with a slightly portly gentleman with white hair and beard who was wearing an Irish football jersey. They were Mountain Momma (she had two kids back at home being taken care of by her husband) and Tipperary (he came from the town of that name in Eire). Todd was fiddling with his sore knee. Mountain Momma offered to check it out and started pushing and pulling Todd's leg in a professional manner. "Orthopedist?" I asked. "Gynecologist," she replied. Mountain Momma thought the knee felt all right, no ligament damage, and she suggested not running with a loaded backpack.

Trail Buddies
Muskrat Creek to NOC:
[Mile 78.4 to Mile 134.1]

Tuesday, April 22. It was very cold, probably in the 30s, but dry the next morning. I folded up my tarp and packed my gear. Originally I had planned to go to Standing Indian Shelter, a 5-mile easy day, but I changed my mind when I learned that Mountain Momma, Tipperary, Todd, and others were headed for Carter Gap, 11.5 miles from Muskrat Creek. I felt good, had few aches and pains, and decided I didn't need a recuperative day. The trail was relatively flat and beautifully sun-dappled as it passed through hardwood forest with several rhododendron tunnels. I saw the year's first open Clintonia lily (also known as bluebead for its late-season fruit), a small nodding

Gnarled oak at Bly Gap

yellow flower that looks best if you lie down on the ground and look up at it. I also walked through stands of beech trees with long pointed red-brown buds getting ready to open. There were many clusters of bluets along the way. The trail made a hairpin turn around Yellow Mountain and then rose gradually toward Standing Indian Mountain.

A mile and a half before the mountain is the eponymous shelter (that means it has the same name – like the REM album – a useful term on a thru-hike that somehow hasn't caught on.) I stopped at the empty shelter, which is situated next to the trail, for a mid-morning food-bar snack, and read the register while I chewed. Shelter registers are usually spiral-bound notebooks in which hikers make witty (or sometimes, snide) comments, leave messages for friends hiking behind them, or just record having been there. (The year after the hike, I had the pleasure of finding a 2003 register in a shelter in Connecticut and reading the little entries written

Millipede with Mountain Momma and Tipperary

there by some of my trail friends.) In this register there was a recent entry by a hiker named Nova who reported seeing a large cat track on the trail; she said her dog went slightly nuts after sniffing it. Bobcat? Mountain Lion? Things like this add zest to the hike (unless you're unduly daunted by the prospect of meeting a large carnivorous animal); however, the odds of actually seeing such an elusive creature are very small.

A short, steep side trail leads to the 5,498-foot summit of Standing Indian Mountain. The summit was not very much higher than the ridgeline that the trail was following, but 5,000 feet means something where I come from. There was a clearing, with lookouts to the west and south. I wasn't sure exactly what I was looking at but the weather was fine, the view was lovely, and I knew I was at the opposite end of the view I had had from Blood Mountain the week before.

I continued along the AT, descending a thousand feet, and I stopped for lunch at

Just Walking

On Siler Bald

a large tree fallen across the trail. Straddling the two-foot tree trunk, I mixed up some hummus from a dry mix and used flour tortillas to it dip up. While I was finishing lunch, Mountain Momma came up the trail and sat down on the log opposite me for a chat. We talked about our lives and our families, and we found ourselves shaking hands and exchanging our real names. Tipperary was not far behind her, and he arrived a little while later.

I left soon after Tip arrived, but we leapfrogged each other over the remaining miles to Carter Gap, where the whole crew from Muskrat Creek ended up. There were two shelters at Carter Gap, old and new ones separated by a hundred feet and connected by a maze of beaten paths leading to the privy, spring, and little tent sites. We wandered around this maze for a while until we happened on the new shelter. After dinner we all huddled in our sleeping bags to stay warm and sang pop songs together. Mountain Momma had sung in the Boston Symphony Chorus while in medical school and was our lead singer.

I had had many preconceptions about what life on the trail would be like. I had imagined it involving solitude, even though I would be seeing other hikers, and the idea of a solitary hike seemed attractive in a way. In retrospect, the friendships I made on the trail turned out to be the most memorable part of the hike. There is a kind of comradeship and even intimacy that forms very quickly between thru-hikers, even though you don't spend all that many hours together (somewhat like Boswell and Johnson). As I walked farther into North Carolina I was beginning to realize this.

On Wednesday, I walked over Albert Mountain (5,220 feet). This is the first steep, rocky section of trail that requires a bit of scrambling – using your hands to climb up difficult pitches. I ate a bowl of granola atop the summit lookout tower, once part of a system of fire lookouts, and chatted with a woman named Mother Nature, who had thru-hiked a few years before. At Glassmine Gap I had lunch with four people from the UNC admissions office. It was hot by then.

At Rock Gap, one of the people at the shelter was a man named Algonkin Buffalo – not a trail name – who was a graduate student at SUNY Stonybrook and had been running a food pantry there. He wasn't thru-hiking but seemed to be on a mini-odyssey of his own. He talked about herbalism, and together we tried to identify a new wildflower with an umbrella-like leaf (not a May Apple, which appears later in the spring). After a chatting for awhile, he picked up his tiny pack, said so long, and walked off southbound on the trail. A mystery man.

It was another cold night. Mountain Momma and Tip had gone on to the highway to stay in a commercial campground. There was a mixture of familiar and new hikers in the shelter, crowding together for warmth. Nova, who had left the note about the cat track, asked if I minded if her dog Bosco slept between us. Bosco, who had his own foam sleeping pad, snuggled up to me during the night and helped keep me warm. (Hikers don't snuggle unless they know

Valley clouds below Wayah Bald

Just Walking

each other well.) By morning Bosco and I had bonded, and I was sorry to see the two of them leave the trail for Franklin, North Carolina next morning.

On Thursday, after a short distance on the AT, I took a blue-blazed side trail to see a natural wonder called the Wasilik Poplar. The trail descended into a moist cove which was already looking pretty and green with new vegetation. I finally came to the tree – a big one all right. It was over eight feet in diameter and was seeing its last days, a sort of a tower with a few branches remaining high above the ground. It had been subjected to ritual abuse by idiots with pocket knives seeking immortality. The *Appalachian Trail Thru-Hiker's Companion*[7], a trail guide I had broken into sections and put in my mail drops, informed me that this poplar (called a "Tulip Tree" up north)

Morning on Wesser Bald

had survived logging early in the century when an even larger companion tree was cut down and proved harder to haul away than the loggers had reckoned on.

Back on the main trail, I passed through a deep cove filled with hemlocks – the metaphorical green cathedral. I came up behind Mountain Momma and Tipperary at Siler Bald, about eight miles from the shelter. This was the first true southern bald on the trail: a round-topped mountain with an open grassy summit. I walked the couple of tenths of a mile up to the top while my friends took a break in the saddle below. The weather was cloudy but the views were good in all directions. I descended, and the three of us continued to Wine Spring campsite, sharing my water supply on the way after theirs ran out.

We set up our tents and tarp, had dinner sitting on a log, and then retired to

---
[7] Complied by the Appalachian Long Distance Hikers Association and published by the Appalachian Trail Conference, this is one of the three basic guides most thru-hikers carry, either whole, or broken into sections to save weight. The other two are the *Appalachian Trail Data Book* and Wingfoot's *Thru Hiker's Handbook*. See the reference section in the Appendix.

Tip's tent when it began to sprinkle. We sprawled inside the tent, talking and feeling very pleasant and intimate in a platonic sort of way. One of the interesting things about the trail is that you are often very physically close to other hikers, many of them women, and just arrange not to let it take on a sexual overtone, which would interfere with the comradeship. After a while, I went back to my tarp, which was pitched low to keep things dry, and wrote in my journal. The rain stopped before I went to bed. A red sun was visible at the horizon.

The next morning I left before my companions and stopped at Wayah Bald (5,342 feet) to look down on the clouds filling the valleys below. The view toward the Smokies 50 miles to the northwest was partially obscured but inspiring nonetheless. I had come 117 miles from Springer, farther than I had ever hiked before. It was another cloudy afternoon and chilly when I reached Cold Spring Shelter, a great name on a hot day but small comfort on this one. The little lean-to was nearly fully occupied by a group of Boy Scouts and leaders from South Carolina. However, there was a nice string of small campsites on the ridge just above the trail. Mountain Momma, Tip, Todd, and I found places there to pitch our shelters.

After dinner we hung our food bags together. This is a good idea in most places to keep mice and other critters from climbing into your food or chewing holes in expensive gear. It is essential when there are bears about, which we thought might be the case. The usual method is to throw a weighted line over a high branch, fasten the food bags to one end and hoist them above a bear's reach. An even better system uses two lines over branches on separate trees, which you then tie together, hanging the food bags at the knot where they join. This puts the food farther from either tree than the single line method; however, you need to find two good branches and toss two lines with some accuracy.[8] After many misses and a tangle, Tip finished the job with an elegant underhand toss that suggested expertise in pub darts.

We gathered around the fire pit and built a campfire for warmth and cheer. Tip made us cups of excellent Irish tea, sharing the precious supply he was carrying, and he told us stories about Ireland. One story concerned driving from Tipperary town to Belfast with three young men. This was during the Troubles, and they were searched exhaustively by the British troops at the border crossing into Northern Ireland. As a soldier rummaged in the engine compartment, one of the lads suggested he might check the oil while he was in there. A burly sergeant got in his face and said menacingly "You're a long way from home, aren't you, boy?" The young man answered, with an innocent expression, "Not half so far as you are, Sir."

[8] As bears learn to overcome these stratagems, the next step in the arms race is to tie a bag to each end of the line so they counterbalance at a height out of a bear's reach, a tricky procedure that requires some pushing and pulling with sticks and string.

Just Walking

By now, Mountain Momma, Tip, and I were well beyond the acquaintance stage and had become friends in the few days we had hiked and camped together. She had just gotten her discharge from the Army, had a husband still in the service and two young boys who were being taken care of by her husband and a nanny. She was hoping to hike a substantial chunk of the trail but didn't have the time for a thru-hike. Tipperary was in it for the duration. I asked him more about himself and was surprised to learn that in addition to being a fanatic for Irish football, he is a Catholic priest, a missionary who had spent years in the poor neighborhoods of Sao Paulo and Lagos as well as an assignment in the Vatican. Counting Gaelic, he could speak five languages.

The weather began to threaten, and we split up to make things tight before the storm came. It turned out to be a thunderstorm with a high wind and heavy rain. I had pegged down the windward edge of the tarp and stayed dry, enjoying the drumbeat of rain and the crash of thunder as I lay warm and cozy in my sleeping bag.

Saturday was the last lap to the Nahantahala Outdoor Center, or NOC. The trail climbed from Cold Spring, rising a little over 400 feet to Copper Ridge Bald, (5,342) then down to Tellico Gap (3,850), back up to Wesser Bald (4,627) and over a few more knobs to the Jumpoff, where it plummeted to the Nahantahala River, which it crosses at 1,700 feet. The day started out foggy and drizzly with an occasional glimpse down to the pastel greens of spring in the misty valley below. As I descended, things became greener and warmer, and there were wild blue dwarf iris clusters, wild geraniums and clumps of ferns everywhere. I was pushing hard to reach NOC in time to buy a cheeseburger while lunch was still being served. In fact, I thought I could smell burgers cooking as I covered the last mile down the ridge. I passed through a small cove, bypassing Rufus Morgan Shelter and stepped out onto the highway next to an NOC building.

After arranging for bunk space in a four-person unit, I unpacked and headed back to the restaurant. On the way I met a guy named Gene, a retired general practitioner from Bermuda who was out looking for birds. In exchange for some information about the trail south of NOC, he treated me to a can of cold beer from a cooler in his car. NOC is in a dry county (i.e., alcoholic beverages are not legal) and that beer was an elixir from the gods. Mountain Momma and Tip arrived, and we had lunch together with Gene. It turned out that Mountain Momma's husband had pulled an assignment that would take him out of town, so she had to return home for a while. Her nanny arrived late in the afternoon with her little boys, and we all had dinner together. As I headed back to the cottage, the boys raced back and forth across the long footbridge over the river.

○ Last Leg

NOC to Fontana Dam:
[Mile 134.1 to Mile 163.1]

Sunday, April 27. Things even out on the trail. My mail drop was not at the NOC outfitter's store when I checked for it, but someone else had received way too much food in his package, and he distributed it to other hikers. This, and a couple of items bought at the store would last the three days to Fontana Dam, the entrance to the Great Smoky Mountains National Park.

At NOC, thru hikers gathered around the map and profile[9] for the next day and boggled at the first really big climb of our hikes: the trail rises steadily from a low point of 1,700 feet at the Nahantahala River to Swim Bald, elevation 4,700 feet. (Anything more than 1,000 feet of elevation gain is likely to attract your attention.) It was indeed a long steep climb, but on a pretty trail bordered by big red pines and carpeted with their long needles, two to a cluster. Despite the sunny weather, I realized on the way up that I was feeling blue. I missed Mountain Momma, whom I had met only five days before. I passed some time composing a haiku poem, counting the syllables on my fingers.

The Nahantahala mountains form a rugged bridge that the AT crosses from the north-south ridge that includes Standing Indian Mountain to a parallel ridge located further west that runs through the Smokies. There are many steep ups and downs. On the first day out of NOC, I noticed that the blazes along the trail had changed again.

> Red pine: big bark scales,
>   2-pronged needles underfoot.
> Yesterday, friends left.

These were outlined in black, which made them look especially crisp and bright. On the way up Swim Bald I met the trail maintainer who was responsible for them, an exceptionally fit looking guy in his 70s (I mean fit, not just fit for his age.) I thanked him for his labors, which made my hike so much easier. I stopped at Swim Bald for lunch and then went

---

[9] The map shows an overhead view of the trail as seen by a bird at high altitude. The profile is a sort of side view as if the trail were stretched out in a straight line. This is what hikers consult most often to orient themselves in terms of ups and downs and to prepare for the climbs and descents ahead.

Just Walking

Looking toward Fontana from Cheoah Bald

down to Sassafras Gap Shelter with Tip, where we stopped for the night. We had a long conversation with Ken and Tony, section hikers from South Carolina, who were headed to Fontana with three other friends. Apart from the usual gear talk, they told me about growing up in South Carolina, part of the first generation to go to integrated schools. As Tony described it, it was a revelation to learn that the black and white kids each had their share of great people as well as assholes. I could see that he took some pride in being part of a culture that aspires to see all folks first and foremost as fellow humans, and I told him we should do so well in the north.

On Monday I climbed out of Sassafras Gap to the top of Cheoah Bald (5,062 feet), the last leg of the big climb out of NOC. It was a sunny, slightly hazy morning. I could see the entire ridge as it zigzagged off toward Fontana Lake, whose location could be inferred from the fog bank in a distant valley. I had a great look at two chestnut sided warblers, the birds whose call sounds like "Pleased to meet you!" The trail passed through large expanses of ferns dotted with their sporangia, like an array of poppy seeds under each frond. I stopped for a break with Tip, took some pictures, and pushed on down to Stecoah Gap (3,165 feet), where a highway crosses the trail. (Until you become a thru-hiker, you might say the trail crosses the highway.) I had a snack at a picnic table by the side of the road and started the climb from the gap to Brown Fork Gap Shelter.

It was a killer climb of about 700 feet up the Cheoah Mountain ridge (distinct from Cheoah Bald). I was feeling energetic, and I ran my pulse up into the 150s while maintaining a fast pace just for the fun of it, at one point reaching 50 feet of elevation gain per minute on my wrist altimeter. This turned out to be a mistake, as I was dead on my feet later that afternoon on the sun-baked ridge heading north from Brown Fork Gap, despite a nice long lunch break at the shelter. It was sunny and warm all day, too warm, compounding my fatigue as I plodded along that ridge. I finally made it to Cable Gap Shelter, which I shared with a pair of serious 40-ish light-pack hikers named Ken and Chris, who had made it from NOC in one day(!) 15.4

Birch trees on Cheoah Bald

miles was enough for me. Todd arrived around 5:30 pm.

There were miniature orchids (Showy Orchis) on the path that ran past the outhouse to the tenting area. As we collected water from the nearby spring, a big black salamander swam out from under a rock and challenged Todd's filter float as if it were a rival salamander. There were several smaller brown ones in there as well. I was glad salamanders don't carry any pathogens that humans are susceptible to. At least I hoped so.

The light-packers were up before dawn cooking Cream of Wheat on their alcohol stove. I got up as well and left early, covering the seven miles to Fontana Dam Shelter (1,800 feet) in three hours. I had arranged to stay at a motel called the Hike Inn, so I called the owner, Jeff Hoch, from the pay phone at the dam. In the meantime, I met a thru-hiker named Froggy Pete who was around 60 and lived in Wells, Maine. He carried a little stuffed frog toy, a tribute to his wife

Just Walking

who had passed away a few years before. Froggy Pete had left the trail in 2002 after he became weakened from weight loss, and he was on his second try.

Jeff picked me up and said, "Well, you've passed the physical – from here on it's all mental." In fact, I felt pretty good. If my knees were going to fail, I thought, they should already be hurting. At least once a day, though, I warned myself to be careful, avoid overstressing my knees, watch where I stepped. I didn't want it all to end prematurely. Jeff took me to his motel and then to town for lunch, passing through Stecoah Gap on the way, which seemed incongruous, given the long hours it had taken to cover the distance on foot over the past two days. The other guest at Hike Inn was a guy named Ken who is legally blind but manages to find his way well enough to hike solo. He was out for a few days in the Smokies. That night whippoorwills were calling near the motel.

Taking a break on a sunny morning

3 Enjoying the Scenery

Enjoying the Scenery

Zen is an ancient branch of Buddhism that is still widely practiced, both in Asia and around the world. Its basic tenet has been borrowed to sell merchandise: "Just do it." Or, as it is sometimes put at greater length: stop striving, stop wanting, and stop thinking. When sitting, just sit. When eating, just eat. When walking, just walk.

Zen sitting is usually practiced in a quiet room without many distractions. However, Zen can also be practiced while walking. The end of Zen practice is attaining a Zen mind, but of course, you can't attain it by striving for it.

What does this have to do with thru-hiking? For one thing, Zen derives in part from the even more ancient idea of the tao, a Chinese word that is sometimes translated as "Way" or "Path", or as the aphorism "Go with the flow." So, while walking on the AT you are engaging in a grand scale metaphor for the tao, and since there isn't all that much to do for

From Fontana Dam

hours on end, you unwittingly begin to practice the principle of "just walking."[10]

By the time I reached the Smokies, my initial nervousness about being able to succeed at my thru-hike had faded. Success was really about simply hiking every day, not thinking months ahead to Katahdin, or to the next month in Virginia... or tomorrow. There's not much planning involved once you actually start hiking. I sometimes became impatient to reach the top of the next hill or the next milestone listed in the *Data Book*. But I was now walking for eight hours a day, more or less, and a lot of the day just involved watching the trail flow under my feet. Before I knew it, I found I was just walking.

[10] Among the myriad questions hikers like to debate is whether one should listen to music while hiking. My own feeling is that whether it's Brahms, bluegrass, or Black Sabbath, wearing earbuds isolates you from the trail.

Just Walking

The Smokies
Fontana Dam to Hot Springs, NC:
[Mile 163.1 to Mile 270.9]

Wednesday, April 30. The Smokies are one of the delights of the Appalachian Trail. The trail follows a ridge which is also the state line between North Carolina and Tennessee (state number three). The mountains are high. Clingmans Dome at 6,643 feet is the highest point on the trail, roughly 350 feet higher than Mount Washington. The Smokies are an area of exceptional beauty, with distant views, lovely woods, and many wildflowers. Despite the elevation, the mountains are covered by hardwoods as well as coniferous trees. They are more comparable to the valleys between the White Mountains than their summits.

The ridge followed by the AT is high enough to pose some major problems for hikers who walk this section early in the spring when snow storms are common. But when I arrived there, the snow I had seen when I flew over the mountains on the way to Atlanta was gone.

During my years of dreaming about someday hiking the AT, I often visited the National Park Service's live webcams and admired the view of the Smokies from the camera position at Look Rock. So it was with special anticipation that I started across the rim of Fontana Dam on a sunny morning after Jeff Hoch dropped me at the Visitor Center.

I left the park road, self-registered at the little Park Service kiosk, and started up the trail. It was a long climb to the 4,500 foot ridge from a starting elevation of 1,800 feet at the top of the dam. On the way I met a ranger with a chainsaw. He asked me to stop and watch while

Tipperary at Spence Field Shelter

44

Enjoying the Scenery

he sawed up a fallen tree, just in case he amputated something (Park Service policy, I guess). I stopped at Birch Spring campsite for a break. Horses are permitted in the park (but not dogs) and a bucket was hung on a tree near the spring so riders could water their mounts. A while later I looked back and saw something bright red on the trail; I thought it might be someone's gear but it turned out to be a pair of scarlet tanagers – lipstick red, Life magazine red.

A side trail led to Shuckstack Mountain (4,019 feet) where I climbed the lookout tower and was rewarded with a view of Fontana Lake and the mountains to the south that I had hiked over a few days before. While eating a food bar at the base of the tower I saw two ovenbirds hopping around in the underbrush. They are brownish birds, much less gaudy than most of their warbler cousins, and somewhat elusive; everyone in the woods hears their call, though: "Cheer, Cheer, CHEER."

The trail continued up to the top of the ridge where I ate lunch sitting on the ground next to the trail. Clouds were forming, and thunder rumbled. Thinking it a good idea not to get caught in a thunderstorm up there, I hastened along to Mollies Ridge Shelter (4,570 feet), arriving well in advance of the storm.

This fieldstone shelter, and several like it in the Smokies, were built by the Civilian Conservation Corps, "the CCC," a New Deal program of the 1930s that produced hundreds of still extant improvements across the U.S. The shelter slept 14 and had an indoor fireplace. Its open front was covered with chain link fencing to keep the bears out. These ugly barriers are now being removed because some morons have taken to feeding the bears through the chain link, defeating its purpose and endangering both bears and hikers. (Once fed, a wild bear will approach campsites for food, and the proximity inevitably leads to the bear being deported and sometimes destroyed.)

The new strategy is to keep the food out of a bear's reach, and accordingly, bear cables had been installed at Mollies Ridge. These devices are a wonderful invention: a horizontal steel cable stretched tight between trees perhaps 30 feet apart, with loops of lighter cable attached at pulleys in the middle of the span. Clip your food bag to a D-ring on one of the cable loops and you can easily pull it up to the main cable, where the bears will have a hard time getting to it. Of course, there are many stories of ingenious bears boosting up cubs to grab the food

---

About Bears

Eastern U.S. bears are all black bears, the species with a straight nose. Unlike grizzlies, black bears in their wild state are not aggressive and will generally just run away when they see you. An exception: mother bears with cubs will vigorously defend them from hapless hikers. A mother bear once chased my friend Leaf far enough down the trail to suit herself and then stopped. Make no mistake, she could have caught him in an instant if she had wanted to. Humans can't outrun bears downhill, uphill, or on the level, and we certainly can't out-climb them. A ranger at Shenandoah National Park, which has lots of bears, once told me she had been there for many years and the only people ever injured by bears were a ranger who ran into a tree while trying to reverse direction when he came face to face with one on the trail, and a man who was swatted when he tried to pull his picnic cooler away from a bear who was dragging it into the woods. This raises the other caution about bears: they like your food, so don't sleep with it near you. Hang it from a tree, or a bear pole when in Shenandoah, or a bear cable in the Smokies.

Just Walking

The great Smoky Mountains from the National Park Service webcam at Look Rock

bags or diving out of the trees and swatting down the bags as they swoop past them, but the system looked pretty close to bear-proof to me.

Several familiar hikers arrived at the shelter: Todd, Dale and Emily ("Vermont Maid" and "Nine Toes"), Mark ("Spitz") and Marcie ("360"). Marcie elected to move on to the next shelter. Late in the afternoon Tipperary arrived.

At 4 am I got up to pee. I held my headlamp so only a thin sliver of light escaped between my fingers. I tried to quietly open the gate in the chain-link front of the shelter but the rusty hinges squeaked and groaned like the door to a crypt. Sleeping hikers stirred and rolled over. Outside, a large patch of stars was visible above the clearing. I found a suitable place not too close to the shelter without tripping on something in the dark. Then I crept back into the shelter, turned off my light, found my own place without making an embarrassing mistake, and slid back into my sleeping bag.

I woke up for good around 7 am. It was cool, breezy, and partly cloudy, and it stayed that way for most of the morning. The area along the trail was blanketed with white/pink flowers called Spring Beauties that, from a distance, look like snow. At Russell Field Shelter, which is located near a beautiful old orchard, I took a granola break before beginning the climb up Rockytop (5,500 feet). The views from this summit and from the adjacent Thunderhead Mountain were superb – you can look down into the

Enjoying the Scenery

valley toward Look Rock. I waved to the Park Service web camera and moved on.

The rest of the day's hike had many ups and downs, including a steep climb of a couple hundred feet up Briars Knob, which looks like a pimple on the tiny profile on the Park Service map but kicked my butt. Another park ranger happened by. While the one I had met the previous day carried a chainsaw, this one was toting an impressive rifle with a scope and a silencer. He was hunting wild pigs that he said had escaped from local farms in years past; their constant rooting was doing a lot of damage to the vegetation along the trail. In fact, I began to notice that patches of Spring Beauties along the trail had been torn up.

I was fairly beat when I arrived at Derrick Knob Shelter. Tip, Todd, and David ("Thermo") from Kentucky were at the shelter for the night. Some clouds had gathered in the afternoon, but it was sunny again by 6 pm. I washed some clothes and hung them out to dry.

The sky was still clear at 4 am – Scorpio and the Milky Way were visible – but it was mostly cloudy when I rose for the day. A bear was sitting up in the ferns a mile from the shelter, a small one maybe 50 yards ahead, just looking blissed out. I clicked my hiking sticks together to get its attention, and it took off downhill from the trail.

By now, I had been hiking every day for more than half a month. That's a lot of

Spring Beauties line the trail

time walking mostly by myself. So, what was going through my mind for all those hours? Lots of things.

Daydreaming, thinking about my life and what I might do after the hike. Thinking about family and friends. Grooving on the scenery and views when they were available. Looking forward to special places like summits where there would be such views. Keeping track of progress, checking the elevation and time on my wrist altimeter watch and estimating where I was and how long it would take to reach the next landmark noted in the *Data Book* – streams, trail junctions, roads, shelters. Sometimes worrying about an ache or pain or blister – would it become worse and force me off the trail to recover? Occasionally the worry was more immediate, like a thunderstorm threatening me on a long exposed ridge; these dangers stimulated a little burst of adrenaline to give the day spice and were followed by a feeling of euphoria when all turned out well.

47

Just Walking

Trail sign at Buckeye Gap

But I may as well confess that a long distance hike is a type of drug experience. A hiker's brain produces endorphins just like a runner's. The endorphins create a very mild high which helps to suppress the discomforts that often accompany hiking (opiates like morphine and heroine latch onto the brain's endorphin receptors). I had been living a stressful life for years before the hike; it's unavoidable when you live and work in a city and have a fast-paced job with deadlines, clients who sometimes become unhappy, and so forth. Psychological stress causes your body to release a different kind of drug – hormones like cortisol, whose level in your blood can be measured and whose effect is the opposite of euphoric. By this point in a thru-hike, your cortisol level may be at an all-time low – I'm sure mine was. The result of all this is a different kind of mental focus, especially when you work your way up a long hill cooking up more endorphins. When the footing is good, you cruise along and watch the scenery go by as you might do on a long train trip. When the footing is bad, you become focused on where to put your foot down at every step.

The Smokies have their own Silers Bald, which was not extraordinary compared to Rockytop. The walk up Clingmans Dome (6,643 feet) was an interesting trail through Fraser fir trees, which are being ravaged by tiny insects called wooly adelgids but didn't look as bad as the reports would lead you to expect. When I reached the summit I walked up the spiral ramp of the concrete observation tower and talked to a young guy who had driven up. The view was nice despite lowering clouds.

On the trail between Clingmans Dome and Mount Collins Shelter a full-fledged thunderstorm hit. It was rumbling for a while, and then the temperature dropped suddenly as the wind picked up. I rummaged in my pack for my raingear and had just gotten it on when

Millipede on Clingmans Dome

View to the south from Clingmans Dome

Path through hemlocks

the storm started pelting me with small ice pellets, cold wind, and horizontal rain. I passed two hikers huddled like wood gnomes under the canopy of a huge fallen hemlock's roots. I hurried to get out of the storm before one of the lighting strikes zapped me and reached the shelter just behind two brothers from Louisiana.

In the shelter, I changed clothes and made soup and tea to warm up. The Louisiana brothers, both in their sixties, were hilarious, livening up the place with a string of jokes. Someone farted: "Bad dog!" Another fart a while later: "That dog still in here?" They also shared some of their tasty Andouille sausage with Todd and me. The sun was back out by 5 pm.

On Saturday I awoke at 6 am and walked through damp woods to the highway in Newfound Gap (5,045 feet). I hitched a ride from a pretty female park ranger who took me most of the 15 miles to Gatlinburg, Tennessee. This fabled town is everything it's cracked up to be – daiquiri bars, commercial wedding chapels, and wax museums; in other words, everything you need for a wild weekend next to nature. Gatlinburg is almost exactly like Niagara Falls except with mountains instead of waterfalls.

When I reached town, a nice couple drove me a couple of miles to the post office, waited while I claimed my food drop, and drove me back downtown. I transferred the food to my backpack

Just Walking

> **Blisters**
>
> Hikers are wary about blisters, which can hurt like the devil and keep getting bigger until you're crippled. Consequently, we carry all kinds of stuff to prevent them and treat them, as soon as possible after feeling a hot spot. This stuff includes: Moleskin (not really made from moles), a soft fabric backed with stickum to shift the friction from your skin to the face of the patch; Molefoam (thicker sticky stuff you can cut into a donut to surround the blister), J&J Compeed patches, Second Skin, and that old stand by, duct tape.

and stuffed the empty box into a trash can and then had a mid-morning snack at a Panera. I considered waiting around until noon so I could have a beer at one of the many bars, but decided not to waste the time. I ran into Brian (whom I had met at Muskrat Creek Shelter), and we hitched a quick ride, first to the NPS visitors' center, and then a second ride back up to the gap, both in the backs of pickup trucks. I called my 18-year-old son Matt from Newfound Gap on the cell phone my wife had persuaded me to carry.

Another 10 miles on the AT brought me to Pecks Corner Shelter, with a stop on the way to climb Charlies Bunion, a trail icon. It's a pretty walk from Charlies Bunion to the shelter, over a knife-edged ridge trail. I took a breather at one of the countless overlooks, tended to a blister with moleskin, and soaked up the view in the afternoon sun. At the shelter Cheryl and Sharon, two women my age from Florida, shared some of the homemade dehydrated chili they were cooking.

Sunday morning was beautiful and cloudless. I left at 8:30 am and hiked over Eagle Rocks, Sequoyah Mountain (named for the genius who invented a system of writing for the Cherokee language) and the steep-sided Mount Chapman. I met a thru-hiker named Grunt, a nice guy who had started at Springer more than a week after I did. Grunt was planning to hike both the Appalachian Trail and Pacific Crest Trail in the same year. He had already hiked the southern desert section of the PCT before coming east to do the AT.

At Tri-Corner Knob Shelter Thermo, Grunt, and I took a break lying in the sun. Later, from the shoulder of Mount Guyot (6,200 feet at the trail) there were views of the valley through a layer of haze below a temperature inversion, with clear skies above. I stopped for the night at Cosby Knob Shelter, where Sharon and Cheryl later arrived. I did some laundry and washed my hair below the spring with my water bottle.

Walnut Mountain Shelter

Enjoying the Scenery

Colorful clothesline at Walnut Mountain

Rain and thunder began at 7 am the next morning. After waiting an hour for it to stop, there was no improvement, so I left at 8 am. At first I used raingear, then unzipped my rain jacket for ventilation and used my umbrella as I walked up the side of Mount Cammerer. There was a big wind blowing at a rocky hairpin turn in the trail, so I folded the umbrella and relied on the raingear the rest of way to Davenport Gap (1,975 feet). The rain stopped around noon.

The trail down to the gap followed swift streams and was very pretty. I stepped over a box turtle on the trail. I met Thermo and a hiker from Pennsylvania named Kathy under the Interstate 40 bridge. Hiking on, the woods were scenic going up Snowbird Mountain – pale pink mountain laurel and orange flame azalea were blooming, and there were trillium of various types and colors as well as beds of tender red poison ivy shoots glistening with toxic oil. The climb was a real trudge, though: long, steep, warm, and humid. Snowbird Mountain (4,263 feet) had an open summit with an FAA directional antenna, and there were nice views of the ragged clouds hanging over the Smokies. I cruised into Groundhog Creek Shelter (2,900 feet), happy to be going downhill. Marcie and Froggy Pete were there, and Brian, David, and Kathy soon arrived, so the shelter was full to capacity. My pack was a little damp inside, but my camp clothes and sleeping bag remained dry. There was more rain during the evening. I had hiked 17.6 miles, and I was tired.

It was raining again on Tuesday morning. I walked in the rain from 7:45 am to Walnut Mountain Shelter, arriving at 1:30 pm. I had passed through the Smokies and was curious to see what the trail would offer next. Deep blue and purple wild delphinium grew along the trail. There were many stream crossings and long sections of trail with flowing or standing water, so my feet were wet. The bald top of Max Patch (4,629 feet) afforded some nice views of nearby hillside pastures

Leave No Trace

AT thru-hikers are an independent lot, but most of us adhere to a little code of outdoor ethics known as "Leave No Trace." Everyone should. Briefly, we are guests in the outdoor environment, and there are seven simple rules to preserve it:

- Plan ahead and prepare.
- Travel and camp on durable surfaces.
- Dispose of waste properly.
- Leave what you find.
- Minimize campfire impacts.
- Respect wildlife.
- Be considerate of other visitors.

Details on how and why can be found at the website of the Center for Outdoor Ethics - www.lnt.org

Just Walking

and the distant cloud-topped Smokies. The sun came out around 3 pm, and I put up a long clothesline full of damp clothes in front of the shelter.[11] Brian passed by with three other hikers, but I was still alone at 4 pm. Thermo arrived a while later to share the rickety old shelter.

Thunder rumbled during the night, and I jumped up to take the clothes off the line. The rain arrived sometime before 6 am. I finally got up for good, dressed, put on my damp socks and boots, and headed out at 7:45 am, thinking that there had been a lot of rainy days in a row. Little did I suspect what lay ahead.

It rained steadily on the way to Kale Gap, but it began to lessen on the thousand-foot ascent of Big Bluff Mountain (4,626 feet). I stripped off my raingear to cool down. The sun was shining by Garenflo Gap (2,500 feet). As the AT approaches Hot Springs, yellow and red sandstone replaces the granite of the preceding mountains. I ambled into town (elevation 1,326 feet) and found a room at Elmer Hall's Sunnybank Inn, a Victorian house with period furnishings and books everywhere.

After lunch at the Paddler's Pub down the street, I went to the laundromat wearing only raingear and carrying all my funky clothes in a bag. Back at Elmer's a shower in the little shared bathroom next to my room completed the ablutions.

Dinner was vegetarian, much of it from Elmer's organic farm – pureed vegetable soup, a beautiful salad with tamari-sesame dressing, pasta with pesto sauce, mint tea, and pecan pie. Elmer presided at the dinner table conversation. Afterwards I browsed the large library. Posted on the wall in the kitchen was a list of the greatest country/western song titles of all time, including such classics as "I've Got Tears in My Ears from Lying on My Back and Crying Over You," "She's Actin' Single and I'm Drinkin' Doubles," and "If the Phone Don't Ring You'll Know It's Me."

Elmer Hall's Sunnybank Inn

---

[11] As noted in the sidebar, I take the seven principles of Leave No Trace seriously. However, one slightly over-zealous interpretation leads to the idea that you shouldn't wear bright colors while hiking, as if it might detract from someone's enjoyment of the woods or leave a trace on their retina. I, on the other hand, like brightly colored gear, so my brick red shorts, bright blue T-shirt, red bandanna, magenta windshirt, and blue raingear made for a very cheerful clothesline.

Enjoying the Scenery

Southern Hospitality

Hot Springs NC to Erwin TN:
[Mile 270.9 to Mile 338.8]

Friday, May 9. After a zero day at Elmer's I hiked out of town, stopping at the lookout on Lovers Leap, later at a fragrant meadow, and again at a fish-filled pond at Tanyard Gap. Painted trillium grew in profusion on Rich Mountain (3,650 feet). I pitched my tarp next to Spring Mountain Shelter and lay under it listening to the patter of tiny flies against the sil-nylon fabric and the buzzing of a wasp that couldn't figure out how to fly out from under it. I had left my bear bag hanging cord at Walnut Mountain Shelter, where it served as a clothesline, so I tied miscellaneous pieces of cord together, along with my bootlaces, to serve the purpose. A nice short-term hiker couple were singing and playing a guitar at the shelter.

I had one worry – the cuticle of my right big toe was tender and red, and when I pressed on it a drop of pus emerged; sometimes hikers just have to endure these things.

The toe felt better the next morning. I met a hiker named Water Witch at Allen Gap and walked with her for a while up the hill toward Camp Creek Bald, then stopped for a rest while she went on. I saw her again at Little Laurel Shelter where we both made lunch stops. Two miles south of Little Laurel the angry buzz of a rattlesnake on the trail brought me up short. It was the first time I had encountered a rattler, but there was no mistaking the signal it was sending: "Back Off!" The snake was maybe eight or ten feet ahead of me and had perceived me as I came clomping along; it did this well before I became aware of it, so it was coiled to strike. I backed off as requested, then took a picture and bushwhacked around it.

By afternoon, I was getting tired of the stickiness and bugs (mostly black flies or their southern equivalent), and the tendon along the front of my ankle was getting cramped and sore. I took ibuprophen and soaked my foot in a cold spring. The last miles to Jerry Cabin Shelter (4,160 feet) were a slog along a rocky ridge. However, the weather became less humid by late afternoon, and a little

Hiking Sticks

Without my hiking sticks I couldn't have made this hike. Two sticks (also called "poles" by some) are vastly superior to a single hiking staff because you center your weight between them when descending steep trails, and you can always have three points of contact with the ground (one foot and two sticks) forming a stable tripod, which is what mountain goats do.

Hiking sticks have many uses, the most important being to reduce impact on your knees when going downhill. They can also give you a push with each step going uphill, they help you keep your balance on bog bridges and stepping stones, they give you an extra fraction of a second to place your feet more carefully on rough terrain, and you can use them to pitch a tarp or fend off hostile dogs. A majority of thru-hikers use them, even many of those with young, strong legs.

Just Walking

breeze dispelled the bugs. The piped spring near the shelter had a weird way of cycling between a slow trickle and high volume gush, sort of a water witch itself. I was alone, I had no more miles of trail to cover, and it was pleasant and peaceful. I pitched the tarp with one side folded over to let me contemplate the sky; this also avoided capturing a menagerie of flying insects as it had the night before. The first quarter moon was almost at the zenith. I was happy to observe that my big toe felt and looked OK. A long distance section hiker came to the shelter after dinner, and we talked for a while as daylight faded.

It was a cloudy Sunday morning, but dry. However, at the top of Big Butt Mountain (4,750 feet) thunder sounded again. I had my raingear ready but used only the umbrella through a couple of hours of rain. (You can hold the umbrella in place with your backpack's sternum strap and still have hands free to use two hiking sticks.)

There were hundreds of white trillium, pink trillium, and painted trillium near Big Butt. I passed a turtle on the trail and stopped for lunch in a dilapidated abandoned barn. The sun came out, and by Hogback Ridge it was a beautiful afternoon with breezes to discourage the bugs. Slo-Poke, Shankadelic, Half-Pint and MacGyver were at Hogback Ridge Shelter. Shankadelic was reading *Lord of the Rings*, and we agreed that Tolkien must have been an avid walker because his descriptions of trails and terrain ring so true.

It was mostly sunny on Monday morning but cool and so windy I had to keep my hat strapped on. (Although foolish looking, my Tilley hat has several advantages over a baseball cap, including a back band and a chin strap that can be used when it is windy.) My nose ran with allergies stirred up by windblown pollen. I crossed the road in Sams Gap (3,800 feet) and met Marcie 360 going up Big Bald. There was a beautiful carpet of little yellow daisy-like flowers on the way as well as tiny white-fringed-phacelia and purple delphinium.

The trail emerged from the trees to the bald top (5,516 feet); it was one of those stunning moments when you go from being enclosed by the woods to a spectacular panoramic view. Two hikers were lying prone on the grass, trying to smoke

Countless trillium on Rich Mountain

Enjoying the Scenery

cigarettes in the high wind. I could see the trail winding down Big Bald and up the next hill a mile ahead, and Marcie was visible on the path, now far in front of me.

I had lunch on some rocks at Big Stamp after checking for imaginary rattlesnakes. The cool weather was energizing. The towering rocks on Little Bald were awesome – bedding planes near vertical and rising 80 feet above the trail. The AT rolled down to Spivey Gap (3,252 feet), where there was a fallen tree studded with glossy orange trumpet shaped fungi. Marcie was camped near the trail.

Having decided to stop in Erwin the next day, I kept going to No Business Knob Shelter, hiking over 20 miles for the first time. I walked from Spivey to No Business Knob between 4 and 6 pm. This section of trail was very beautiful – almost like a western canyon walk, with red pine needles underfoot and warm sunlight slanting through the trees. A magnolia tree with gigantic leaves grew in front of No-Business Shelter. There was no privy, and one of the short-term hikers who were there for the night had stepped in shit out back and spent a long time cleaning his boot. (Leave No Trace, dammit!).

On Tuesday it was a short hike from No Business Knob over Temple Ridge to the switchback trail descending to the Nolichucky River (1,700 feet) and Erwin, Tennessee. It was a sunny morning. On the way down I could hear trains on the track that follows the river gorge, and there were several overlooks at the turns, with views of the river and the industrial buildings at the outskirts of town. I emerged near the river and passed Uncle Johnny's hostel and outfitter store, which had signs sprouting all over it to lure hikers in. However, I had already decided I wanted to stay in the middle

Approaching Big Bald

Just Walking

Marcie 306 crossing Big Bald

of town, so I crossed the bridge and stuck out my thumb. I was worried at first about the lack of traffic on the road into town, but needn't have. I soon was given a ride by a guy who did a lot of hiking and worked for an outfitter. He had Gene Ammons cooking on the tape player. He dropped me downtown, and I walked a couple of blocks down an attractive, tree-lined street of handsome Victorian houses, soon arriving at Miss Janet's hostel. It was recognizable by the thru-hikers sprawling on the porch.

Miss Janet was out, but one of the hikers showed me how to sign in, and I found a bunk, took a shower, and walked a few blocks to a restaurant called the Burrito Factory. After a pleasant lunch I bought a twelve-pack of Bud at a convenience store and shared it with the other hikers at Miss Janet's. Among them were Reason, Lumberjack, Mr. Pumpy, and Very Small Animal, a French woman with the Little Prince tattooed on her shoulder, who was on her second thru-hike. I spent the rest of the day picking up my mail drop, sending flowers to Sheila for our wedding anniversary, and picking up lunch items and other odds and ends, including a new line for hanging my food bag. Miss Janet returned and took us to Johnson City where we saw *X-Men II* at the Cineplex and had an AYCE pizza-feed.

Gaps, Knobs, and Humps

Erwin TN to Damascus VA:
[Mile 338.8 to Mile 457.3]

Wednesday, May 14. Breakfast at Miss Janet's is no simple thing. Janet deputized guests to break eggs, fry bacon, and make fruit salad while she made French toast. A dozen of us sat at picnic tables in her back yard, including a couple of hikers I didn't know at the time but would later travel with. Janet proposed a go-around, asking what music we would like to hear while summiting Katahdin. My response was *Stairway to Heaven*, although it turned out a little differently.

After the usual confusion of a dozen people packing up, Miss Janet drove me back to the trail, where I promptly took a wrong turn and had to backtrack for ten minutes. Finally on the AT, I climbed up to Curley Maple Gap Shelter (3,070 feet) and walked on through a recently burned-over area to Beauty Spot, a pale yellow-green meadow from which I could see Unaka Mountain and Roan High Knob. Tiny black grasshoppers jumped up like popcorn as I walked through the meadow. Lumberjack and two other hikers from Miss Janet's passed me slackpacking south. (Slackpacking means day hiking with a light load with the aid of a host who drops you off and/or picks you up at the end of the day.)

Iron Mountain Gap

The trail passes through Deep Gap (4,100 feet) and then climbs Unaka Mountain (5,180 feet), whose dark summit was wooded with red cedar trees, ferns, moss, and lichens and resembled a bleak White Mountain col.

I walked on to Cherry Gap Shelter. At the shelter I met a couple of thru-hikers from Florida, Chilly Willy and Kilroy, both around 40, and Hot Dog, a man in his 60s who was thru-hiking with a Manx cat named Stubby (what else?). Hot Dog told us stories of growing up in southern Virginia and eating many kinds of fowl and game, including a favorite, robin pie. Meanwhile, Stubby, who rode atop Hot Dog's backpack during the day, was busy rounding up mice and voles around the campsite, inside a hollow tree, and in the rafters of the shelter. He continued to prowl at least until I fell asleep.

Thursday morning started sunny, but the clouds increased over the day. I walked through Iron Mountain Gap, which was carpeted with yellow flowers, and over

Just Walking

Little Rock Knob, which was fogged in. It was spitting rain in Hughes Gap and on the 2,200-foot climb up Roan High Knob (6,285 feet). For once, I was actually happy about the rain, which cooled me on the long ascent. The top of the mountain was in the clouds as I walked into the shelter, a dark and gloomy cabin. It had a second floor that felt like it might collapse at any moment, and the columns that held up the overhang in front were leaning at alarming angles. Marcie 360 arrived, and near dark a trail angel stopped by with cans of beer and Pepsi for us. We both declined his offer of a ride to the Trail Days festival in Damascus; I was really getting into my hike and didn't feel like taking time off to attend this hiker extravaganza.

On Friday morning I slacked back to the overlooks at the top of the trail; they had been fogged-in the previous afternoon, but it was now sunny, and there was a clear view to the hills and valleys below. I returned to the shelter, picked up my pack, and started going forward on the

From Roan High Knob

trail at 9 am. I moved at a leisurely pace to Carvers Gap and the other balds associated with Roan High Knob. It was a pretty morning. I chatted with three women who were dayhiking with cameras. I took a break sitting in the ferns along the side-hill trail and then

hiked down to Overmountain Shelter – a real gem of a converted barn – and had lunch there alone. The shelter is named for the Revolutionary War militia that came "over-mountain" to a big battle in South Carolina. After lunch I climbed up the trail in a hillside meadow

Enjoying the Scenery

and could look down on the shelter, now shrunk to the size of a postage stamp.

The AT went up and over Little Hump and then Hump Mountain (5,587 feet); the 360-degree views from these balds are spectacular, and you can see the trail far ahead and behind. There was a big storm in the distance over Grandfather, a jagged mountain ridge. The trail descended over difficult footing to Doll Flats. My left arch was aching from all the walking in U-shaped ruts on the balds, which causes extra pronation of your feet. After collecting water at the spring I decided to continue down to Apple House Shelter (at roughly 3,000 feet), near Highway 19, which goes through Elk Park, North Carolina.

There were many stories circulating in the hiking community about some people in this area who were apparently aggrieved by a trail relocation on land they considered theirs and who played dirty tricks on unsuspecting hikers. The worst stories concerned stringing fish hooks across the trail and stopping for hitchhikers only to zoom off after the victims had put their packs in the back of the truck but before they could climb in. I was skeptical, but I found myself hoping no yahoos would show up during the night. In fact, one of the reasons I had pushed on was that I was concerned about Marcie having to stay there alone. Visitors did show up during dinner – a couple of local college professors who were walking three dogs.

Overmountain Shelter in the distance

Hump Mountain

On Saturday I made it quickly to the road and caught a hitch to the Country House Restaurant from a young guy in a pickup. I had a big breakfast of country ham, eggs, grits, and their famous dinner-plate-sized biscuit, all for $4.50. The place had a nice atmosphere, with many folks talking to old friends and pleasant waitresses. After breakfast I walked to the post office. A gentleman gave me two apples while I was repacking my food bag. I walked to a gas station/

Just Walking

Hitch Hiking

People who live near cities, especially women, would never think of hitch hiking; it's dangerous, right? However, unless you hitchhike you can't thru-hike. How else can you get to post offices and food stores which may be miles from the trail? The good news is that in rural America there are many kinds of people, not necessarily hikers themselves, who will give hikers a ride. Some will even reverse direction to do it. You end up meeting real people and having a pleasant chat, and everyone leaves with a smile on their face.

Women, who really do have more to fear, often hitch in the company of another hiker. Since my thru-hike, I always stop for hikers with their thumbs out, and I've learned that you have more options on shorter hikes if you start by hitching a ride from the end point to the starting point. The typical time to get a ride is probably ten minutes. Strangely, people with all that room in their SUVs hardly ever stop.

Jones Falls

convenience store for crackers, cheese, and cookies and hitched a ride back to the trail with a man who was interested in history – we had a pleasant discussion about the economic origins of the Civil War, a topic I had a feeling he liked to bring up with Yankees. He also warned me about those "bad people" along the next leg of the trail.

> White petals on the trail
> Dogwood.
> Are there really
> People to fear here?

It is an understatement to say this day was one long walk – 17.3 miles including a recent trail relocation – and I added more miles to that by going the wrong way from Jones Falls (which was a very pretty place with a Louisiana Waterthrush walking around on one of the ledges). By the time I had convinced myself I was going the wrong direction I had backtracked for a half hour – a 2 1/2 mile detour. Going forward again, I came to a grassy section along the Elk River around 3 pm and crossed

Enjoying the Scenery

Laurel Fork at 5:25 pm. This was a nice surprise, because I wasn't sure I'd passed an earlier milestone yet, and I was getting tired. My legs held out on the long climb into Moreland Gap Shelter, but I was running on vapors when I arrived, around 7:30 pm. I had also developed a little blister on the outside of my left heel despite applying moleskin and duct tape around noon. It hurt when my foot pronated.

There was rain during the night, but only a sprinkle on Sunday morning. The shelter was jam-packed, and three guys actually slept on a ground cloth with their legs tucked under the sleeping platform, which made it kind of difficult to sit on the edge of the platform to put on my boots.

It was an easy hike to Dennis Cove and Laurel Fork. There was plenty of rock to pick around near the famous staircase cascade of Laurel Falls. The trail edged along the river gorge below the falls on a narrow shelf of rust-brown rock.

Laurel Falls

I stopped for lunch at Laurel Fork Shelter, which is perched on the steep opposite side of the gorge, and chatted with another hiker who happened by. There was then a steep 2,000-foot climb up Pond Mountain (3,800 feet) that had me sucking air. It was warm and sunny for most of the day, and it was pleasant walking along the river but too hot going up the mountain. Finally, I made an easy descent to Watauga Lake (2,100 feet), where I dropped my pack, removed my boots, and kept walking right into the lake with my clothes on: refreshment and laundry in one easy step.

Several people were at Watauga Lake Shelter including Happy Feet, a welder from Cambridge, Massachusetts, and Pokey, woman in pigtails about my age who lived in Jackson, New Hampshire, where she ran a B&B and kept a few cattle. Happy Feet filled me in on Trail Days, which sounded both fun and instructive. He received a lot of useful information from gear manufacturers who were providing individual evaluations and advice and sometimes exchanging broken gear on the spot.

The trip into Damascus was unremarkable except for the mileage – 21.6 miles on Monday and 18.3 on Tuesday. The molefoam patch over my left heel blister was working well. I met a southbound

Just Walking

birdwatcher who was interested to hear about the waterthrush at Jones Falls. There was also a couple in their 60s at Double Springs shelter who were getting acquainted on a 7-day hike, an acid test of their compatibility.

I awoke early, packed quietly, and hit the trail at dawn. I coasted into Damascus around 1:30 on Tuesday, May 20. The trail followed rolling ridgelines ranging from 3,500 to 4,000 feet except for a final downhill run into town (elevation 1,928 feet), so I was able to make it by lunch. On Wednesday I had a restful zero day at the Maples B&B, doing errands and reading *Pride and Prejudice*, which I had broken up into sections and included in my mail drops. I had reached the fourth state along the trail.

Dawn from Double Springs

4 Marathon

Marathon

Virginia contains the longest stretch of the Appalachian Trail, more than 500 miles – almost enough to wear out a new pair of boots. The Trail Companion talks about the "Virginia Blues" which afflict some thru-hikers – the feeling that, despite the long miles you are able to hike each day, you really aren't making much progress. In short, Virginia doesn't really repay striving to get ahead. Hikers who drive themselves onward toward their goal sometimes end up leaving the trail here.

Non-hikers sometimes say they are impressed with all the guts and determination it must take to thru-hike. The truth is, not much of that is necessary – or useful. You just need to feel like hiking when you wake up each day.

This all gets back to the Zen concept of just walking, and the idea (maybe it's just another way of saying the same thing) that it's unbelievably cool to be able to go from here to way up there, just by walking.

By Damascus, each day had become a little routine. Walk, sit and rest, walk, stop for lunch, walk, stop to camp and eat, sleep, get up, and walk. Simply sitting was an activity that felt wonderful whether on the ground along the trail or on the wooden floor of a shelter.

Setting up camp was a practiced ritual, and so was repacking in the morning. This was both utilitarian (so I could find things in my pack when I needed them) and pleasant to do in itself. Sleeping on a wooden floor with a half-inch of plastic foam for a mattress may seem like a hardship, but I had come to find it unbelievably comfortable. True, it helps if you are tired and have learned the trick of how to lie on the flat parts of your body instead of the parts that stick out.

But getting up and feeling like hiking again, day after day, is mostly about just sitting, just eating, and just walking.

Rhododendrons on the trail near Lost Mountain Shelter

Just Walking

○ Pastoral
Damascus to Pearisburg VA:
[Mile 457.3 to Mile 619.5]

Thursday, May 22. After a couple of excellent breakfasts and a zero day at The Maples B&B, the white blazes led me out of Damascus and up the wooded trail to the Grayson Highlands. It was cloudy and damp again, and my clothes were soon wet from dripping foliage. I looked around for Lost Mountain from a place called the Lookout, but the low clouds were disorienting; perhaps that's why it's lost. The trail next to White Laurel Creek was pretty, and there is a cool bridge on a segment of the rail trail where one railroad passed over another at the creek junction. Many people were at Lost Mountain Shelter, including Pokey, Primitive, Lumberjack, and Snotrocket, but only three of us slept in the shelter itself.

The highlands were very pretty, mostly open pasture with grazing cattle and rocky outcrops from time to time. The

From Thomas Knob Shelter

dominant colors were gray, pale green, and the color of rhododendron blossoms in the fog.

By 11:30 am on Wednesday I had made it over Whitetop Mountain (5,080 feet at the trail) to Elk Garden, where there was a cooler of beer, courtesy of a trail angel. I drank an Old Milwaukee and moved on. Lunch was spent sitting on the ground at the side trail to the summit of Mount Rogers, Virginia's highest mountain. Afterwards I ran up to tag the summit (5,729 feet), which was in a grove of spruce and looked very much like one of the lower White Mountain peaks of New Hampshire (even though its absolute elevation was equal to one of the Presidentials). Walking on to

Marathon

Thomas Knob and Grayson Highlands, the trail was very rocky and cobbley.

A group of school kids on a camping trip scurried around Thomas Knob Shelter, and several older photo students were tramping the highlands with their cameras. Fog made the scenery interesting and an occasional glimpse of blue sky was visible. The trail went over and under big rocks in one place. Lumberjack and I saw several of the famous ponies who graze the highland meadow and also a couple of deer. Periodic trail markers on short square posts held up by cairns of rock marked the way across a sort of moor on the ridgetop. Scenes from Thomas Hardy novels came to mind.

I ambled into Wise Shelter an hour before a thunderstorm cloudburst hit. Eight hikers were already there, including Lumberjack, a guy named I.B., and a hiking family known as the West Virginians: Slim Jim, Dormouse, and Nic-Nac. Slim Jim was cooking on a little tin-can wood stove, and he went around the site breaking dead branches off the trees to use as fuel. I was too tired to cook. It rained like crazy a couple of times during the night, and water poured off the roof in torrents.

The weather cleared after the midnight deluge – the stars were shining at 3:30 am. Dormouse was up most of the night chattering to Slim Jim, who was amazingly tolerant of being awakened repeatedly – it must be love. My opinion of Dormouse went up several notches when she kindly provided a light to help me find my way back into the shelter after getting lost in the dark among scattered copses of trees while finding a place to pee.

The sky was blue at 7 am the next morning. The trail crossed a high pasture full of steers and calves. Some big clouds floated above, but it was mostly

Pasture north of Wise Shelter

67

Just Walking

On the way into Groseclose

sunny. New ferns were unfurling their fiddleheads, glowing yellow-green in the early morning light. The trail continued across Scales Gap, past Balanced Rock, then up Stone and Pine mountains. Some people were saddling up with a horse guide at Scales Gap.

At Old Orchard shelter a group of thru-hikers, looking dissipated and hung over, were recovering from a feast the night before, which reportedly included cheeseburgers, beer, and a large bottle of Jim Beam bourbon that a trail angel (perhaps one of Lucifer's) had brought them. Three people were standing around the smoldering remains of the campfire, which they had blown back into a little flame. One of them was trying to dry a pair of sneakers dangling from a pole and looked sort of like a fisherman. Following the Lucifer theme, one of the hikers wore a baseball cap with little brass horns attached – this was Greenman, who turned up a couple of more times along the trail. I decided I didn't really like their style.

Raccoon Branch Shelter was my destination for the night. It was in a pretty spot, with a little braided spring percolating down the hillside out back. A small weir had been constructed to concentrate the flow so you could collect water.

Lumberjack and multiple-time thru-hikers AT Addict and No Pain were there, as well as a couple from Columbus, Ohio, and a young guy named Indiana Slim. AT Addict was in his fifties and had thru-hiked the AT three times and section-hiked the entire trail three more times; he was working on the fourth section hike.[12] He had also thru-hiked the Pacific Crest Trail and Continental Divide Trail and considered the AT the most difficult of the three, owing to its terrain and rough footing. No Pain was on his third thru-hike; he was the

Millipede next to a stile at State Road 610

---

[12] About as many hikers complete the entire Appalachian Trail by doing it in sections over several years as those who thru-hike it in a single year. There's no important difference.

Marathon

only African American thru-hiker I had met so far. We talked for a while before bed about places and people along the trail, behind and ahead. Lumberjack kept asking them questions after I grew sleepy and turned in.

Everyone but No Pain was up at 6:30 am. It was a nice morning with some thin overcast. The trail came down through a meadow where a small herd of cows grazed and then climbed the ridge next to a horse pasture. I arrived at Partnership Shelter around noon; it is located about a hundred yards from a ranger station with a pay phone that can be used to order deliveries of pizza and beer. Lumberjack had warned me that the party animals were planning an even bigger bash for Memorial Day, so I made plans to avoid this place except for lunch. Stopping at Chatfield Shelter about 3:45 pm, it was just me and a guy named Pockets, although Boilerplate slacked by, waving his arms as if he were about to start flying without the pack weight he usually carried.

The next morning was Memorial Day. After a bowl of granola, a leisurely walk brought me to Groseclose, Virginia, and the Village Motel, which was run by a very nice Polish couple. The weather report for Poland was on the satellite TV in the office. Lumberjack, Pokey, Happy Feet, and others also showed up at the motel. The nearby Red Barn restaurant provided a hearty second breakfast and recent baseball standings in the weekend edition of *USA Today*. In the afternoon I sat in my room watching Tim Wakefield and the Red Sox beat Roger Clemens and the Yankees on ESPN; later that day Lumberjack, a hard-core Yankees fan, was gracious in defeat.

On Tuesday I caught the "shuttle" for a couple of miles to a diner in Atkins with Lumberjack and Spitz. The owner of the diner, who looked like Tommy Lee Jones, was transporting hikers in his minivan to drum up business. After breakfast, his son took us to the post office and waited while we shopped at the nearby grocery store. Waiting in line with us to check out were two local farmers, whose problem with the frequent rain was bigger than ours: they can't mow hay when it's wet, and if they let the grass grow too long, its nutritional value as a livestock feed diminishes.

Returning to the motel in time to see Pokey saddling up for the day, I packed my stuff, crossed the little creek, walked past the Dairy Queen and across the Interstate ramps, and was back on the trail passing through the rural landscape at 9:30 am. It

> **Stiles**
> *The AT crosses many pastures where cattle graze. The pastures are fenced in with barbed wire to keep the livestock inside. Rather than a gate, which someone is bound to leave open, access is most often provided by means of a pair of ladders straddling the fence in an A-frame. You mount three rungs, step over the top strand of wire, and down the opposite side. In some places there is an alternative design with a little maze that a hiker can squeeze through but a cow can't.*

Just Walking

Looking down to Burkes Garden

was the usual humid, overcast morning, but the sun peeked out by noon, and it was partly sunny for the rest of the day. The early going was dull, but the trail later crossed some beautiful meadows on hillsides with views across the valley to a wooded ridge. There was a great rest spot next to a stile in the shade of a tree at State Road 610; I took Thermo's picture there and he took mine. The trail then ran along the North Fork of the Holstein River, through yellow flag iris and pink phlox, and past a ruined old mill. The day's hike wound up at Knot Maul Branch Shelter, which was occupied by Spitz, Pokey, Strider and a family of southbound section hikers.

Earlier in the day, someone had been hollering from down the horse trail that crosses the AT at Tilson Gap, so I turned off to investigate. Instead of an injured person calling for help, I found a man trying to summon a young hunting dog who had strayed despite his impressive array of electronic tracking equipment – a briefcase console and multi-pronged directional antenna. The missing puppy was one of three expensive Korean hunting dogs he was training with electronic collars that both sent and received radio signals. The dog was at the shelter that evening, 10 miles north of Tilson Gap. One of the southbounders at the shelter used his cell phone to call the number on the dog's collar and arranged to take it to State Road 42 the next morning. However, after we were all long asleep, the dog's owners showed up with their electronic squawk-box and Coleman lanterns and took him away.

It was partly cloudy Wednesday morning. The climb up Chestnut Knob (4,410 feet) was not too bad, and there were pretty views down into the lush valley known as Burke's Garden, but I was tired by the time I reached Chestnut Knob

Marathon

Shelter, a stone cabin on the ridgetop. It was also chilly because of a brisk wind and a deck of clouds following a cold front. After a hot lunch of granola in the cabin I pushed on to Jenkins Shelter. This was a long haul, owing in part to very stony, rocky trails. The idea that the AT in Virginia is a piece of cake is not true: the trails are not always smooth going, and there are plenty of ups and downs. At the shelter that evening were Marcie, Spitz, Lumberjack, Wounded Knee, Smokey and Bandit, and two section-hiking guys who had been at Wise Shelter.

It started raining again in the wee hours and continued until 9 am Thursday. I woke up late and left at 8:45 am, using my umbrella to ward off lingering showers. The regular AT crossed Little Wolf Creek about ten times. There is also a high water trail, but it wasn't needed. Cans of V8 had been left by a trail angel at the first road crossing, where Lumberjack and I took a morning break. At the interstate highway interchange there

From Brushy Mountain

was a very welcome second occurrence of trail magic for the day: a cooler with fresh strawberries and bottles of Miller Highlife. Along the highway roadcut were tall outcroppings of Devonian shale and sandstone, warped and fractured like a bent baklava.

I reached the side trail to Helveys Mill Shelter, my original target for the day, around 3 pm. Chatting there for a while with Strider and two fellows my age, one pointed out the mud on my legs, thereby establishing himself as a non-thru-hiker. After weighing the options, I said "What the Hell," and decided to keep going.

Cranking it up to 3 miles per hour for the next 9.5 miles, mostly on a gentle down-grade, I arrived at Jennys Knob shelter about 6:45 pm. On the way three northbounders passed slacking south – Flatlander, 2 Dog Night, and Pushing Up Daisies. A group of women were camped near the road a mile south of the shelter. They were doctors and nurses from a nearby hospital (who else would camp in surgical scrubs?); they fed me Pringles and wished me good luck. I declined to share in the tequila they were planning to open, and from the look of the young woman who was clearly the doctor in charge, it was a good thing.

Marcie had stopped and camped a few miles before Jennys Knob Shelter. Thermo ended up at the shelter later. Also at the shelter were two women with dogs, a guy named Pops who couldn't handle my name (he kept calling me "Millipod" or "Millidew"), and a woman named Firefeet.

A flycatcher sang on a tree branch opposite the shelter – probably a wood peewee – and as I lay in my sleeping bag, barred owls called. It didn't take long to fall asleep on the comfortable wood floor.

On Friday it was a quick hike down to Lickskillet Hollow (great name), then an easy climb up to the ridge of Brushy

Millipede takes a dip at the Falls of Dismal

Mountain, and down again to Kimberling Creek, where Firefeet happened by while I was sitting next to the trail taking a break. As she was taking my picture on the suspension bridge over the creek, two sheriff's deputies came through with a young bloodhound they were training. The dog followed a scent trail to find another officer who was squatting beneath the bridge, and he was smothered with hugs and kisses by his trainers.

We detoured from the trail crossing at State Road 606 to a country store, where we met Thermo. I feasted on a L'il Debbie Raisin Crème Pie and a Dr. Pepper, comforts available at this outpost of civilization. The store was a classic – ammo for sale, a gallery of photos of guys holding up dead bobcats and other game they had shot, and even a shelf of spices and breading products made specifically for cooking game. I have no problem with hunters if they eat what they kill, but what about those bobcats?

Dinner time visitor to Wapiti Shelter

We all walked back to the trail and up the ridge again. Firefeet and I took a detour to the Tolkien-esque "Falls of Dismal" on the mis-named Dismal Creek (it's actually a beautiful trout stream). I swam in the green pool below the falls during a sunny break while Firefeet took photos with her camera and mine, including some flattering shots of me in my dripping skivvies. It may have been the cold water or the idea of swimming half naked with a man of recent acquaintance that kept her out, or maybe just good sense.

The walk from Dismal Falls to Wapiti Shelter felt longer than it was (about six miles). Back on the AT there were long stretches of flat trail meandering through the woods with no landmarks. The skies were mostly cloudy now, with intermittent sunny breaks. I was getting tired and kept looking at the map, trying to identify my position in relation to the little brooks we were crossing on the south side of Dismal Creek. Finally, much later than we had hoped, the trail crossed the creek on a bridge and came to a signed junction. There was still a ways to go and a couple more streams, now flowing from north to south, to cross.

On the walk Firefeet told me about herself. She had recently served a hitch in the Navy as a flute, piccolo, and saxophone player, and her boyfriend had thru-hiked the previous year. We finally reached Wapiti Shelter and found

Just Walking

From Angels Rest

Pops, who was acting a bit thick again. Thermo was there but opted to go on past the shelter before stopping for the day. We were joined later by Bubbles, a slim woman with a Slavic face who was unfortunately suffering from blisters and heat rash, and her trail companion, a woman named Cougar, who gave an interesting demonstration of hammock rigging. A deer walked around the shelter during dinner. (Wapiti means "deer".)

I rose early Saturday and left at 6:45 am, just as it began to rain. Pops continued to struggle with my name and upset his coffee pot, which was percolating on his stove. I later felt bad about my hasty goodbye to Firefeet who didn't expect to keep up with me. I never did see her in Pearisburg but learned months later that she had completed her thru-hike.

My umbrella was again useful going up the steep climb to the Sugar Run Mountain ridge. The rain stopped in an hour or two. Trucking along the ridgetop, impatient to arrive in Pearisburg as early as possible, I kept checking the map to follow my progress. Marcie was resting by the trail where it makes a big loop around a radio antenna on top of the mountain. By then it was just sprinkling on and off, with clouds drifting low across the ridge.

The sun showed itself briefly around noon, and the day became pleasantly warm and humid. The way was brightened by many pink azaleas and honeysuckle bushes, which have a sweet fragrance you can pick up several feet away. The view from Angels Rest, a high bluff above town, was a scenic but messy cloudscape with some gaps open to the pretty green countryside below. The final descent of nearly 2,000 feet was very steep, and much of it was covered with particularly sticky, slimy mud. The rate of descent on my wrist altimeter hit 70 feet per minute, and I literally boot skied on the muddy trail at times.

I decided to pass up the motel at the base of the mountain, which was not in a very scenic spot, in favor of hiking the half mile up to Pearisburg, where laundry, post office, restaurants, and stores were more accessible. The second motel at the top of the hill was my destination. It had outdoor walkways, and there was muddy hiker gear parked outside many of the rooms. After a shower, I walked to the nearby gas station/convenience store and then to a Hardee's for lunch. Returning to the room, I took off all my clothes and put on my raingear and walked the half mile or so to the laundromat, which is on a street parallel to Pearisburg's main street.

The rain showers continued while I did the laundry. Walking a couple of blocks during the wash cycle, I enjoyed a Bud at a venerable local beer bar (no liquor). Several more blocks' walk led to the public library, which is down a side street off the highway north of the town center; unfortunately it is closed on Sundays and Mondays, so there would be no email at this stop. Back at the laundromat attending to my drying clothes, I talked to a local guy who was there because his power had been knocked out by a storm.

Back in the room I changed into clean clothes and then had dinner at a sports bar next to the motel. At the bar was a black man named Bob who had lived in Dracut, Massachusetts, for 22 years and then moved back to Pearisburg when

Mountain laurel in the rain

Just Walking

he retired. We had a long interesting talk. Far from being a Red Sox fan he had become disaffected by the peculiar shortage of players of color the Sox always seemed to suffer from (until the current owners bought the club); trading Ellis Burks was the last straw for him. (Happily, Burks returned in 2004 and received a World Series championship ring.) He agreed with me that the Red Sox's "Curse of the Bambino" was mostly due to the club's unwritten policy of limiting the number of black players on the roster, thereby excluding themselves from a great pool of talent.

I called home; Sheila was out, but I chatted with Greg and Matt. Late in the evening Sheila and I had a nice talk. She was very cordial and asked if I had received her email.

Most of Sunday was spent resting in the motel room and strolling around town, which has a lovely courthouse and a statue commemorating a Confederate victory over Union forces. That afternoon, I learned there was an internet terminal in the motel office and so was able to retrieve my emails after all. There was one from my business partner Skip and one from my friend Gordon, who was on a tour of minor league baseball parks.

And there was the email from Sheila, a long one that I replied to and then spent the rest of the day thinking about. My absence had been harder on her than I expected. She was angry at my selfish behavior in deserting our household for six months. In my reply, I offered to come home if she needed me.

Introspection

Pearisburg to Waynesboro:
[Mile 619.5 to Mile 844.8]

Monday, June 2. I didn't fall sleep until 2 am, tossing and turning. Rising at 7 am, I had breakfast at Hardee's, and picked up my mail drop and a surprise package from my friend Debbie, aka Medusa, who had thru-hiked in 1996. It contained carefully bubble-wrapped chocolate chip cookies, fruit bars, and a squirt gun. I bought a few groceries at the Food Lion across the street and stove alcohol at an auto supply store. After packing all of this carefully I checked out of the motel at 9:30 am. It was a warm, sunny morning going down the hill to the trail. No Pain passed me, headed up into town.

The AT crosses the highway bridge over the wide New River (elevation 1,600 feet) and then heads up the hill behind the big Celanese cigarette filter plant, whose clanking and whirring remained audible for a couple of miles. The trail climbs up the nose of Peters Mountain and follows the ridge until it opens up to pasture at Rice Field Shelter (3,500 feet). On the way a lot of time was spent thinking about Sheila.

Debbie's cookies made a hit with four hikers who were sitting at an overlook with a panoramic view of West Virginia. There was a lovely prospect before Syms

Cloudscape from Sinking Creek Mountain ridge

Gap, looking across to Pine Swamp Knob. The walk down to Pine Swamp Branch Shelter was longer than necessary because of the nearly level trail segments between umpteen switchbacks. I passed Pokey and a woman named T-Bird, both of whom stopped at the shelter.

Also there for the night were Nemo, Gus, Twigs, Moose-Munch, and James. Gus turned out to be a social worker who had worked with Sheila the previous year. Small world. Gus and her buddy Twigs were hiking from Springer Mountain to Harpers Ferry. Twigs was a slender young woman with big eyes and salt-and-pepper hair trimmed short; she had a droll wit. Nemo was a small woman with a salty and slightly insane sense of humor that kept us all laughing. Moose Munch was a big guy, about 30, with red hair and beard who became the leader of the group. T-Bird was a Union College pal of Nemo's, who wore her blond hair in dreads. She sang very well and played a small Montana guitar that she carried strapped onto her pack. The shelter had two sleeping shelves on each side with a central fireplace which we put to good use. A nice evening.

There was rain during the night and again in the morning. I started hiking at 8:45 am, under the umbrella again. Bailey Gap Shelter, about four miles ahead on the next ridge, was still full of people when I stopped for a rest. The rain was getting on people's nerves. It finally stopped, but the ridge was cold and windy, an unusual state of affairs for Virginia in June. There were a couple of pretty sections with rock outcrops and

Just Walking

mountain laurel in full bloom. After having soup and tea for lunch at War Spur Shelter around 3 pm, I decided to stay. The crew from the previous night showed up, plus Blueberry and Pinot, a couple from Colorado.

On Wednesday the skies were fair. It was a long haul over John's Creek Mountain to Laurel Creek Shelter – I arrived there at 10 am and was glad not to have tried for it the day before. The AT continued to Sinking Creek Valley, which was well-named. I walked down a sloping pasture that became progressively more squishy underfoot and stepped ten inches deep into a pond of mustard-brown slime right in front of the stile. A group of hikers who had just had the same experience were hanging around to watch the next victim. Reportedly, a couple of hikers, depressed by all the rain and with their boots full of muck had made a decision then and there to hitch to town and get off the trail for good.

There were more clouds by this time, and showers soon began, but it was a

Descending Dragons Tooth

warm day, and my shirt was already wet from my having rinsed it out in a brook, so there was no need to bother with the umbrella. Pushing Up Daisies passed coming down a steep meadow; she was feeling sick and was turning back for the day.

Tom from Birmingham, a southbound section hiker with an American flag headband, warned me about the steep, muddy trail up Sinking Creek Mountain just ahead, probably much like the crazy descent into Pearisburg, but it wasn't as hard going up as it had been for him coming down.

In the 1800s the Sarver family had cleared an enormous number of rocks while farming the ridgetop and piled them up in strange looking mounds which have remained over the years. A side trail to Sarver Hollow Shelter drops about 200 feet down the flank of the ridge over a quarter mile. I slipped on the steep, muddy trail and fell on my ass going down, but soon reached a beautiful new shelter and its lovely spring. The path kicked my butt going back up, and I cursed polysyllabically to the merriment of some hikers taking a break at the junction with the AT.

The ridge walk had many broad sloping ledges with wide-screen views of the valley and the opposite ridge. By now the afternoon sun was appearing, and scattered castellanus clouds made an awesome cloudscape – "castles in the air." Surviving a few slips on the lichen-slick ledge I reached Niday Shelter around 4:30 pm, intact except for a section of one of my hiking sticks that I had fallen on and bent over like a hairpin. The same gang showed up again, plus Smokey and Bandit, Flatlander, and some others. T-Bird sang beautifully and entertained us. Moose Munch produced a pint bottle of Dickel's bourbon which we savored in small sips.

After eating some granola on Thursday morning I worked my way 1,500 feet up the Brush Mountain ridge beyond Craig Creek. The morning was sunny, breezy, and very pleasant, as a June morning should be.

Pokey was at the top of the ridge, and we took a rest on a real bench the trail crew had provided. We talked about how the climb up the ridge illustrated why it is so favorable for an army to defend high ground, as Lee's army did at the Battle of Fredericksburg, inflicting over 12,000 casualties on the Union forces whose misfortune lay in being commanded by Burnside (and attacking from below).

The AT continued along the ridge, past the memorial for Audie Murphy (the most decorated WWII infantryman). After a glimpse of Core Mountain and Dragon's Tooth, the trail crossed Trout Creek and started climbing them.

Seventeen-year cicadas had been emerging over the previous couple of

Morning in Beckner Gap

Just Walking

days. They are weirdly beautiful creatures the size of your thumb, with beady red eyes flanking a wide forehead. They leave their empty exoskeletons on tree trunks after climbing up from their underground burrows. An individual cicada makes a loud buzz to attract a mate during the two-day adulthood that follows 17 years of underground adolescence, and on this stretch of trail the collective sound of thousands of them was a sort of surreal, pulsing, high-pitched drone, like the sound track to a 1950s Japanese sci-fi movie.

Reaching 2500 feet, there was a view north and a little later a view to the many-toothed ridge. A sunny spot along the trail under some 2-needle red pine trees provided a nice setting for lunch.

It was a tough climb over Dragon's Tooth (3,020 feet), with many rocky outcrops, each of which looked like the final tooth, only to be followed by another and then another. (As Nemo said, you thought you'd reached the incisor but it was only

Tinker Cliffs

the bicuspid.) The descent followed a series of steep bare rock ledges, some of them narrower than your boot.

From the ridge the din of a motorbike without a muffler was audible; someone was riding up and down the long driveway of a suburban house on the road below. From the road crossing it was a short way to Four Pines Hostel, where many of my recent acquaintances were staying, including Chilly Willy and Kilroy, whom I had last seen at Cherry Gap Shelter south of Roan High Knob. Lone Wolf was there and also the famous Baltimore Jack, who was on his fifth thru-hike. The hostel turned out to be behind the suburban house, and the motorbike rider was the teenage son of the owner.

Four Pines Hostel was a big three-bay garage whose floor was covered with mattresses and cots; it had a fridge with cold drinks and other comforts of home. A playboy foldout was stuck to the wall, which struck me as odd, considering the many female hikers who stay there. Most of the places on the garage floor were already taken, and I settled in on a broken cot.

After consuming a couple of 75 cent beers from the fridge, it seemed a good time for a shower. As I was drying off someone started beating on the door, complaining that I had been in the little bathroom too long. It was Baltimore Jack, who had to pee. Chilly Willy made me feel better afterwards, telling me that BJ was clearly out of line, but as a middle-aged man I could feel his pain.

We shuttled to the Home Place restaurant in Catawba for a terrific all-you-can-eat meal; it was barbeque night to boot. I called Sheila after dinner and, over the din of the motorbike, which the kid was riding up and down again, cleared the air between us after having obsessed about her email message for four days. I told her again that I was serious about coming home if she wanted me to. This was not an easy decision, having come this far, but I meant it. She told me she was getting used to being on her own and wanted me to finish my hike. I felt a lot better afterwards.

At dawn on Friday pink clouds were visible through the open garage doors while Lone Wolf and Baltimore Jack hustled around getting their gear ready. The trail went up and down a small hill in the woods, crossed a steep pasture, and entered the Catawba Mountain ridge at Beckner Gap, which I had seen the previous day from Dragon's Tooth. The grassy hillside was luminous in the morning sun. I passed Lone Wolf, a big man who carries a huge load and draws a howling wolf's head around his entries in the shelter registers. At the site of the former Boy Scout Shelter, a side trail led down to the spring; several foot-long lizards were sunbathing along the way, their heads toward the trail.

Back on the AT, I stopped to chat with three older hikers, then continued up to McAffee Knob (3,197 feet), a superb overlook. Some other hikers volunteered to take my picture in the standard pose with legs dangling off the overhanging precipice, but I later found that they hadn't depressed the shutter release all the way. Chilly Willy and Kilroy were at the overlook, and we met again later in the day at Tinker Cliffs (3,000 feet), which is one of the great spots on the trail (although everything seems nice when the sun is shining).

Leaving McAffee Knob, the ridge curves to the north, and along the way the trail passes over a series of knobs from which there are successive views of the cliffs getting closer and the ridge turning right toward Daleville. Lunch was spent lounging on the bare rock ledges with Chilly Willy and Kilroy, Hoops (a Nets fan), and Stonehenge. Hiking down the Tinker Mountain ridge, I collected water at Lambert Shelter and met Slip and Trip, a young couple from Columbus, Ohio. We feasted together on three cans of trail magic soda left in a stream by an angel.

Just Walking

Having by this time decided to go all the way to Daleville, I steamed ahead at a fast pace. The trail was good at first, followed by some steep, eroded sections. The weather continued sunny, breezy, and warm all day. It was an endurance hike for the last three hours, through the hairpin turn at Angels Gap, past the enormous graffiti-covered Hay Rock, and finally down to a muddy bottom near Tinker Creek (1,165 feet). On the final leg into town a live opossum was lying on its side in the trail. (Perhaps it was actually playing 'possum – I'm not sure why this is an effective survival tactic, but in any case it seemed better not to mess with a critter with teeth like his.)

I emerged onto U.S. Highway 220, feeling totally spent. A Best Western motel was almost next to the trail, and after 25.5 miles, a personal record, it looked too inviting to pass up. The rest of the day consisted of dinner at the Chinese restaurant across the highway and early bedtime.

Chilly Willy and Kilroy at the Guillotine on Apple Orchard Mountain

Marathon

Friday had been a high energy day owing both to my talk with Sheila and the good weather. On Saturday, heavy rain was predicted, so it was a good opportunity for a zero day at the motel. The night clerk was coming off her shift and gave me a ride to Troutville, where I walked up and down the sidewalk waiting for the post office to open. After picking up the mail drop and trying to hitchhike back to Daleville, no rides were offered for half an hour, and finally I decided to walk the two miles. This would be more than a bit annoying in the workaday world, but here there was no reason to lose my equanimity – nothing special needed to be done soon, except to eat breakfast, a big plate of hash and eggs at the counter of a truck stop near the highway interchange, listening to the conversation of the truck drivers around me.

My Merrill boots had developed a gaping hole that let in water from the puddles we were so often walking through, so I strolled over to the nearby mall and bought a pair of heavier duty Vasque Sundowners from the very good outfitters there. They also had a replacement for the bottom section of the hiking stick I had bent double a few days earlier. Having taken care of that, the middle of the day was occupied with a takeout lunch from the Bojangles BBQ, eaten while watching Roger Clemens lose to the Cubs. Sweet.

I called home around noon and talked to my older son Matt; Greg was at a track meet. After more BBQ for dinner from a different restaurant at the mall I sprawled on the bed watching the movie channel: first "Cabaret" and then "Guys and Dolls." At 11:30 pm Sheila and I had a really nice phone call. There was no internet at the Best Western, so I would have to wait to read the next email she had sent.

Upon leaving the motel on Sunday, light rain and low clouds lingered, so I walked under the umbrella for a while, traversing meadows and crossing the highway in Troutville before mounting the ridge. The new boots seemed OK but the sole was stiffer and therefore more slippery than the Merrills' on smooth rock.

The last stop for the day was Wilson Creek Shelter. Lone Wolf was leaving as I arrived, but he soon returned with a faun(!), probably a few days old, in his arms. As he told the story, the faun tumbled down a steep embankment when its mother bolted, and when she didn't return, he decided to bring it back to the shelter. A bad decision, we all know now. The faun hung around through the night, bleating and waking us up again and again. Unfortunately, it died the next day despite efforts by some of the hikers to revive it. Please don't mess with wildlife.

On Monday, after having listened to the faun all night, I crawled out of my sleeping bag and onto the trail at 6:30 am, feeling a bit groggy at first but soon enjoying the sunny day. The AT crossed the Blue Ridge Parkway several times.

Just Walking

Two indigo buntings, spectacular iridescent blue birds, were perched near the trail, shining in the sun.

I'm one of those people who have an internal juke box that is rarely silent. The indigo bunting has a distinctive "low-low-high-high" song, like the intro to the 60's R&B classic "I Like Bread and Butter," so for the rest of the day that song played in my head.

Moose Munch was on the trail this morning, as well as a new acquaintance, a young guy with a thick reddish-brown beard right out of the Civil War, whose name was Sleepy Floyd. We chatted awhile and caught some rays during a granola break at one of the overlooks. There were views to the Tolkien-esque Peaks of Otter a few miles to the east.

Stopping for lunch at Cove Mountain Shelter, I met Moonshadow and learned she had been at that breakfast at Miss Janet's in Erwin, although we had never talked there. I hiked on ahead and swam at Jenkins Creek in a big eddy. This dip in the cool clear water also helped relieve some pain in my left foot and left shin, which was probably due to the stiffer sole and higher heel of the new boots. However, the boots were also protecting my feet from sharp rocks, of which there are many on the trail in this area, contrary to the shibboleth about Virginia trails being easy.

I reached Bryant Ridge Shelter around 4:30 pm. It was a beautiful new shelter with a loft. A brook out front provided the water supply. 2 Dog Night was there with her two dogs and her mother, who was paying a trail visit. Sleepy Floyd, Moose Munch, Moonshadow, Indigo, Cruiser, and later, Lone Wolf also stopped for the night. We collected wood and had a nice campfire before turning in.

North of Marble Spring

Marathon

The James River

Tuesday was mostly to partly sunny all day, becoming clear by dinnertime. Half an hour from the shelter a small bear was sitting in the ferns by the trail up Floyd Mountain; it ambled off into the woods when it heard me coming. There was more climbing up Apple Orchard Mountain (4,225 feet) and the smaller High Cock Knob. I fiddled with the lacing of my left boot to soothe the metatarsal pain I was having.

Low on water and feeling hot and tired, I pulled into Thunder Hill Shelter for a break; two section hikers were still lying around at noon. Just as I was about to refill my water reservoir their dog waded into the walled-in spring, stirring up the mud, so I went on without refilling, smoke coming out of my ears. Jim from Birmingham passed by again on the way to Marble Spring, where the group camping there for the night included Chilly Willy and Kilroy, Moonshadow, Slip and Trip, Indigo and Cruiser, and a guy who was pulling 30-mile days trying to thru-hike the trail in three months. My tarp and the mosquito net bivy that hangs under it provided a bug-free zone for reading and journaling. It was a warm night.

Waking up at 5 am on Wednesday and unable to go back to sleep, I lowered the cluster of food bags we had stretched between trees the night before, packed up, and left camp at 6 am. It was a beautiful, warm, humid morning with delicious breezes. From the ridge there was a great view down the valley to the west and a little later a panorama of the James River. The trail continued down and across Matt's Creek, past the shelter and onto a mega-footbridge across the James (elevation 678 feet). The bridge was guarded by legions of mosquitoes.

Just Walking

At the highway on the opposite bank I waited in the hot sun for 40 minutes for a hitch to the post office in Big Island and was joined by Hoops, Stonehenge, and Brew before a helpful driver in a pickup truck took us all to town. After claiming our mail drops and repacking our food bags on the front step of the post office, Brew and I walked to an Amoco/grocery store and stopped for lunch at a hot dog stand. We yogi'd a ride back to the trail[13] from a guy who ran a cabinetry shop and liked hikers.

Back on the trail, I walked along a lovely swift stream but didn't swim – I was covering miles again and didn't want to stop so soon after the side trip to Big Island. At the next rest break at John's Hollow Shelter, Moonshadow and a section hiker named Virginia Creeper were there. It was hot and humid, and as we talked I mixed and drank three cups of Tang sitting on the wooden floor,

Pedlar Dam

boots and socks off, my feet stretched out before me.

After lunch there was a grueling 2,000-foot climb in the heat to Big Rocky Row – "grueling" means you feel like gruel afterwards. On the long traverse through pretty woods to Bluff Mountain (3,372 feet) thunder was rumbling and it rained for ten minutes, which felt good; it was surprising to enjoy the rain after grousing about it for weeks. I made it down to Punchbowl Shelter before it started to rain hard. Two section hikers from Gaithersburg, Virginia were there, as well as Virginia Creeper, Moonshadow, and Sleepy Floyd. We cooked in the shelter as the rain fell outside, listening to the frogs in the nearby pond. The bugs were bad all day.

On Thursday morning it was very humid, and I was feeling low on energy, but there was trail magic ahead to give

---

[13] Thru-hikers don't like to beg for food or rides, but we're friendly folks who often strike up conversations with strangers who sometimes make spontaneous offers that are gratefully accepted. This is called "yogi-ing" after the TV cartoon bear.

me a lift. At the road crossing Dan and Judy Williams from Parrott, Virginia, were cooking a complete, deluxe, sit-down, multi-course breakfast for thru-hikers, and it was all good! After breakfast, the AT passed Pedlar Dam, where a huge sheet of water cascaded down a wide spillway; the whole surface of this inclined plane seemed alive as it shimmered in the morning sun. The trail wrapped around the reservoir to Brown Mountain Creek and the eponymous shelter, where I chatted over lunch with Virginia Creeper. He was in his late 60s and was getting in shape for a long hike out west. In the small spring, a resident crayfish ran playfully around the bottom of the pool as I dipped in my water bottle. Having an arthropod trail name myself, I felt an ancient kinship.

It was still hot and sticky after lunch, so I ascended the 2,500-foot climb to Bald Knob (4,100 feet) in small increments of 250 feet with at least a standing blow or a sit-down after each chunk. A lizard with bright blue patches flashed out of sight behind a rock. The climb turned out to be easier than expected, and I made it over and down to Cow Camp Gap Shelter, which is a quarter-mile off the trail, at 4:30 pm. I washed all my clothes in the stream, sponged off and stood around naked while I air dried, and felt a lot better.

Moonshadow arrived a while later, and she was the only other person at the shelter. Before the hike, Moonshadow had worked at an association of regional governments, so she understood land use planning. She was in her twenties, and like many female thru-hikers (and some males), she hikes in a skirt. We talked for a while, and I felt a little bit proud that this woman trusted me enough to stay at this out-of-the-way shelter with a man she didn't know all that well. (It might have been a little different if she had arrived 20 minutes earlier when I was

The trail on Tar Jacket Ridge south of the Priest

Just Walking

walking bare-assed from the brook to the shelter.) My entry in the shelter register described how Dan and Judy must have dosed us with acid, hence the psychedelic sheet of water crawling down the spillway, the dancing crayfish, and the lizard with fluorescent blue markings. I shared my book of Gary Snyder's poetry with Moonshadow, but she preferred his translations of Miyazawa Kenji's poems to his original work.

Another typical thru-hiker moment: realizing too late after leaving the shelter that you had forgotten your food bagging line: thus, Friday morning began. Moonshadow and I hop-scotched a couple of times during the morning as the trail passed over the balds; she was hustling to meet the shuttle to the Dutch Haus hostel. It was an overcast, cool, humid day with some low clouds in the valleys. There was a series of ups and downs along Tar Jacket Ridge, but nothing remarkable.

Later in the day two groups passed on the way to The Priest Shelter, some camp counselors in training, and members of a large family group who were going up to Spy Rock with no raingear while thunder rumbled. The rain began just before the shelter appeared around 4 pm. It was indeed full of the family's stuff as they had warned me. Crouched on the edge of the floor watching it rain, I decided to cook dinner before they returned. When the rain slackened I spent ten minutes tramping around the area searching for a decent campsite and finally put up my tarp in a little thicket nearby.

The group of counselors and two of the family members soon showed up, and I retreated to the mosquito net bivy under my tarp, wriggled into my dry clothes with some contortions, and stayed there rather than join the cramped chaos inside the shelter. It had been a buggy day with a few more black fly bites.

From the Priest

Marathon

The family disappeared sometime before nightfall (I was under the tarp, pitched low, and didn't see them decamp), and the counselors moved into the shelter. Cuddled up to a rock under my ground cloth that was too big to move, I managed to sleep soundly. It's amazing how well a tarp keeps you dry even in steady rain.

Saturday morning was humid. Half a mile beyond the shelter the AT passes over the summit of The Priest (4,063 feet), the last 4,000-footer until Killington in Vermont. The trail was easy but monotonous as it went steeply downhill to the Tye River, 3,000 feet below. After crossing the footbridge the AT regains most of this elevation as it climbs the Three Ridges (3,870 feet). Sweat dripped off me and my energy slowly faded. It felt good to stop every 250 feet for a blow. A new kind of trail magic awaited at the junction with the Har-Mau Trail: a former thru-hiker named Seneca was sitting there reading the day's newspaper, and he had the up-to-date baseball stand-

The Three Ridges

Just Walking

A damp day in Shenandoah National Park

ings (the Red Sox were hanging in there). I climbed up to the South Ridge and ate lunch on the rocks.

Later, at Hanging Rock, a couple of day hikers took my picture and I returned the favor. Seneca was taking a break on Bee Mountain at the other end of the Har-Mau, and he had good news – the shelter was just over the hill. Arriving at Maupin Field Shelter by mid-afternoon, I cleaned up, hung my tarp and sweaty clothes on the bushes to dry, and relaxed on the boards. Hikers named Jason and Sarah stopped for dinner and then went on; two guys named Here's Johnny and Wu stayed for the night. Indiana Slim also stopped by. He was compiling a list of interesting trail names and had a couple hundred already. It is difficult to address someone named Here's Johnny.

I didn't sleep very well – it was warm inside the net bivy, which I was using inside the shelter to keep the bugs off, Wu kept breathing loudly – not an actual snore but just as annoying – and a nest of wasps somewhere kept buzzing every few minutes. No wasps actually appeared, but the sound is enough to wake you up if you're not sure where they are.

The weather was nice on Sunday morning, but it was not destined to last. Light rain started around noon, resulting in poor visibility at the overlooks on Humpback Mountain; nothing new about that. It was warm, so there was no point in using raingear or an umbrella. A trail crew of three women were doing an inventory with a measuring wheel. At a quick late lunch stop at Paul Wolfe Shelter the trail register contained a fanciful account of cannibalism on the trail. I reached Rockfish Gap (1,902 feet) at 4:15 pm, having covered 21 miles. There is a wonderful group of people in Waynesboro who run shuttles into town for the hikers, and one transported me directly to the motel without hitching. Those folks have my everlasting gratitude!

Marathon

○ Imaginary View

Shenandoah National Park to Front Royal VA: [Mile 844.8 to Mile 951.9]

Monday, June 16. Shenandoah is one of the featured attractions on the trail. My family and I had car-camped there a few years before and we were wowed by the views from the ridge down to the verdant farmland in the valley below. Seeing thru-hikers relaxing in back of Big Meadows Lodge was one of the things that helped inspire me to take my own hike and one day be sitting there as a thru-hiker.

I rose early and walked from my motel in Waynesboro down to the laundromat, put all my clothes, except the raingear I was wearing, into a washing machine and crossed the street to the famous Weasie's Restaurant for breakfast. The pancakes were good, but I decided not to go for the stuff-yourself-silly challenge advertised on a wall placard. After breakfast I finished the laundry, donned my regular hiking clothes in a utility closet, and went to the post office and the library for my food drop and email. Greg had sent my summer quilt, so I mailed the 3-season sleeping bag back home in same box. Sheila's email provided food for thought about our relationship, but in a positive way. I purchased some lunch supplies, called one of the shuttle angels for a ride to the trail, and started hiking around 12:30 pm. It was way too late for the 20 miles my itinerary called for.

The terrain in Shenandoah is not extreme, but there are many little ups and downs between the gaps, which are at 2,000 to 3,000 feet, and the high points, which range from 3,000 to 3,800 feet.

It was drizzling for most of the afternoon – poor views but not enough rain even for the umbrella. The day was actually pleasantly atmospheric, as shreds of fog blew across the summit of Bear Den Mountain, and clouds filled the gap beyond it. It dawned on me after a while that my planned destination, Blackrock Hut, is 20 miles from Rockfish Gap, not from the previous shelter, and that it would take until 9 or 10 pm to reach it. Around 8 pm I decided to stealth camp near the Flip Flop Trail junction.

There was a flat but somewhat rocky place to pitch the tarp on top of the ridge as the fog rolled in. I walked the prescribed 100 yards from the campsite and hung a bear bag, which is definitely called for in Shenandoah.

Though the summer solstice was near, it was becoming hard to see in the failing light. There were no trails in the area and few memorable trees to use as landmarks, so it took some care not to forget the location of the bear bag, or, worse, to lose the way back to the tarp. It all worked out, but these preparations left no time to cook before it was completely dark, so dinner for the night was a food bar and some m&ms, and (since it was impossible to find the bear bag in the dark) I put the wrappers in a baggie and stuffed it in the crotch of a tree

Just Walking

away from the tarp, hoping it would not attract visitors. It was undisturbed the next morning.

My routine is to pitch the tarp high enough to sit up beneath it, but as the night grew colder I lowered it to the ground to stay warm. Unfortunately, it was now a bit too low, and by the middle of the night droplets of condensation spattered onto my face every time a raindrop struck the tarp. I climbed out and raised it six inches to allow some ventilation (which is the way it should have been pitched in the first place) and things were fine after that. Even fully dressed in all my spare clothes, though, it was cold under the light quilt, and the rocky site didn't make for a good night's sleep.

On Tuesday, I retrieved my food bag and the baggie of trash, packed up, and hit the trail in raingear. There is not much to say about the day, except that it was an endurance hike in the rain, which continued all day. The rain, wind, and cool temperatures (probably never exceeding 50), all made for potential hypothermia in the second half of June in Virginia. Around noon I walked a half-mile off the trail and down 450 feet of elevation to buy a hot lunch at Loft Mountain Wayside, only to find it closed owing to a power failure caused by a thunderstorm. I returned, grumbling, to the trail and soldiered on. Around 6 pm, feeling myself getting cold, even while hiking steadily in full raingear, I stopped, added an insulating layer, and

Friendly deer next to a Shenandoah mile marker

ate a Snickers. At 7 pm Hightop Hut finally came into view, 24.5 miles from the previous night's campsite.

The day did have some highlights: two wild turkeys, one of which stayed just ahead of me on the trail for a couple hundred yards, moving up twenty yards at a time. The first Shenandoah bear, a small one that jumped out of a tree not far ahead of me, landed with a crash, and disappeared into the underbrush.

Several thru-hikers were already at Hightop, including Morph, Blink-Blink, Sea Eagle, and Odwalla. All of them were trying to stay warm. I cooked and ate quickly and went up to an empty space in the loft, removed wet shirt, shorts, undies, and socks, and put on dry clothes. While climbing down from the loft for something, I rammed my head into a solid beam that served as a lintel across the front of the lean-to; it didn't hurt much but made a resounding boom that made the bystanders wince. When it became obvious that my camp clothes weren't going to be sufficient for warmth, I put on my damp fleece sweater and raingear over them. The quilt (which is the zip-off extra top from the Golite sleeping bag) was simply inadequate for the nighttime temperatures, which must have fallen into the low 40s. Trying to huddle in a fetal position without one's butt sticking out from under the quilt is basically impossible to do. Finally, at 3 am I tried crawling halfway into a large trash bag, which warmed me up a little, in a damp way.

Wednesday was my 56th birthday (the Beatles' "Birthday" was playing in my head all day). I woke up at 5:15 am, damp from the condensation inside my trash bag but no longer chilled to the bone. Judging from the other inhabitants of the shelter, I wasn't the only one who had spent a cold night: some people were wrapped in cocoons made out of their wet tents. I packed quietly and started hiking at 6:10 am. I had lost my warm hat somewhere in the chaos of the shelter but didn't want to fuss around too much and wake up the others.

The weather at the start of the day was overcast, but it began to brighten, and there was an actual glimpse of the sun by 9 am. It was an up-and-down trail, and my body felt as though it had walked a marathon the day before, which was close to the truth. Odwalla and Blink-Blink overtook me, and we talked about hammocks and other gear while walking together for a while.

We pulled into Lewis Campground around 11:30 am and bought lunch at the camp store. We were joined by Supastar and Treebeard (a great name borrowed from *Lord of the Rings*, very appropriate given his size, long beard, and interest in forestry). Lunch was a sandwich and a Ben and Jerry's ice cream bar enjoyed while sitting in the sun (for a change) on the wooden bench outside the store. A tiger swallowtail butterfly perched on the bench next to us.

Going on alone, I made good time up the little hills on the trail as the partly cloudy skies cheered me along. The trail crossed a road and passed an old cemetery, but there were no familiar landmarks from the family driving vacation. I made it to Big Meadows Lodge by 3 pm, having motored 2.4 miles in 45 minutes from Laurel Prong Trail to Milam's Gap.

There were no problems checking in at Big Meadows Lodge. I'm one of those people that always expects my reservation to be lost, although it never happens. Several of the hikers enjoyed a good meal in the dining room accompanied by the featured Virginia wine. Morph was kind enough to bring my hat with him after it turned up in the shelter.

Just Walking

The oddity of the day was a large, pointed, pink egg, maybe two inches in diameter, just lying on the trail near a parkway crossing. Wild turkey? A 5-inch-long Luna moth hung motionless on the side of the lodge, its lime green wings spread on the dark brown surface.

That evening I went to the tap room to sip Wild Turkey and hear a very good musician sing and play folk and pop tunes on guitar and harmonica. The bartender joined him in a passable version of "Me and Bobby McGee." Who should walk in but Nemo, who had gotten off the trail a few days before to skip over a long section she had previously done and continue hiking from Lee, Massachusetts. Talking with her and her boyfriend made it a pleasant evening.

A zero day at the lodge on Thursday began with a hazy view of the valley, but the clouds below us soon returned. Above, it was partly sunny. Morph, who is about my age, and Double Dare, who might be in his thirties, both breakfasted with me in the dining room. Much of the day was spent lounging and reading a great book from the gift shop, *Geology Along the Skyline Drive* by Robert L. Badger, which I left behind as a donation to the lodge's library. It wasn't worth walking the short distance to Blackrock to see the non-existent views. I wrote postcards to friends and family and talked on the phone with my business partner Skip, making plans to meet in Front Royal. Near dinnertime, some of us went down to the bar and watched the weather report on a DC TV station: more rain in the forecast, extending the string of rainy weekends they had been having; since the winter there had only

Finally, a view from Shenandoah

Marathon

Sleepyheads at Pass Mountain Shelter

been a handful on which it didn't rain on either Saturday or Sunday.

On Friday I sat in the lodge's big lounge chatting with Sketch, an architecture student who had just graduated, and we ate breakfast with three other new acquaintances: Martha Graham (a trail name taken from a Triumph motorcycle she once owned), Gazelle, and Hopeful. It began to rain so hard during breakfast that I had to borrow an umbrella to fetch mine from my room.

By the time the rain slackened I had already decided to leave at 10 am regardless of the weather, but it stopped within the first hour of hiking. During lunch at the next lodge, Skyland, a deer just outside the window was also eating lunch, which consisted of most of the leaves of a small mountain laurel bush. The wait staff – European students – complimented me on my blue raingear, which I wore into the dining room.

After lunch, a man and his 13-year-old daughter who had been staying at Big Meadows chatted with me for a while at a picnic table near the Pinnacles. A little later a small bear climbed down a tree maybe 100 feet from the trail and ran away. At the outlook near Mary's Rock, the view of the sunlit valley below opened up for a while, the first distant view in Shenandoah. A medium-sized bear was standing 30 feet from the trail near the lookout; he seemed to be indifferent to my presence, or maybe he was waiting to see if I'd offer a handout. All he got was his picture taken.

Arriving at Pass Mountain Hut at 7:15 pm, I settled in with section hikers from Seattle named Shannon and Blue, thru-hikers Beav and Blaze, and some Boy Scouts. These Shenandoah huts use a system of bear poles to keep your food out of greedy paws. The trick is to raise your food bag on the end of a long pole to one of the hooks at the top of a 12-foot upright, and transfer it to the hook; it would make a great birthday party game for children.

Bear pole hung with food bags

Just Walking

Saturday, June 21, was Naked Hiking Day, a venerable institution, but no one was likely to bare any skin on this cold day with morning showers starting an hour or so out of camp. I had slept well in dry clothes. The day's hike was mostly unremarkable – a few white-clustered lily-like flowers and some red columbines. There were no views, but the trail passed through some nice shady green areas of mature trees and bright short-leaved grass. There were deer along the trail, some of them letting me approach within five feet before shying away.

At Elkwallow Wayside I had a BBQ pork sandwich and their trademark blackberry milkshake while sitting on a ledge in the little gift shop area. The wayside is one of the park's original drive-ins and has no indoor seating. Several motorcycle riders were standing around trying to warm up. It stopped raining after lunch, but the cold weather called for a fleece top under an open rain jacket.

Jim and Molly Denton Shelter

Reaching Gravel Spring Hut at 3 pm, I had a nice chat with a couple from DC who were day hiking; they returned a couple hours later while dinner was cooking on the alcohol stove. A trail angel named Craig paid a visit; his son, Scubaman, was thru-hiking. We talked baseball and football while drinking cans of Budweiser. He left as it started to rain again, and thru-hiker Scott showed up after having done big miles from Big Meadows.

After an early start on Sunday there were glimpses of the sun at first, then increasing clouds, but the day became partly sunny again just after noon when I reached Chester Gap and U.S. Highway 522, which runs into Front Royal. A guy in a beat-up little car picked me up; (hitchhikers love to see those beat-up little cars coming). He told me about some strange animals they keep at the Smithsonian zoological research station just outside town; (the facility was behind a high fence covered with dense poison ivy on the last leg before the highway). Another of the mysteries of the trail.

After checking into a Quality Inn, I did my laundry and had a cheeseburger at the restaurant in an old converted grain mill across the street from the laundromat while my clothes dried. Back at the motel there was time to take a nap and then sit in the sun by the swimming pool – had summer finally arrived? Skip showed up around 6:30 pm. He was the first person from my "regular" life I had seen since mid-April. We went back to the restaurant where I had eaten lunch and had a wonderful dinner together, beginning with a little sippin' whiskey. Our architecture office was breaking up. (Skip is an urban designer and I'm a land use planner.) This news strengthened my tentative decision not to return after the hike to what was left of the office. After Skip left, I watched the Mets blow a lead to the Yankees and fell asleep.

Despite the disappointing weather in Shenandoah, we hikers had remained in good spirits thanks to a measure of self-deprecating humor. And now the sun was shining.

○ Sunshine

Front Royal to Harpers Ferry WV:
[Mile 951.9 to Mile 1005.8]

Monday, June 23. I was up by 6 am, walked downtown, ate breakfast at a little restaurant on Main Street, walked back to the motel and then up the highway to the post office, and finally back to the motel to pack up. It all added up to a couple of miles before even starting the day's hike. After a half-hour of thumbing by the busy road out of town, the father of a former thru-hiker picked me up. Back at the trail, which crosses the highway at 950 feet elevation, I took the advice of a note pinned onto the trail crossing sign and walked along the shoulder to the next gate, bypassing the half-mile-long water-filled trench that this piece of trail had become in the recent rains. I rejoined the AT where it crosses a mowed meadow and enters the woods.

Sunny, sunny, sunny! There were trail magic Cokes at Manassas Gap Shelter. The deck of the Jim and Molly Denton Shelter was a nice spot for lunch. The shelter was new and beautiful, and the privy was also pristine, except for a wolf spider next to the seat. It was so big that at first I thought it was one of those rubber joke spiders, but then it moved. I gently coaxed it out the door with a broom but no longer felt like sitting on that seat. Walking again, I tired after climbing a few hills in the heat but was happy to accept the sun in preference to the rain for a while. Fifteen miles from Front Royal was the shelter called Dick's Dome, whose occupants included Green Turtle, Seabee, Mothman, Stonehenge, and a local kid named Sam who just wanted to see what it was like. We had a nice dinner chat while Green Turtle constructed a Pepsi-can stove with the small tool kit he carries. GT also carries a

Just Walking

rubber stamp and leaves a cartoon turtle with his entries in the shelter registers; I'd been seeing them for weeks.

> Sweating up the hill, then
>   one of earth's great wonders –
>   a cool summer breeze.

Tuesday was just past the solstice, and now that it had become sunny, people were waking up earlier. I rose at 5:20 am and was on the trail at 6 am. It was warm, with clear skies. At U.S. 50 a pinned-up note advertised Doc's BBQ, 0.8 mile down the road. It sounded better than a food bar, and I enjoyed a good eggs-and-bacon breakfast prepared by a lady who reminded me of my late grandmother.

Two stops at shelters during the morning to replenish my water supply were an indication of the amount of sweating I was doing. The big challenge of the day was climbing the seven ridges known as the "Roller Coaster". There was a welcome sign from the "Merry Trail Crew" saying they hoped we'd enjoy the ride. Below this message, someone had written, "Does this mean the mudbowl ride is over?" Although each climb was only about 500 feet, it was hard work in the heat and humidity, but I was determined not to complain. The trail crossed little clear streams at the low points in the roller coaster, and I dunked my head at one of the crossings and then sat down in a pool to cool my posterior. The trail had had many muddy stretches since Front Royal, but as it went on the mud gave way to more rock.

It was only 82 degrees at 5 pm, but it felt worse. We thru-hikers this year had been lucky in one respect – the temperatures had been cool and, apart from the rain, comfortable for hiking, whereas in most years the temperatures in Virginia in June would have been in the 90s.

Bears Den Hostel

Marathon

The final destination for the day was Bear's Den hostel, a beautiful stone mansion run by Potomac Appalachian Trail Club. At the hostel I met Granite (from New Hampshire, naturally), a Red Sox fan with Ted Williams' number 9 on his cap; Journey, whom I'd seen but not met at Big Meadows; and Scubaman, whose father had given me a beer at Gravel Spring a few days before. Seabee was also there. I helped the hostel staff update their reservation book, cooked a frozen pizza in the kitchen for dinner, and lounged in the living room looking at the photos in a coffee table book about the trail. I went downstairs to the bunkroom, talked for a while with the other hikers, and conked out before 9 pm.

On Wednesday Seabee and I got up at 6:30 am. We packed up, trying to not disturb the people still sleeping, and were out the door by 7 am. There was a nice view to the west from the nearby Bear's Den Rocks, a pretty pink haze obscuring the urban sprawl in the distance. The

"1,000 miles!"

Just Walking

Shenandoah River near Harpers Ferry

1000-mile point with large numerals made from stones arranged in the middle of the trail. The payoff for my effort was a steep descent to the wide, beautiful Shenandoah River (elevation 300 feet) with its many staircase rapids. The white blazes were soon crossing the bridge carrying U.S. 340. Ahead was a wooded hillside with a house or two peeking out.

After climbing up a wooded trail on the hillside, first on the AT itself and then on the blue-blazed side trail, a thru-hiker emerges on the pretty campus of a former African American college, now serving as a National Park Service training center. It was a city block from there to the Appalachian Trail Conference headquarters, a major milestone that we had all been looking forward to for a long time. Moose Munch was there talking to Carolina Cruiser, who was making a film about hiking the AT. He took some footage of my boots (which didn't make the cut). The ATC staff took my picture on the porch and

trail went over two more humps in the roller coaster. At Route 7 in Snickers Gap, the wait was a minute or more for a large enough gap to cross the morning commuter traffic headed for DC. The AT climbed the ridge on the opposite side of the gap on a decent rolling path.

At the PATC's beautiful Blackburn Center (1,650 feet), the caretaker offered a blackberry soda that was delivered by her little girl. We chatted on the deck with PATC's trail manager Chris. Heading north, there was a long ridge walk through pretty woods, with some rocky sections and moderate slopes. The trail crossed WV Route 9 and climbed Loudon Heights. I was getting very tired now. Someone had marked the AT's gave me the Polaroid snapshot on which I recorded my trail name, starting date, and other information, and submitted it for entry into the year's hiker album.

I walked up the street to the Hilltop Hotel, registered, and dropped off my pack, and then walked a mile or so in the late afternoon heat to the library in nearby Bolivar, West Virginia, to read and reply to Sheila's email. There were many beautiful old houses along the way, including one that Stonewall Jackson had used as his headquarters after capturing Harpers Ferry. I walked back down to the lower town at the other end of Harpers Ferry, only to find that they roll up the sidewalks at 5 pm. However, the keeper of a local pub that had just closed for the night took pity and let me in for a glass of wine. I crawled back to the hotel (tired, not drunk) and had dinner at the buffet in their dining room with Seabee and a hiker named Tom Grandstaff. We talked in my room until 11.

Thursday morning was very warm, and it turned into another seasonally hot day. I picked up my mail drop at the post office and stopped at the ATC to look at the photo albums. There was a picture of my friend Debbie (Medusa) in the 1996 album. I weighed myself on the scale in the bathroom: 154.5 pounds in my undies – a loss of only 6 pounds, which surprised me.

Among the hikers checking in at the ATC headquarters that morning were Thermo, Journey, Granite, Double Dare, and Scubaman. After a stroll around the historic lower town I visited the excellent "Black Voices" exhibit, where I ran into Treebeard and Supastar. Later, back at the ATC office I talked to a visiting group of young people, aged 11-16, from an environmental camp. I had lunch in the lower town and dinner in a restaurant on the way to Bolivar, where I picked up some things at the 7/11. I went to bed ready to resume my hike in the morning.

View of the Potomac River from the Hilltop Hotel

5
Flyin'

Flyin'

By the time I crossed the Potomac, my body was well hardened to the rigors of long miles, and I was going with the flow. Even better, the sun had come out, and the trail was smooth and relatively level. If you depend on spectacular scenery for motivation, this section of the trail can lead to boredom and a hiker syndrome known as "the long green tunnel." But I had immersed myself in the trail experience (just walking) and was deeper into a state of mind where the walking is an end in itself, so it was a pleasure of sorts to watch the miles go by, like a passenger on a train. The rhythm of walking was always present below my conscious mind, and my endorphins were flowing, providing a mild high that lasted all day.

Had I achieved (bad word) Zen mind? Sorry, it isn't that easy. Thoughts came and went, like clouds drifting with the wind, but they were almost always there.

The walking rhythm gave rise to music deep in my head. It's my belief that human beings fall into two categories:

Jefferson's Rock

those with an internal juke box and those without one. If the reader is wondering what this means, you're one of the people without it, and I can only say it's much like having an annoying song (like "Tomorrow" from the musical *Annie*) stuck in your head and not being able to get it out. Except that for me the music is usually not annoying, just persistent. My internal jukebox tended to include a lot of Bob Dylan, some Rolling Stones, a bit of Muddy Waters, R&B, even C&W. After watching the All-Time Top 100 Country Western Songs special on television in the bar at Big Meadows, Johnny Cash's classic "Ring of Fire" (#4 all-time) was with me for the next three days. (Can you hear those horns?)

The music running through my head would stop when I stopped for a rest, and then the same song would resume when I began walking again. It was diverting and entertaining, but sometimes what I wanted was some quiet. This could be achieved by concentrating on my breath going in and out in synchrony with my steps, and then there was a quiet spell of just passing through the space and natural sounds of the woods until thoughts crept back in and the music returned to accompany the rhythm of the hike.

Crossing State Lines
Harpers Ferry WV to Quarry Gap PA: [Mile 1,005.8 to Mile 1,067.5]

Friday, June 27. I checked out of the hotel and started hiking at 9 am. On

105

Just Walking

Leaving Harpers Ferry

the way out of Harpers Ferry, the AT passes (Thomas) Jefferson's Rock, then descends through the lower town and across a footbridge into Maryland. It was a warm, sunny, humid morning as I walked the pretty Chesapeake and Ohio Canal towpath along the Potomac shore. The river was moving a huge amount of water past me.

The trail departed from the towpath and climbed 700 feet up the steep end of South Mountain ridge. On top it was soft, wide, and easy and the weather had become cooler, drier, and breezy by lunchtime. I ate by the side of the trail.

In the afternoon the trail passed some interesting Civil War exhibits in Fox Gap and Crampton Gap (950 feet). There

The Potomac flows by

were important skirmishes fought in these gaps on the day before the battle of Antietam in nearby Sharpsburg, one of the biggest mutual slaughters of all time. (I had visited the battlefield a few years before. It is not much changed from 1862.) There was also a huge, bizarre-looking monument dedicated to Civil War newspaper correspondents, a sort of asymmetrical triumphal arch fashioned from red and brown sandstone. Face, Blaze, and I contemplated it as we sipped Cokes from the vending machine at the state park.

Several of us camped at Dahlgren Campground: Blink Blink, Face and Blaze, Seabee, Tom Grandstaff, Mountain Jack,

Civil War correspondents monument

Double Dare, Supastar, and Treebeard. A 60-ish guy named Stripe struck up an acquaintance; he had grown up in South Boston and now lived in Hyde Park, another Boston neighborhood. We also met a man just starting a flip-flop[14] thru-hike, whom we named Fizz after his can of soda overflowed.

Dahlgren has a large open camping area in which we set up our tents in two rows. It also has a bathhouse with electric lights and free hot showers, courtesy of the state of Maryland. After dinner Mountain Jack called us all to come over and look at the beautiful collection of large moths – Cecropias and others I couldn't identify – that had gathered on the window screens of the building. Mountain Jack is a big man in his sixties who enjoys talking about wildlife and plants along the trail. He always had something interesting to say.

On Saturday there was no dew on my tarp. I awoke early, showered, packed, and started hiking at 7:20 am. Mountain Jack's moth exhibit was still on the bathroom window. Blink Blink was at the (original) Washington Monument, a couple of miles into the day's hike; it is a sort of stone beehive on top of a hill. She was formerly a Capitol Hill staffer for Senator Max Cleland and looked to be in her 30s.

The AT soon crossed I-70, which my family and I had driven on vacation

Above the sprawling plain

---

[14] A flip-flop starts somewhere in the middle of the trail, proceeds to one end and then jumps back to finish the other half, in either direction.

Just Walking

several years before. It was a lovely day – no clouds except some high cirrus. Black Rock provided a lookout to a wide view of the plains of Maryland. I stopped for conversation with three folks working on a PATC trail crew and hiked for a while with Stripe. He is the retired head of the Boston regional office of the U.S. Department of Health and Human Services; he sported a white crew cut and had the gift of gab, a great hiking companion. Fizz came up behind us as we arrived at Warner Gap, where Hoops and his girlfriend were dispensing trail magic. After a beer and a candy bar each, we went on up the last hill of the day, discussing Boston sports teams, and then down the side trail to Devil's Racecourse Shelter. At the shelter I met thru-hiker Ace (a land use planner from Columbus, Ohio), Lightbright, a medical student from Vermont, and section hiker Patti, from Toledo.

Nearly everyone was out of bed before me on Sunday, but we stragglers still managed to be back on the trail by 7 am. A fellow at High Rock took my picture against a panoramic background of Maryland farms and sprawl development. There is a sign there saying that hang-gliders must obtain permission from the Secret Service; it seems the underground Pentagon (and perhaps Dick Cheney's bunker) was over on the next ridge. Batman, take notice!

Before long, I entered Pennsylvania with a whoop and a holler and a chorus of "*Pennsylvania,*" sung to the tune of "*Oklahoma*" ("…And the girls look cute/In their birthday suits/And the wind comes whistlin' through the piiiines…") A sign identified the actual Mason-Dixon Line (elevation 1,250 feet according to the Data Book). It was a pleasant day, sunny and not too humid. The trail passed through dry woods over rolling hills, with a few rocky sections and some neat outcrops called the Chimney Rocks

Quarry Gap Shelter

on the long flat top of Rocky Mountain (2,000 feet).

Ace and I ate lunch at Antietam Shelter with two PATC trail maintainers. Jim Stauch, the volunteer overseer of the section north of Route 30, talked me into going to Caledonia State Park for a swim and then on to Quarry Gap Shelter for the night. It was a long push to Caledonia, but the plunge into the cool, clear water of a real swimming pool was well worth it. After an ice cream cone at the snack bar and a nice phone call with Matt and Sheila, I went on to the shelter much refreshed.

Quarry Gap is a beautiful, newly reconstructed shelter with a breezeway dining area between two sleeping pavilions (one reserved for snorers), a landscaped stream flowing in a gravel-lined channel out front, hanging plants, and solar path lights. Jim Stauch showed up around dinnertime to chat with Thermo and me while we watched the lights come on. Jim was the designer of the rebuilt shelter and the head of its construction crew. Quarry Gap was his pride and joy, and he could explain every design detail. A man and his two sons showed up around 9 pm as we were turning in.

○ Ridge Walking
Quarry Gap to Port Clinton:
[Mile 1,067.5 to Mile 1,199.9]

Monday, June 30. We were up and out of Quarry Gap Shelter by 8 am. (Thinking back on it, I realize that although not every day on the trail was wonderful, there was never a day when I hung around, not really wanting to hike.) The sky was white with a high, thin overcast, though the sun shone through gaps in the clouds and was bright enough to make shadows for most of the day.

It was an easy day of ridge walking typical of the Pennsylvania section of the AT south of Port Clinton: good trail that runs along relatively level ridges for miles and miles at elevations between 1,200 and 2,000 feet, with just a few rocky sections. This topography and

Thermo

Pine Grove Furnace

Just Walking

Walking into Boiling Springs

the preceding day's long hike made for a leisurely pace and several lengthy rest stops. I spent an hour before lunch at Birch Run Shelter shooting the breeze with Thermo and Fizz; this was one of those unhurried, pleasant conversations where you just enjoy the moment. Thermo is a quiet guy who had been hiking with me on and off since the Nahantahalas. He had taken some awesome bike trips, including an 11,000-miler to Alaska from his home in Frankfort, Kentucky. He liked to buy peanut butter, jelly, and sliced bread and make sandwiches along the trail.

We were about to start hiking again when a pair of slackers happened by – it was Chris and Meredith, whom I had last seen in Georgia! We had a nice chat and traded some news about other hikers, including Tipperary, Jug, and Dale and Emily (who had had to leave the trail because of an injury). Lunch was enjoyed sitting on the ground next to the trail surrounded by mountain laurel and ripening blueberries.

Fizz and I walked together in the afternoon. We made it into Tom's Run Shelter at 3 pm. I took a nap before dinner. Stripe, Ace, Mountain Jack, and Lightbright stopped for short or long rest breaks and then went on. Thermo, Fizz and I stayed the night.

Tuesday was another lovely day, not too humid, with a bright blue sky. I walked alone to Pine Grove Furnace State Park, passing the historic Iron Masters' hostel and the stone furnace for which the park is named. No one was around as I passed the lake and walked up the trail to Piney Mountain Ridge. There it was: the halfway sign – only 1,086 miles to go.[15] A fellow in his 60s happened by and told

---

[15] The Appalachian Trail's length changes from year to year as sections are relocated. The mileage sign is updated periodically, but its location remains unchanged.

me that "the hurricane in the Gulf of Mexico wasn't expected to reach us." (I was oblivious to the fact that there was a hurricane.) He also said that they had closed the trails on Mt. Katahdin due to excess heat(!), after a hiker had died, apparently from heat stroke. Was this prudence or paternalism?

At the Green Mountain General Store, Thermo and I both ate the foolish half gallon of ice cream (chocolate peanut butter for me) that is traditional at the halfway point. This store is a competitor for the half-way honors with the one in the state park. Jim Stauch had convinced us to patronize it to keep the original half-way challenge sponsor from jacking up prices. I felt overloaded for the rest of the afternoon.

Going on, we hiked over a mini-rollercoaster with a neat rock maze on top of the first hill. We passed Alec Kennedy Shelter and Center Point Knob and hiked down through farm fields toward the village of Boiling Springs (elevation 500 feet). It was a nice opportunity to catch the breeze, the view, and the blue sky on the ridge above town. Walking through those planted fields was great, a totally different kind of landscape from the woods and even the cow pastures we had seen in Virginia. Fizz was visible about 200 yards ahead of me as the trail passed rows of corn, beans, and whatever.

Thermo, Fizz, Lightbright, and I camped in a mowed grass campsite. I set up my tarp in a little thicket, then we all walked into town.

Boiling Springs is a beautiful village with a row of historic houses and a clear pond right in the center supplied by the (cool) water visibly "boiling" up from the spring. Fizz and I had a good dinner at the local tavern. He is a journalist and had been editing a newspaper in Virginia near DC. We walked back to

Cumberland Valley farm

Just Walking

Boiling Springs village

the campsite, which was next to the railroad tracks. Freight trains passed within 25 feet of our tents. It was fun to hear a whistle miles away and then listen as the train approached and finally went roaring by. Luckily there was no road crossing near the campsite or the trains would have blown their stentorian whistles right next to us.

I woke up around 4 am, lay awake, and finally decided to get up around 5 am. A pink sky arched over the farm fields. I packed up, walked into Boiling Springs, and sat by the pond before breakfast. Fizz came along after a while and sat with me in the morning stillness. After breakfast at a local pastry shop, I stopped at the post office and the convenience store to restock for the next leg of the hike, and then sat in front of the ATC branch office organizing my food bag on a bench.

I finally started walking out of town at 9:30 am on what was becoming a sunny, hazy and warm morning. The trail followed wooded hedgerows between farm fields for much of the way across the wide, flat Cumberland Valley. Crossing over the Pennsylvania Turnpike, seven miles into the day's journey, it was hot and more hazy, and I was tired. It helped to dowse my head under the spigot at the ATC farm where the trail passes over Conodoguinet Creek. It was at this point that Jug walked in. He had been off the trail a couple of times to replenish his bankroll but was keeping up by carrying little and walking long miles every day. True to his trail name, he had a plastic gallon milk jug full of water in his hand.

I pushed on to Darlington Shelter, up on Blue Mountain ridge, and stopped there for the night. Despite a threat of thunder no rain ensued. Ace, Stripe, and I sat around and talked about city planning. Jug was there, and so was Lion King, who took down his hair to display a golden mane when I asked about his

Hay bales

Flyin'

trailname. He was making a video of his second thru-hike and carried a fearsome pack weight, even for a big man. Lion King was also a cornucopia of definitive opinions about every subject from worthy musicians to the best way to dispose of tea bags. Not that I disliked him, but the difference between us was summed up in our trail names.

A group of thru-hikers arrived around 8:30 am, including Jenn, Last Minute, Willow, Tank, Mothman, and Mountain Jack. Ace, Stripe, Jack, and I went to bed around 9 pm and listened to the conversation of the other folks until we fell asleep.

On Thursday we early birds rose together and were on the trail shortly after 6 am. It had rained during the night and the landscape was damp and foggy in spots. We walked down and across a valley, passing through a hay field studded with huge bales. We saw a very large bird (an eagle?) take off. We walked up Cove Mountain ridge and pushed for

Inside the Doyle Hotel bar

Duncannon without stopping, pursued by hungry mosquitoes. This was the first bad mosquito attack since the James River, thanks to the cool rainy weather through Virginia. The sun had burned through the damp haze by the time we came to the Hawk Rock overlook, 800 feet above Duncannon.

The three of us walked down the steep trail into town and went straight to the Doyle Hotel bar for an excellent breakfast of omelets and draft Rolling Rock, which is a great light (not "Lite") lager that is better on tap than in bottles, and better still if you've been hiking for days. You enter the hotel through the bar, which has nine stools, three big tables, and the usual array of beer signs and regalia. The rooms upstairs are funky but clean, and there are two bathrooms per floor. My room was 8 by 12 feet with cracked plaster and no screens on the windows. I stretched my clothesline across its diagonal.

I showered, did the laundry, walked around town, and then returned to my room and napped. I ate Hoppin' John (black-eyed peas stewed with ham hocks) for dinner in the bar and talked for a while with Oopala, a thru-hiker in his 30s from Alaska. In addition to the guys I hiked in with, the guests at the Doyle included Lightbright, Mothman, Fizz, and Mountain Jack, as well as Mr. Pumpy and Very Small Animal, whom I had last seen at Miss Janet's place in Erwin.

Just Walking

After dinner Ace, Stripe, Fizz, and I walked down the main street to an ice cream stand, enjoying the old houses, the day lilies, and the summer heat. I ordered a Moose Tracks cone on the advice of a woman in one of the family groups sitting at the picnic tables out front.

We returned to the Doyle to catch a set by local singer/guitarist Sue Grace while some of the local denizens of the bar whooped it up. Audience response peaked at the lines "If the river was whiskey and I was a duck/ I'd swim to the bottom and never come up." It was good fun and good music too. Bedtime was at 10 pm to get some rest for the next day's hike.

On Friday July 4, I awoke around 5 am, packed up, and went to the restaurant across the street for breakfast – pancakes, sausage, and coffee at the counter while working guys down the line discussed fixing a "big-assed generator" at the local nursing home. The forecasted high was

The Susquehanna at dawn

95 degrees. I took some early morning pictures of the Susquehanna River with the sun rising then went back across the street to check my email at the Doyle. Some customers were already at the bar when I left.

The day's hike began at 8:20 am – down High Street past a row of houses to the Clarks Ferry Bridge (elevation 380 feet). I ascended Peters Mountain, as the next ridge is called, moving slowly. The trail stays pretty level at 1,300 to 1,400 feet. There's a nice view back to Duncannon across the river. I was idly thinking about the good times I was leaving behind and wondering about what was ahead.

At a pipeline crossing, you could see downriver to the historic stone bridge at Harrisburg that was there when Robert E. Lee's army passed through. I collected water and took a breather at Clarks Ferry Shelter with Oopala. Afterwards, I walked alone along the ridge, stopping at Route 225 and at Table Rock, which had a big view to the south and an indigo bunting to boot. Someone in Duncannon had told me that Bounce fabric softener sheets repel mosquitoes, so I hung a sheet from my backpack to see if it works. Results of the experiment: it doesn't have much effect on the bugs, but it sure makes you smell fresh!

It was a nice day with some cumulus castellanus forming in the mostly blue sky. These cloudscapes are one of the joys of ridge walking. I reached Peters Mountain Shelter at 2:30 pm and sat around talking with Jug, Oopala, and Lion King, who showed us some video he had taken of a big diamondback rattlesnake at the spring I had visited earlier in the day.

Jug and Lion King moved on to attend a party at the next gap that they had been invited to. I went down to the spring, which was 300 vertical feet below us, carrying as many of the shelter's water jugs as I thought I could handle and labored back up the stone steps with several liters of water.

Two weekend hikers showed up later in the day, and we sat talking in the still afternoon heat. One of them was in his mid-twenties and was an experienced hiker but a babe in the woods when it came to life in general. He howled with disbelief when we told him how much it cost to pay the rent and buy health insurance in Boston. There was no discernible breeze in the shelter, so I spread my ground cloth under the trees and slept in my net bivy.

I slept pretty well in fact. In the morning I rolled up the bivy on my ground cloth, packed, ate some granola, and was back on the trail at 7:30 am. It was Saturday, warm and humid but not as hot as the day before. After a solitary lunch alone on Sharp Mountain, the next ridge, there were some rocky stretches, but they were not too bad, and the trail continued to run quite level.

The Pennsylvania maps are excellent; (Bill Bryson, who complained about them, must have used an earlier set). They show contours, have profiles that seem accurate, and denote views and other points of interest. I had been wondering about one of these points labeled "The General". Was it a giant tree? A rock formation? After a one-mile side trip to investigate, it turned out to be a huge abandoned steam shovel used for strip mining coal and left to rust in the woods. Worth a one-mile detour, I'd say. Returning to the AT, I had a good look at a hooded warbler, which required no detour at all.

The trail passed through an abandoned mining village, and coal was evident on the trail and in old piles near Rausch Gap Shelter. Before leaving for the hike, I had noted in the Data Book the rock formations the trail would be passing

Just Walking

The General

through, based on the excellent *Underfoot: a Geologic Guide to the Appalachian Trail* by V. Collins Chew. This point in the trail marked the advance from the very old Pre-Cambrian rock in Georgia and Virginia to a unique bit of exposed Pennsylvanian era strata, dating from the "Age of Ferns".

I missed the side trail to the shelter owing to a misplaced sign, a hard-to-see blue blaze, and an inattentive attitude. It cost an extra half-mile, but I finally made it. A high school Spanish teacher and his father, out for a weekend hike, were in the shelter. Rausch Gap has a stainless steel trough that captures the water trickling from a spring out front and makes it easy to fill your water bottle. Oopala and Latecomer arrived and camped nearby. One of the weekend hikers from the day before also camped near the shelter, and we spent more time talking.

My shelter mates left before I rose at 6 am on Sunday. During the previous day I had developed a little blister on the second toe of my left foot, so I cut a little donut of mole foam to protect it, and secured everything with a strip of duct tape from the supply I had wrapped around my umbrella handle. I left around 8 am. A man and his young sons who were bike-camping nearby said they had seen a bear near the shelter.

I walked out of the woods and into the meadows near Swatara Gap (480 feet). A black-throated green warbler sang, and another warbler replied with a rising song like a northern parula's but without the drop in pitch at the end. I crossed the pretty historic iron bridge at the gap and finally stopped at William Penn Shelter for lunch with Latecomer.

Some sections of the trail were smooth, and others were total rock fields with difficult footing, a sample of things to come. I had planned to go to Hertlein Shelter for the night but decided to stop instead at the 501 Shelter, so-called because it is a tenth of a mile from Highway 501. The shelter has a solar-heated cold shower, which I used first

Historic bridge in Swatara Gap

with my clothes on, then without. The cold water felt fine. There were several thru-hikers from Alabama at the shelter. I used my cell phone to order pizza, and two of us walked down to the highway to meet the delivery guy. We spent the evening BS-ing.

On Monday I awoke before 5 am, packed by feel in the semi-darkness and left the shelter at 5:20 am, headed for Port Clinton and a bus ride home. When I reached Hertlein Shelter, two and a half hours later, Thermo was camped by the spring. It was cooler than the day before,

Just Walking

> **About Boots**
>
> Your feet are your fortune on a long distance hike. You also have to pick them up approximately 4 million times between Georgia and Maine. Like most gear decisions, it's a matter of weight versus performance. I have weak ankles that I've rolled a few times while hiking, so it's boots for me. After trying and replacing some medium weight Merrills, I found that I needed a heavier boot to protect my feet from the sharp rocks that were sticking up all over the trail in Virginia, not to mention the infamous Pennsylvania rocks. Boots weigh 1.6 pounds each, so that's a total of 6.5 million pounds lifted step-by-step over the length of the trail. You also need to realize that boots last around 700 to 1000 miles, so you will probably need three pairs to complete the trail, as I did. Many thru hikers these days are choosing footwear that is lighter (and cheaper), which is to say, sneakers. Athletic shoes weigh half of what boots do, and they are designed to cushion your feet from shocks and sharp objects stabbing at you. If you have good strong ankles, you may well decide to choose sneakers. The real disadvantage to athletic shoes is that they're cut low and let in the water and ooze when you step in a mud puddle, so you're less likely to follow the leave-no-trace rule of walking right through the center of the puddle.

View from the Pinnacle

but very humid. Not much climbing was in the itinerary. Sunlight filtered through the thin overcast and gave the woods a pale green aura. The trail traversed both rock fields and sections of good footing.

It was mostly an endurance day. I stirred up a flock of large ground birds with reddish backs and broad fan tails (grouse?). Lion King passed me heading south for the day; he had left a rattlesnake warning note on the trail but the snake was gone by the time I happened by. With three miles to go, it started storming – the first real rain hard enough to demand an umbrella since the day before Front Royal, six weeks before! The trail descended into Port Clinton on steep trail but with good footing and some stairs to make it easier.

The Port Clinton Hotel was closed (because it was Monday – go figure) so I joined Sassafras and her husband Bump on the deck next to Union House B&B, waiting for the staff to show up and open the doors at 5 pm. In the meantime I had a beer and shelled peanuts with Wayne, a house painter who was working on the building. He told me about losing his driver's license owing to a DUI conviction but was unrepentant and spent the evening drinking in the bar.

I registered when they opened and took a shower in a tiny basement alcove and later enjoyed a good dinner with some decent homemade wine being offered by the owner, Hermy. After dinner I chatted with Sassafras and Bump; he manages the Portland, Maine, Civic Center. We were joined by their friend Mountain Butterfly. I went to bed early, having walked nearly 24 miles, happy to have saved a day, which I would spend at home.

I awoke at 3:30 am Tuesday and couldn't go back to sleep. This appeared to be part of a pattern: the same thing happened at Fontana, Hot Springs, Damascus, and Pearisburg and may have had something to do with sleeping in a bed instead of on a comfortable shelter floor or the ground.

At 6 am I retrieved my pack from the basement storage room and walked out the back door and down the street to the Peanut Store (the local candy shop) to catch the bus to Boston via New York City. At the bus stop an older gentleman who lived next door came by for a chat. On the bus, I made a to-do list for my visit home and updated my journal. It was nifty in a way to come off the trail and to emerge a couple hours later from the Port Authority Bus Terminal onto 8th Avenue in Manhattan.

I arrived home late in the afternoon, a world away from the trail. Riding the MBTA Green Line from the Riverside bus station to my regular stop and walking home from there, it felt like any workday walk home, except for the weight on my back. I spent the week buying new Garmont boots, a Granite Gear Ozone Nimbus backpack, which I hoped would be kinder to my shoulders than my Golite pack had been, and food for the second half of the hike.

My long hair and beard made it even harder for Sheila to connect with me, and she had not completely forgiven me for absenting myself for three months. Although we did talk, she wouldn't share a bed with me, so I slept in the spare room. On Friday I drove to Becket, Massachusetts, to spend the weekend with my 15 year old son Greg at his summer camp, where he was part of a crew building a new cabin. The new look was not a problem for him, and we had a great time and were both teary-eyed when I left for home on Sunday.

○ Pennsylvania Rocks
   Port Clinton to the Delaware River:
   [Mile 1,199.9 to Mile 1,276.4]

Monday, July 14. I left home on foot, took the "T" to the bus station, and arrived in Manhattan around 6 pm. A second bus to Reading, Pennsylvania, arrived there just in time for me to catch the last bus to Port Clinton. I walked through the door of the Union House B&B just before 10 pm, when they close.

Just Walking

The next morning there was an excellent breakfast at the B&B, shared with Double Dare and Duff – eggs, potatoes, peppers and onions. I was back on the trail at 9:10 am. It felt like a normal hiking day, with no disorientation from having taken a week off. The new pack felt pretty good – still some shoulder cramping, but not bad considering a load that included a full food resupply and two liters of water. The new boots also felt good, except for a bruise on my left ankle where the stiff collar was pressing against my shin on steep uphills.

There were great overlooks at Pulpit Rock (1,582 feet) and the Pinnacle, from both of which you can see the ridge descending to rich green farmland and wood lots below. There were many rock-strewn stretches on the trail, but none of them was too bad yet. A male-female pair of scarlet tanagers was perched by the trail: the male is bright red and the female is yellow. I hooked up with Double Dare at Gold Spring, and we walked the last two miles of trail together to Eckville Shelter, which is 3/10 mile off the trail. The stretch of trail before the road was on a bull-dozed roadbed, a startling and unaesthetic change from the narrow footpath through the woods.

Eckville Shelter is run by three-time thru-hiker Lazee and is located behind his house. He has a list of rules that some find irksome, but, hey, it's his back yard. Among the hikers at the shelter that night were Blueberry and Pinot, Moose Munch, T Bird, Loser, Charity, 2-Dog Night, Moxie, Spin, and Cheesecake. The sky was lovely and clear as the sun set. Loser was joined by friends who live nearby and brought guitars to join with him and T-Bird in singing and playing. Someone pointed out that this was a night we would all remember and feel nostalgic about some day, and it was truly a great evening. Sadly, Blueberry and Pinot announced that they had not been enjoying the hike for a while and had decided to leave the trail.

Wednesday morning was very humid and cloudy. The trail quickly mounted the main ridge of Blue Mountain, which ranges from 1,360 to 1,560 feet, essentially a level ridge. There were very rocky stretches as well as rock piles, which are actually easier on the feet because you can hop from one large rock to the next. Beyond Allentown Shelter the trail was seriously painful, studded with closely spaced sharp cobbles of fractured

The folks at Eckville Shelter

quartzite. Even the stiff soles of my Garmonts weren't enough foot protection on this. As Wingfoot says about this section in his trail guide, you can't step between the stones and you hate to step on them.

I was hot, and my feet were still in pain as I reached Route 309, where a woman was waiting to rendezvous with her hiking partner. She gave me a Gatorade, which tasted like the nectar of the gods just then. Charity, Cheesecake, and Spin came along, and we rested for a spell on the porch of a nearby restaurant that has an outside spigot hikers may use to fill their water containers. I felt better on the next leg of the trail. There were interesting scrambles at Knife's Edge and on Bake Oven Knob, which had another terrific panoramic view of the patchwork quilt of farmland below. The Pennsylvania section of the trail is exactly what Earl Shaffer meant by the "long, green tunnel", but I found these views out to open farmland especially beautiful.

Charity, Double Dare, Karma, and I camped at Bake Oven Knob Shelter. We commiserated about the state of our feet and discussed the painful trek awaiting us tomorrow. It was a long hike to the shelter's spring, which was down the ridge on a long, sparsely marked side path that took some care to follow. When you're tired and have sore feet, the final indignity would be getting lost on the way to the spring.

Pennsylvania rocks

It was clear and dry on Thursday morning. I was up and out by 5:40 am, planning to do a 24-miler. I filled up on water at Outerbridge Shelter, which had a lovely, cold spring with ample flow. There were blueberries on the ridge above the shelter that I snacked on as I walked. The trail crossed the Lehigh River on the highway bridge (elevation 380 feet) to the foot of a steep escarpment rising to 1,485 feet. I climbed the talus slope and reddish-brown ledges, which included a challenging scramble reminiscent of some White Mountain trails – it was the highlight of the day. (A scramble is just a steep rocky section where you need to use your hands to climb up – this was the first one since Albert Mountain in North Carolina.)

A nice breeze was blowing at the top and the landscape had a sort of above-treeline look at first. The trail then followed a gravel road though a desolate area that had been devastated by zinc pollution from the former smelter in the gap. There were a few living trees

Just Walking

Scramble above Lehigh Gap

along the road and a sea of bare rocks and dead trees on either side, with some hazy views down to the valley. I was expecting Mel Gibson to show up in his leathers carrying a sawed-off shotgun as he did in *Road Warrior*. I ate lunch in the shade of one of the living trees, enjoying the sunny day and odd landscape. A few miles later there was a less extreme climb out of Little Gap (elevation 1,100 feet), where I stopped for a rest and met Stinger.

Pushing on and resting every hour-and-a-half, I talked to Stinger again at a break and met Moose Munch, Beav, and Blaze at Smith Gap. The last three miles were tough, the trail carpeted with small, sharp, painful daggers of quartzite. I reached Leroy Smith Shelter at 5:25 pm and was joined by Stinger, Doc, Llama, their dog Coy, Green Turtle, and two others.

I left the shelter at 7:30 am on Friday, but went down to the spring for water and didn't started hiking until 8 am. The moon had been out at 4 am, but a big raft of gray clouds had come to cover the sky. There were light sprinkles a couple of times before I reached the next shelter for a break. The going was rocky, and there was a long stretch of trail with no landmarks until the Wolf Rocks, which called for some ledge walking.

I had seen five black bears by this time, the last one back in Shenandoah, and the trail was approaching northwest

Flyin'

New Jersey, which is said to have more bears per square mile than anywhere else on the trail, Shenandoah included. On a sparsely wooded ridge, I heard crashing in the woods to my left and turned to see two medium sized bears, probably one-year-olds, galloping parallel to the trail at an unbelievable speed. They seemed to be running in a straight line, penetrating the underbrush as though it wasn't there. I held my breath until they passed, crossed the trail fifty yards ahead of me, and disappeared. Believe me, there is no way you can outrun a bear, so it's a good thing they don't often want to mess with people.

I had arrived at Kirkridge Shelter by 2:30 pm and spent the afternoon talking with Big Wing – an interesting fellow in his 50s who had worked as a hunting guide; he is fluent in Chinese and spent his time in the Navy hanging out in a radio shack in the Formosa Strait eavesdropping on communications from the People's Republic. We were joined by Doc, Llama, Coy, T-Bird, Mr. Pumpy, and Wave. T-Bird and Wave played the guitar and sang. Mr. Pumpy and I discussed old films and recalled favorite scenes from Hitchcock's films, like the great plunging closeup in *Notorious* in which Ingrid Bergman passes Cary Grant the key to the wine cellar where uranium is being hidden by the Nazis. There really is more than gear talk on the trail.

Last to arrive was Anishnabe, a superfast woman thru-hiker who had left Springer on May 11 and had walked from Palmerton to Kirkridge Shelter in 11 hours, which is no mean feat. Coy settled in to cuddle with us for a while and then left to join his human companions in their tent.

We were all feeling pleasantly tired and

Wasteland

Just Walking

content when we turned in, but the evening was not over yet. Kirkridge Shelter faces an unobstructed open vista to the next parallel ridge, and we watched an awesome thunderstorm in the distance. Again and again glowing red tubes jumped from the clouds to the ground on the distant ridge as lighting struck. As if this wasn't enough of a light show, there were several enormous cloud-to-cloud discharges much closer to us. These immense electric arcs traveled horizontally at eye level above the valley and must have been at least a mile long.

I left the shelter at 6:40 am on Saturday morning. The rocks weren't so bad, the weather was good, and the sun, which had just risen, filled the fields below the ridge with warm light and long shadows. From Mount Minsi there were nice views of the Delaware River, one of the big milestones of a thru-hike. The trail went down through rhododendron tunnels and hemlock glades, across a creek and past a lotus-covered pond to Delaware Water Gap. On the way I could see boats on the river, and cars on the highway below. The highway din became increasingly audible as the trail descended.

Delaware Water Gap is a lovely little village. A little restaurant called the Trail's End Café had a breakfast menu that included eggs and pepperoni; Ace and Karma were sitting at another table. I picked up my mail drop at the post office and repacked at a table next to the local church that operates a hiker hostel – God bless them. After lunch with Big Wing at the Trail's End, I resumed hiking at 1 pm.

Early morning view from the ridge

In the Garden
Delaware River to the New York State Line:
[Mile 1,276.4 to Mile 1,350]

Saturday, July 19, 1 pm. The AT crosses the Delaware River on the highway bridge (elevation 350 feet) next to traffic and a bustling picnic area. It passes under Interstate 80 and then follows a steadily rising wide path into the woods on the New Jersey side. An older gentleman was harvesting oyster mushrooms from a fallen tree trunk. The ferns along the trail through the woods were a brilliant emerald green. There were many day hikers on the trail, and many of them stopped to say hello.

The trail soon reached Sunfish Pond (1,382 feet) – a National Natural Landmark. Giant tadpoles and many fish were visible in the clear water. It was still a beautiful day, sunny with some fair weather cumulus. Spin and I swam in the pond while Cheesecake looked on. It was a breach of the rules, but one I was told the rangers wink at. I dried off with my bandanna (who needs a towel?) and resumed hiking. At one point along the edge of the pond there was a sort of environmental artwork of tall skinny cairns assembled from carefully selected shoreline rocks. The trail left the pond and climbed gradually to Mount Mohican, as the ridge is called in New Jersey.

The top of the ridge was open, with lovely views to both sides: the Delaware River and distant mountains just visible northwest. This was one of those stretches where the skyscape was as beautiful as the landscape, and the blue of the sky was reflected in the river and ponds below. In the east, there are not many places where you can see from horizon to horizon, but this is one of them. I caught up to Cheesecake and Spin who were taking pictures of a large bear eating blueberries less than 30 feet from the trail; the bear seemed indifferent to the people standing around watching. The sharp rocks were bad again in this stretch.

Ferns along the trail in New Jersey

Just Walking

Environmental artwork at Sunfish Pond

I made it to Camp Road at 6 pm, walked the quarter-mile to the Appalachian Mountain Club's Mohican Outdoor Center, cleaned up and did some laundry in the shower, hung up the damp clothes, cooked, and ate. A patch of skin on my left heel had peeled off, so I put a J&J Compeed pad on it. Mello Yello was there with Constant Motion, who was resting a sprained ankle. Later, local musicians performed in the lodge. I listened with Ace and others. A trail angel even furnished beer.

I slept alone in the front bunk room. Rising at 5:30 am, I was back on the AT by 6:45 am. It was dry and cloudless until late morning. There were nice views from the ridge and from the Catfish Fire Tower (1,565 feet at its base) where I met Chicken Legs and CC. They had slept in the open near the tower and said the night sky had been awesome.

I felt tired for most of the day. I ate lunch perched on a rock under a gnarled pine tree on Rattlesnake Mountain, which is just a local high point on the long, nearly level ridge. Unintentionally, I blew past the Brink Road Shelter, where I had planned to replenish my water supply, but I was being pursued by a cloud of mosquitoes. (It turned out for the best because the shelter is one of the buggiest on the AT.) Realizing my mistake when I was long past the shelter, I could tell from the lakes that were visible from the ridge that Route 206 was not too far ahead. There were a couple of miles yet to go when my water supply ran out. At 206 I stopped at the Worthington Bakery, filled my reservoir, and washed down two apple turnovers with two bottles of iced tea. Three more tiring miles brought me to Gren Anderson Shelter, which is noted for its unenclosed privy. I do like good ventilation in a privy!

I had dinner with Journey, Mello Yello, Sketch, Gazelle, and others and crashed early. We made room on the crowded shelter floor for Journey, a slender woman of about 50 who lives

Cloudscape over the Delaware River

Flyin'

Bear eating blueberries

near Pittsburg. She was one of the few hikers I had met who was on the trail while a spouse remained at home. Her conversation had the friendly, engaged quality of a person who grew up truly well-mannered, although I sometimes suspected she'd rather not talk at all.

Before crawling into my sleeping bag on the shelter floor, I stowed my food bag in the steel locker provided to keep it safe from bears. The shelter register had an entry about a hiker who had stopped the day before to find water there, leaving his pack at the trail junction; a bear ransacked it in the short while he was gone.

Monday was a nice morning. I ate granola, packed, and then used the open-air privy; privacy is provided by the mutual agreement of all – one simply keeps track of who is out back. It soon became cloudy above and foggy below the ridge. Journey, Mello Yellow and I took a long rest at the "Parthenon" – a sort of Doric picnic pavilion on top of Sunrise Mountain (1,653 feet).

The trails continued to be rocky. We took another rest at Mashipacong Shelter and ran into Anishnabe there. We had lunch at the High Point State Park headquarters area and were joined by Gazelle and Sketch. The trail passes High Point (1,803 feet) a couple hundred feet below the summit, which we were too lazy to climb on this hazy day. The AT turns eastward here and, thankfully, leaves the rocky regime we'd been treading on since Port Clinton. We walked through woods and pastures and were joined again late in the afternoon by Anishnabe, who caught up with us (naturally) as we took a rest break by the side of the trail.

All of us stopped for the night at the "Secret Shelter," a collection of nicely crafted rough wood buildings made available by a thru-hiker benefactor, but not listed in the trail guides until recently. It even has an indoor hot shower and

The privy at Gren Anderson Shelter

127

Just Walking

Journey and Mello Yello

a clothes dryer. It was a very pleasant evening as we ate and chatted, enjoying the breeze and watching the clouds go by. CC and Chicken Legs arrived after a while.

A strong thunderstorm broke around dusk. Rain and wind forced us off the porch of the building where we had been sitting under the little overhang. Thunder and lightning continued for at least two hours, and a couple of close-by lightning strikes literally shook the ground. I eventually climbed into the loft with Anishnabe, Gazelle, and Sketch, while others tented or hammocked, and CC and Chicken Legs curled up on the cramped first floor.

We were all slow to start hiking on Tuesday. Journey's tent had taken on some water and Mello Yello got wet in his hammock despite securing its tarp as well as possible. The weather showed some signs of clearing but remained humid. I walked around a wildlife refuge (and mosquito hatchery), and saw two great blue herons and an indigo bunting.

The trail climbed up and over Pochuck Mountain (800 feet) to a shelter, which Journey and Mello Yello were just leaving when I arrived. I caught up with them again at a new boardwalk crossing a large wetland, an awesome piece of trail relocation which saved a couple of road miles and reportedly took 20 years from conception to completion. The boardwalk goes through a lovely cattail marsh with only one loose-strife plant

Boardwalk through cattail marsh

visible; (although pretty, purple loosestrife is invasive and will soon take over the whole wetland if not weeded out). We made it to Route 24 at 2 pm, and immediately went to heaven – Heaven Hill Farm – for ice cream and baked goods. Who should I meet there but Leaf, an old trail friend whom I first camped with in Georgia and had last seen in the Smokies.

Hitching into Vernon I scored an eagle, i.e., picked up by the first car that came along. It was driven by a trail maintainer who told me about the boardwalk as we drove into town. I checked into the Appalachian Trail Motel at the edge of Vernon, then walked another mile to pick up a mail drop and groceries. Returning to my room, I sat around pondering the hidden meaning of an AT thru-hike. Is there a spiritual destination comparable to the physical goal of reaching the summit of Katahdin? And, once you've reached it, can it be revisited again and again, or is it like an enchanted spot in the forest that you can find only once?

It was sprinkling early Wednesday morning but it had stopped by the time I left the motel. I gave hitching a try, but after standing there for 10 minutes with my thumb out it seemed easier to walk back to the AT. Anishnabe blew past me at her customary walking speed. I reached the trail and climbed up a rocky section to the summit of Wayawanda Mountain (1,340 feet) where I met up with Blink Blink, Scubaman, and Granite. The morning continued damp, and much insect repellent was needed. The mosquito density in this part of the trail seemed as noteworthy as that of the bear population. We rested at Wayawanda Shelter, then climbed over Prospect Rock.

Blink Blink, Scubaman, and Granite

The AT runs along exposed rocky ledges in this area, and we ate lunch sitting on the bare rock near the State Line Trail junction. The first southbound thru-hikers, Bojangles and Wheel, passed through as we were getting ready to pack up.

The trail turned north on a long stretch of the exposed ledge with many little scrambles up and down as it paralleled Greenwood Lake. This was very enjoy-

Just Walking

able, but also tiring. At Route 17A, I stopped at a dairy bar for a hot fudge sundae. The afternoon brought nice partly cloudy weather, although some castellanus clouds were growing into thunderheads in the distance.

The day wound up with a hike over the Pinnacles (1,294 feet) to the Cat Rocks, which were each visible from the other. I arrived at Wildcat Shelter at 5:30 pm and had a reunion with Moonshadow and Morph, whom I hadn't seen since Virginia. Also arriving were Skittles, Rubberband Man, Mello Yello, Journey, Sheep Stuff, CC and Chicken Legs, Sketch and Gazelle. It was crowded, but we made room for everyone who wanted to use the shelter. Morph to Journey: "Were you a hippie in the 60s?" "No. Were you?" Morph, holding up two fingers: "Peace, Man!"

Reunion
East of the NY State Line to the Hudson River: [Mile 1,350 to Mile 1,384.5]

Thursday, July 24. It was raining when we awoke on Thursday, but it soon stopped. There were many ups and downs during the morning with hordes of mosquitoes at the low points. I kept reapplying repellent (20% DEET), but it soon ran off with my sweat, and speed was the only refuge. There were tough climbs on the steep rocky ridge and also good views from Mombasha High Point (1,280 feet), where I ran into Sheep Stuff. She is a sheep farmer from southwest Pennsylvania who ministers to the homeless in her own home, and she was not happy about having been evicted from the church hostel in Vernon which has (overly?) strict rules about the number of hikers who can stay there.

I hiked over Buchanan Mountain (1,142 feet) and past Little Dam Lake, then up and over Arden Mountain (1,180 feet), another series of steep climbs, albeit short ones of less than 500 feet. The

Mountain Jack inside Lemon Squeezer

trail went down a long steep slope to Route 17 and the bridge over the New York State Thruway (elevation 560 feet) into Harriman State Park. The climb in the southbound direction is identified on the trail sign as "Agony Grind," a different approach to public relations than the "Roller Coaster" in Virginia.

The park has a very attractive wooded landscape without much understory, and a short distance into it is the Lemon Squeezer, one of the famous spots along the AT. The Squeezer is a slanted narrow crack followed by a 6-foot step. Inside it I met Mountain Jack for the first time since Maryland. We both made it up the step with a little bouldering technique and then traded photos. I stopped at Fingerboard Shelter for a rest with Mello Yello, Buttercup and Oreo. Mello and I took a detour to Tiorati Circle for water; it came out of the tap rusty and began to clog my in-line filter. It was windy, and the lake didn't look very inviting despite the nice beach, so swimming was not in the cards for the day.

Hudson River

Keeping the faith, I backtracked to where I'd left the AT instead of blue-blazing directly to William Brien Shelter. Jack was there again where the AT crosses the road, and he offered the surprising news that my old friend Tipperary was only a half-hour ahead. I quickened my pace, excited at the prospect of our reunion, and sure enough, there he was at the shelter, without his beard and 50 pounds lighter than when I had last seen him, in the Smokies. We hugged and caught up on what had since happened to each of us. Also at the shelter were Cornpatch, Mello Yello, Sketch and Gazelle, Mountain Jack, Morph, and Indiana Slim (last seen in Virginia), who played '40s and '50s R&B and blues on a portable tape player.

I sat up on my sleeping shelf at 5:30 am on Friday. The stars had been visible, although not brilliant, at 2:30 am, with Jupiter very bright in the south. (There

Just Walking

hadn't really been many clear nights on the trail when there was an open area big enough to see the sky.) After packing quickly, I said goodbye to Tip, who is also an early riser. I was looking forward to getting home again for a couple of days before going up to Waterville Valley, New Hampshire, to lead two hikes for the Appalachian Trail Conference meeting.

I mounted the rock pile next to the shelter, climbed over Little Black Mountain and down to Beachybottom Brook (great name) to collect water. Palisades Parkway was less busy than expected, and I made it across in one piece and continued up West Mountain. It was a lovely clear morning. From a high overlook, a piece of the Hudson River was visible, and in the distance, reflections from the buildings of Manhattan. The tranquility of the scene was occasionally interrupted by sounds of ordnance being detonated at West Point's practice range, not far to the north.

132

The trail followed West Mountain's ridge, providing several views ahead to Bear Mountain and its observation tower. After hiking down into the gap and then up Bear Mountain (1,305 feet), I climbed the stairs inside the recently renovated stone tower, which resounded musically with the echoes of the voices of other visitors, and took in the view. I went on down the hill past a group of kids to the Bear Mountain Inn, where I changed clothes and caught the bus to New York City and Boston.

○ **An Interlude**
Home and Mt. Mooselauke
[Mile 1772.7 to Mile 1782.2]

After visiting my family for a couple of days in Boston, I drove up to Waterville Valley, New Hampshire, starting about 4:30 am Tuesday and arriving at 7 am at the hike staging area for the biennial Appalachian Trail Conference meeting.

Before deciding to thru-hike the AT, I had promised Ed Hawkins, a member of the host committee, that I would lead two hikes on portions of the AT in the White Mountains. The first day's hike was over Mt. Mooselauke, which, at 4,802 feet was quite a contrast to the little ridges the trail had been crossing from Maryland to New York. The other leader and I decided to hike in opposite directions and exchange car keys to avoid a lengthy shuttle around the mountain. I drew the north-to-south traverse, which was good, because the AT follows Beaver Brook Trail, which is very steep, rising by steps, handholds, and scrambles up rock ledges in a mossy gorge next to a lovely series of cascades. Up is my preferred direction on trails like this.

It was a beautiful day, and it was a good group of hikers. With only a day pack on, I had to hold back on the climbs to stay with the group. We stopped for a rest at Beaver Brook Shelter where we met some thru-hikers, both northbound and southbound. We stopped for lunch on Mooselauke's summit, where the views

On top of Mount Mooselauke

were great and the alpine vegetation was beautiful as always. We then hiked down to Glencliff village and through another mile of woods to Oliverian Notch (1,180 feet). A long stretch on the downhill side was spent in conversation with a man in his 70s, who was an active trail maintainer in North Carolina. He said he expected to be sore the next day, but he had no trouble keeping up with the rest of the group.

Many AT hikers like to find opportunities to slack-pack sections of the trail with the help of friends or hostel owners who shuttle them ahead so they can walk with a minimum of gear and food on their back. This traverse of Mooselauke turned out to be the only slack of my hike.

After the day's hike, I had dinner at the resort restaurant and later sat around with my friend Debbie, a hiking/backpacking leader in the AMC Boston chapter. We were camped at Osceola View Campground which is surrounded by Osceola, Tripyramid and other mountains and is absolutely beautiful.

Those mountains looked even better in the glow of sunrise on Wednesday. I led a second day hike 2,200 feet up the Gale River Trail to Galehead Hut (3,780 feet), where it joins the AT, then steeply up to South Twin Mountain (4,902 feet), down to Zealand Hut, and out Zealand Road (2,000 feet). On the way out we saw a beaver swimming in Zealand Pond. It was another nice group of people, including a 1988 GA-ME thru-hiker. After the hike I drove home, and on Thursday morning I was on a bus headed back to New York City and then Bear Mountain Inn.

6 Homecoming

Homecoming

I made the claim in the Virginia chapter that thru-hiking is about wanting to hike every day, not about gutting it out. Nonetheless, it's also true that in most outdoor activities there is discomfort, and to enjoy the experience you have, from time to time, to be able to ignore being cold, wet, tired, in mild pain, etc. It's all a state of mind: focus on the positive, not the negative. Better yet, find some good in the negative, some beauty in a rainy day. It is also a big help if you have learned some techniques to stay a bit more comfortable and to prevent little pains from turning into big ones. All this would soon come into play.

Crossing the Hudson River marked my return to New England, which is my home. I would be walking on several sections of trail that I had hiked in the past and knew to be beautiful and interesting. Although my side trip to lead two hikes at the ATC meeting in New Hampshire gave me a taste of what was to come, it was too soon to look far ahead to the White Mountains. Still, I knew it was only a few more days to Connecticut and the Berkshires. Harriman State Park had already showed some signs of the rocky terrain that is common throughout New England and makes hiking there both interesting and difficult. It was fun to hear fellow thru-hikers who hadn't been to New England before talk about how the trail had changed from the level ridges of Pennsylvania.

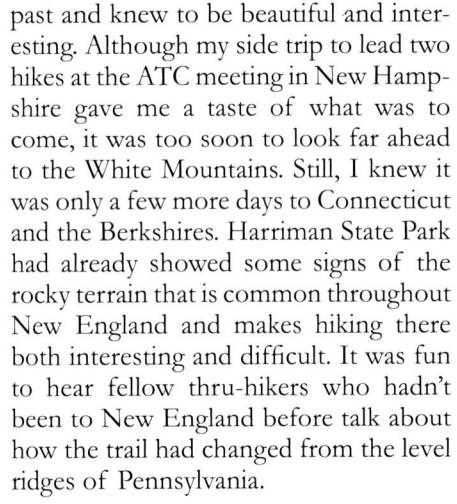

I had looked forward to getting home to see my family, first on the way to Port Clinton and then in the days leading up to Bear Mountain. It was still a long way to my last planned break from the hike, in Hanover, New Hampshire, where I would leave the trail for a few days to take my son Matt to college. So I was ready to re-immerse myself in the daily business of walking, resting, eating, and sleeping, and the rhythm of the trail.

Crossing the Hudson

Just Walking

○ **A Wet Walk**
   The Hudson River to Mount Everett MA
   [Mile 1,384.5 to Mile 1,495.7]

Thursday, July 31. The bus from Manhattan stopped at the Bear Mountain Inn at 4:30 in the afternoon. I had a glass of wine at the bar with Mountain Dew and Dirty Frank. After dinner at the Inn, I walked across the Hudson River bridge in the afternoon sun and up Anthony's Nose to Hemlock Springs campsite; no one else was there.

Rain began during the night and continued as light drizzle on Friday morning. There was no need to hurry, so getting up and repacking my gear and wet tarp was done at a leisurely pace. The day's hike didn't begin until 9:30 am. At a break near Graymore Monastery, I regretted not staying there for a night as many thru-hikers do. The trail made many minor ups and downs. The weather continued to be gray all day, with drizzle and condensation dripping from the trees and rubbing off of the wet bushes; soon I was wet and stayed that way.

Lunch on the trail

While having lunch on Canopus Hill, Chilly Willy and Kilroy, last seen at Tinker Cliffs, south of Daleville, Virginia, stopped for a chat. They convinced me to go past Dennytown Road to Fahnestock State Park for the night. On the way I had a nice talk with a local hiker named "Just Greg," who had left cans of soda at the Route 301 crossing. I walked up the road to the park, pitched the tarp, showered, cooked, and ate, while mosquitoes buzzed around. It started raining again after I went to bed, so I lowered the tarp a bit.

Late the next day, Saturday, I was sitting under the tarp, pitched high, with a slight breeze and no bugs for the moment. It was 6:05 pm. A large group of less experienced adult weekend campers had filled up the Morgan Stewart Shelter and several of the tent sites, but luckily there was a piece of flat open ground in a grove of trees to camp on (and later share with Chilly Willy and Kilroy). I was drinking lemonade by the potful – humid-day thirst, augmented by an Italian sub I had eaten earlier in the afternoon. I reviewed the day's events sitting cross-legged on my sleeping pad, writing the day's journal on the usual half-size, loose-leaf page with a ballpoint pen.

New hikers encountered during the day included a southbound sectioner named

Homecoming

Rapids in the Housatonic

Uncle, a woman who was thru-hiking southbound, and a northbound section hiker named Just Leslie. I also had run into Double Dare, who was slacking south. There were no views in the morning, but a decent one around lunchtime at Canopus Lake, and the prospects were better still from Hosner Mountain and Depot Hill, where the shelter was. It seemed like a long day since packing up in the post-precipitation tree-drip, and heading out onto the highway at 8 am to return to the AT.

There were a few intermittent showers and one heavy one, which occurred while I sat under the overhang at the Mountain Top Deli, a short detour from the trail crossing, eating the aforementioned loaded sub. In the afternoon a crayfish came walking down the trail, a startling sight, but these things happen after a few days of rain.

I spent a comfortable night inside the net bivy under my tarp near Morgan Stewart Shelter. There was heavy dew Sunday

Just Walking

morning, but no rain. Some sensitive chafed areas had appeared in my crotch and under my arms, the result of hiking in wet clothes, but it wasn't to be avoided. I put on my wet shirt and shorts, and my second pair of socks, which were dry going on. During the day's first rest stop at the invitingly-named Nuclear Lake, the sky was still cloudy but a few rays of sun were breaking through. Alas, it just raised false hopes.

After taking a peaceful noon break in the light rain on top of West Mountain, the rain became heavier during lunch at Telephone Pioneers Shelter. It didn't matter, as I was wet all day anyway. In the afternoon there was a nice bit of trail through a hemlock grove. A cheerful ME-GA hiker named Waldo stopped to chat, and a weekend hiking group that was looking a bit soggy and dejected stepped aside to let me pass.

The trail emerged onto Dover Road, and I stopped to replenish my water supply from the faucet at a nicely landscaped house next to the AT that was listed in the *Trail Companion*. Across the road, the footpath followed the edge of a pasture where several cows were grazing. The rain became heavier, and thunder rumbled as I walked over a wooded hill. Finally, I opened my umbrella to avoid going from damp to soaked.

A pretty section ran over board bridges across a swamp.[16]

Slip and Trip and two of their friends, who had joined them for a few days, were at the next road crossing. The friends didn't look too enthused about hiking in the rain, which grew heavier as the day wore on. I decided to bail out at Route 22 and go to a motel. Next to the road is a commuter rail station named for the AT, which crosses its platform. Several hikers sat on the porch of a nearby building housing a landscaping business. The landscaper gave us rides to the nearest motel in his station wagon. The motel was owned by a young couple with a small baby. They were nice enough to do my laundry for three dollars. Chilly Willy and Kilroy were also there, so we walked down the shoulder of the road to a local restaurant and had dinner together.

On Monday the owner of the motel gave me a ride back to the trail, and I started hiking under an umbrella at 7:20 am. It was a nice walk through rolling fields and over stiles much like the ones in Virginia. I stopped at Wiley Shelter for a break from the rain; it was full of giggling teenage girls and a couple of older hikers. Going on, the trail passed the Gate of Heaven Cemetery; it had

---
[16] Swamps are wetlands with trees growing in them, in contrast to marshes, which are grassy, and bogs, which are their own thing.

Homecoming

a large ornamental gate worthy of the name, but the graves were overgrown.

I soon came to Hoyt Road and the Connecticut border. Hurrah! And to make this state line crossing even better, the sun began to appear. The AT went over 10-Mile Hill and down to the 10-Mile River, which it followed to the Housatonic. I began to feel I was really in New England. The trail was wide and passed through an attractive fragrant stand of hemlocks. The space under hemlocks is lovely and green, covered above but open and free of most understory below. It was a contrast to the morning's dripping, weed-choked section.

The white blazes followed the shore of the Housatonic River, which has some impressive rapids in this stretch. At the next road a short detour took me across Bulls Bridge, a covered bridge leading into the village of the same name on the east bank of the river. I bought a sandwich and cold drink at a little deli and ate at a picnic table outside.

Connecticut trail through the pine woods

Just Walking

Cloudy weather

Leaving Bulls Bridge, the trail climbs steeply up Schaghticoke Mountain (1,300 feet). A group of teenage boys was hanging out at an overlook, and one of them took my picture. The climb felt good. Rain held off until I had passed Indian Rocks, then began again, light but with distant thunder. I reached Aldo Mountain Lean-to around 5 pm. There was a nice stream in front, providing the water supply. No one else was at the shelter. I enjoyed a pasta dinner and drank the rest of the instant lemonade I had mixed up in my liter bottle while on the trail.

On Tuesday I slept until 8 am on the shelter floor using my net bivy to keep the mosquitoes off. I walked the fifth of a mile to the road and was headed into Kent when an attractive woman, about 60, picked me up unbidden and took me the rest of the way to town. I thanked her and had breakfast at the restaurant she recommended. Kent is a nice town – a bit rich, but no franchises or touristy stores. There's a large private school near the AT. In the restaurant I saw Lumberjack and Geo for the first time since central Virginia.

After breakfast I walked to the post office for my mail drop, then to the library, where I killed time looking at nature guides while waiting for an internet terminal, and finally checked and replied to my email. At the nearby drug store the pharmacist recommended hydrocortisone cream for the various pack rashes I had going, and Balmex diaper cream to protect my skin from new ones. It worked, and I'll never hike again without Balmex. I'm in his debt.

I walked back to the trail and started hiking around 12:15 pm, up to the ridge

Homecoming

and then over Caleb's Peak – an easy climb. There was a hazy view of town from the overlook where I had lunch. Beyond a second overlook there was a difficult climb down St. John's Ledge to River Road. This section was a long flat walk next to the Housatonic, first on a gravel road, then on a woodland trail, and finally through a field. It was nice to have the river views and even nicer to pass through hemlocks here and there. I met a couple of groups, one with a counselor exhorting a tired teenager to go another five minutes before resting. "Follow through!" she yelled as she pulled him by the hand.

When I started uphill from the road it was raining again. I was low on water and what I had was a little silty (no wonder considering all the rain running off into the brooks over the past several days). Where had all the huge biting flies come from? They were like greenheads, about the size of a yellow jacket, but with brown eyes. I was swatting them away all afternoon as they alighted to suck my blood. I finally came to Caesar Brook campsite and set up my tarp in the rain about 7:15 pm. It was pleasant under the tarp during dinner except for the mosquitoes.

I had a good night's sleep in the net bivy. Awaking on Wednesday to (surprise) light rain, I folded the bivy, ate granola, and sat under the tarp reading for a while, to try to wait it out. The rain eventually diminished, and I wiped the excess water off the tarp and packed up. I felt low on energy and was moving slowly during the morning, which was damp as usual and plagued with mosquitoes, deer flies (the little ones with delta wings), and those brownheads. I had forgotten to include the next section map in my Kent mail drop and really missed it.

Looking north to Race Mountain and Mount Everett

Just Walking

A southbound thru-hiker named Jeremy was sitting at Hang Glider overlook; he planned to detour to New York City at Bear Mountain. As had become a pattern by now, the weather turned partly cloudy and pleasant by lunchtime, which I spent at Belter's Bump, an open ledgy spot. After lunch I descended to Route 7 and met a man and his 13-year-old daughter who asked questions about me and the trail and gave me a little bottle of water. It was nice to walk along roads and fields for a change.

I took a side trip at what I mistook for the Mohawk Trail (damn, I missed that map), and eventually came to a house where a guy in a Patagonia shirt was sorting gear in his back yard for a trip to the San Juan mountains of Colorado with three teenage boys. After talking for a while about hiking I declined his invitation to go swimming with them at Great Falls and returned to the trail. It passed the hydro station and the falls, which truly were great, and continued past houses and up into the hills.

Sage's Ravine

The wet weather had yielded a variety of colorful mushrooms sprouting from the leaf litter along the footpath, as attractive in their own way as spring wildflowers. Their colors ranged from brown to bright yellow, orange, and red, as well as some with pale lavender caps. A thunderstorm arrived at about 4 pm when I was on top of Prospect Mountain, but after some wind, noise, and more rain, it had passed over by the time I reached the Limestone Spring Shelter trail, which descended 300 feet over a half-mile. I lay in the shelter, listening to the patter of rain on the roof and the calling of a great horned owl somewhere close by. Monkey and Iron Chef, both from Massachusetts, arrived late.

It was a steep climb back up the side trail on Thursday morning. It was hazy and damp as usual, and the views were fogged in when I reached the AT around 8:45 am, but the weather became mostly sunny as I walked into Salisbury. Double Dare came out of the White Hart Inn to greet me. He had jumped forward a

Homecoming

Cliff edge walk on Race Mountain

hundred miles to get away from a bad-news bunch of belligerent thru-hikers who were making shelter life unpleasant with their smoking, drinking, and general rowdiness. DD and I ate omelets at the Thyme-Enz Café. I bought stove alcohol (isopropyl was all they had) at the village's auto supply store.

I returned to the trail at 11:30 am for the second climb of the day, a long one to Lion's Head, territory I had covered on a fall day hike a few years before. After collecting water from the excellent Riga Spring, I walked over a series of rocky ledges to Bear Mountain (Connecticut's highest point at 2,316 feet) and ate lunch

there around 2:30 pm. Hopeful, Foxie, and Monkey soon arrived. There was a hazy view ahead to Race Mountain and Mount Everett, which marks the Massachusetts border.

The descent to Sage's Ravine (1,350 feet) was steep and sometimes slippery. Hopeful and Foxie were picking their way carefully down the steep ledges. At the bottom of the lovely ravine, which is animated by a brook with little cascades and verdant with foliage and moss, I met a ridge runner (a park ranger who patrols the trails) and a section hiker from Worcester, Massachusetts. I walked part way up to Race Mountain (2,350 feet) with the hiker.

The climb out of the ravine was yet another long and steep one for the day, followed by a great cliff-edge walk.

Once, when I hiked this stretch of trail on a nice spring day a few years before, a dozen vultures took off from just below the lip of the cliff and flew at eye level only a few feet away. This time there was almost no view, but it was still nice to pass through the clumps of little wind-gnarled trees with ledge rock underfoot.

The trail went down steeply and then up again to the summit of Mount Everett (2,602 feet), followed by a final runout to Glen Brook Shelter. The side trail to the shelter was really just a series of blue blazes on the large oak trees. It was a pretty spot, but there was not much understory to define the path, so I meandered through the woods looking for blazes until I found the shelter. There was a nice spot between two pine trees, a short distance from the shelter, to pitch the tarp on a bed of pine needles. I ate at the shelter with southbounder Zagat, a nice guy in his twenties, and then retired to my tarp.

It wasn't the best of nights. My stomach was a bit out of sorts. I had had a bout of the runs earlier in the day and needed to visit the privy once during the night. I awoke a second time at 2 am to find a mouse inside my net bivy; I cornered it at the foot end and gently evicted it. In addition, everything kept sliding sideways and twisting on the slightly sloping site; pine needles don't provide much friction to hold things in place. By morning, the gear that I'd systematically arranged within the bivy for easy retrieval was a jumble.

○ **The Berkshires**
Glen Brook Lean-to to the Vermont state line: [Mile 1,495.7 to Mile 1,579.3]

Friday, August 8. I slept late (until 8 am) and slowly got re-organized. I put a Compeed patch on some tender skin on the side of my right heel. The red patches on my feet from days of walking in wet socks hadn't fully healed. I was feeling tired and sub-par. Thinking back a couple of days, I remembered having noticed too late that I had installed my in-line filter backwards after cleaning it. My gastrointestinal problems were doubtless the result of drinking water that was contaminated by unintention-

Last Battle of Shay's Rebellion was here

ally drawing back-flow from the filter, but it was evidence that the filter was actually removing pathogens.

I hiked to Jug End and down the steep trail to the road, passing Last Minute, Hopeful, and Foxie on the way. I left the trail at Route 41 and hitched a ride into South Egremont with an 83-year old lady driving a maroon 1988 Olds. "My late husband always warned me not to pick up hitch hikers," she said, but she did, and I was grateful.

By the time I retrieved a mail drop from the post office, my appetite had improved, so I ordered a meatloaf plate at Mom's Restaurant next door. In the restaurant a fellow about my age came over from another table to ask about my hike.

After lunch I checked into the Egremont Inn. It is a historic inn from the late 1700s, and I was given a lovely "stagecoach stop" room with a four-poster bed covered with a hand-sewn quilt, a tiny bathroom, and pedestal sink in the corner of the main room. Unfortunately the room soon stank of my wet gear, but at least my stuff was drying.

I sipped a glass of wine at the little bar, chatting with the staff. Dinner was outstanding, and the staff were very pleasant, professional, and friendly. During dinner they brought me a telephone, which surprised me, as no one knew I was stopping there. It was Dirty Frank, who had asked for any hiker who happened to be at the Inn. He had cut his foot and wanted me to leave a note at the trail telling his friends where he would be.

I woke up Saturday feeling better, took two Immodium, bought lunch fixings, ate breakfast at the Inn, and left at 9:50 am. No one offered to pick me up, so I walked a mile or so to the trail, where I posted the requested message from Dirty Frank.

The trail went through mowed hayfields at first. There was a notice at the next road, warning that some bog bridges ahead might be under water. They were – some by a foot or more, but this stretch lasted only about 20 yards, so I plunged on, being used to wet feet by now. (My socks had dried by the time I left the Inn, but the boots hadn't.)

It was sunny as I walked along the Housatonic, past rows of corn loaded with ripe ears. I stopped at a garden center on Route 7 for a bottle of iced tea. There were jugs of water in the cooler for hikers. Walking on, I came to another section I had hiked before – up June Mountain and East Mountain (1,750 feet) to Tom Leonard Shelter, where I ate lunch; it was very buggy.

The AT crossed Route 23 and headed up the next mountain. It was by then a cloudy but warm afternoon, but there was no rain. Around 5 pm I stopped at Benedict Pond and took a dip. Refreshed, I pushed on for the final lap to North Wilcox Shelter, set up the tarp as it began to sprinkle, and cooked and ate under it. Hopeful, Foxie, and three

Just Walking

weekenders were in the shelter, which was buggy. It rained hard during the night, but everything stayed dry under the tarp.

By Sunday morning the rain had stopped, but water was dripping from the trees. This section of trail seemed familiar at a couple of places. There were large groves of hemlock and white pine, and the trail crossed several streams. On Tyringham Cobble I took a break sitting on the ground in an old field among goldenrod and Queen Anne's Lace while it rained softly. It was very pretty. In Gary Snyder's poems some of the most beautiful images involve rainy days or nights.

I crossed Jerusalem Road and Main Road and climbed up Baldy Mountain on pretty sections of trail. I wasn't feeling super-energetic but kept going. My gastrointestinal problems seemed to be over. I ate lunch sitting on a boardwalk over a wetland with a stream passing through it. It began to rain again just as

Along the Housatonic

I was putting things away, but it soon stopped. I skirted the Goose Ponds and passed the shelter side trail.

A footbridge carries the AT over the Massachusetts Turnpike. I always hope to see a hiker when driving under this bridge, which is labeled "Appalachian Trail" for the benefit of motorists, and had often imagined myself hiking across it. So it was a moment of glory, and a couple of passing cars even honked in salute.

Last Minute and Pony Boy were at the Route 20 crossing a short distance north

Homecoming

of the Pike. LM had yogi'd a ride to the nearest store from a day hiker, so I asked him to buy me an iced tea. PB and I sat and talked by the side of the road. LM returned after a while with not only the requested items but also three McDonalds Big Mac meals, which we devoured hungrily.

With seven miles to go, I climbed Becket Mountain (2,178 feet) and then walked on level trail through several wet meadows and past abandoned beaver ponds. A rickety split-log bridge covered with slippery algae crossed a slough. After warning myself to be careful I took a couple of steps. The thin logs sagged under my weight and racked and twisted. My feet came loose, and I fell backward into two feet of standing water. A pair of muddy waves closed over me before I could scramble to my feet. It was such a spectacular fall I found myself wishing someone else was there to see it.

After staggering out of the mudhole I went on and made it to October Mountain Shelter at 7:30 pm. Alpha and Trench (and Cadbury the dog) were there. We talked about Maine's 100-mile Wilderness, which they had previously hiked. Dinner was unnecessary after the Big Mac feed, so I made lemonade and retired to the tarp at 8:30 pm and went to bed. I try not to be impatient when I hike, but I wondered when the weather would change. It had rained part of every day since crossing the Hudson River ten days before.

Cheese Monument

On Monday I woke up to a dry morning. I left without breakfast around 8 am and munched on a food bar while walking. It was hard to start a rhythm going – the trails were both muddy and root-y. During the morning I covered a stretch south of Warner Hill that I had day-hiked early in the spring a couple of years before. There were a couple of southbound thru-hikers at Kay Wood Shelter at lunchtime.

I walked into the town of Dalton around 2:30 pm, bought an iced tea, and yogi'd a ride to the laundromat from a local guy who was thinking about hiking the 17 miles from Dalton to Mount Greylock. I was packing up my dry laundry when heavy rain began, accompanied by copious thunder. I went next door to a sub shop to sit on the porch and watch the storm, a pleasant experience when you're under cover.

I had intended to complete the last five miles I'd planned for the day, but instead decided to stay at a motel for the night.

Just Walking

It was just too discouraging to face the idea of getting all those nice dry clothes wet again, so I begged a ride to the Shamrock Motor Inn. Days of hiking in wet boots and socks were taking their toll. The Balmex was helping but there were raw red patches on top of my toes on both feet and underneath a couple of them.

On Tuesday I awoke at 5:30 am, showered, and started the day's hike with a backtrack from the motel to the last blaze I'd passed on the way into town. The AT continued down Dalton's High Street and into the woods. It was a good section of trail, attractive and easy on the 1,000-foot climb past the Crystal Mountain campsite, which had been the original objective for Monday. There were some wet areas on top of the hill, but I kept my feet fairly dry by hopping over puddles and finding stepping stones. Part of Leave-No-Trace hiking is to avoid stepping on the soft margins of puddles, which just makes them larger, but it's tempting to cheat now and then when you're desperately trying to keep your socks dry.

The trail headed down a long hillside into the town of Cheshire, past the brand new Ashuwillicook rail-trail, to the post office, where I claimed my mail drop from a very nice clerk. I went up Main Street looking for groceries, which I found at the Shell station on Route 8. I drank a Sobe green tea and backtracked on the AT from its Route 8 crossing to the Cheese Monument opposite the post office.

This is one of the better public monuments I've ever seen. It is dedicated to a local Baptist clergyman, John Leland, who worked with Thomas Jefferson to

Clouds over Mount Graylock

Homecoming

secure religious freedom in the Bill of Rights amendments to the Constitution. The town sent a huge cheddar cheese to Jefferson on his inauguration, and the monument represents a giant cheese press. This may be where the expression "he's a big cheese" comes from.

Having returned to the point where I left the AT in search of food, I hiked on across Route 8 and up a section that was familiar from a previous day hike, along the edge of a meadow, and onto the foot of Mt Greylock (3,491 feet). While climbing over the stile at the edge of a fenced-in field, I remembered looking at it a few years before and imagining what it would be like to do it on a thru-hike.

The trail up Greylock is a lovely one, at one point passing through a huge grove of towering hemlocks on a steep hillside. However, once atop Saddleball Ridge the footpath ran through a long series of unavoidable mudholes, bogs, and deep puddles, and water was flowing copiously down the trail itself, so my earlier

From Glastenbury fire tower

efforts to keep my feet dry were in vain. I met a short-term hiker, two SoBos, and some day trippers near the summit.

Despite the usual worries about not being able to get a room, the Bascom Lodge staff had my reservation and were friendly and helpful. They even provided a towel and shampoo, and treated me to the novel experience of having hot showers two days in a row. I sat alone in a bunkroom before dinner, enjoying the view of the shifting clouds below as the sun shone in. As the clouds skimmed over the mountain, the top of the tall summit monument seemed to dissolve and rematerialize.

Mountain Jack arrived around 5 pm. We had an excellent dinner, thanks to the cooking staff, two women from Venezuela and Zambia, respectively. Jack and

Just Walking

I shared a table with a friendly couple from Barcelona and some other nice folks.

I went outside at 4 am on Wednesday, just to take a look around, and watched the moon come and go through the warm drifting fog. The same group of folks was present again at breakfast, which was large and sumptuous. I left the lodge and started hiking at 9 am.

It was the usual overcast foggy morning. After passing over a spur called Mount Williams (3,116 feet), the AT descended steeply to the Hoosic River valley 2,300 feet below. The sun was out before I reached the base of the mountain, and I followed the white blazes down roads through North Adams, across Route 2, and back onto a trail running alongside Sherman Brook and up the ridge on the opposite side.

A very rocky steep section led up to the junction with the Pine Cobble trail (2,100 feet). A pediatrician from San Diego was also on his way up, and a large group from Fort Wayne, Indiana, was taking a break at Eph's Lookout. I crossed the Vermont state line with a cheer. Three states to go.

○ On and Off the Long Trail
The Vermont State line to Hanover NH:
[Mile 1,579.3 to Mile 1,729.3]

Wednesday, August 13, continued. The trail became muddier. I crossed County Road and began the section of the AT/Long Trail that I'd hiked with my son Matt's Boy Scout troop nine years earlier. There were little ups and downs, all between 2,000 and 3,000 feet elevation. Thunder rumbled, but the clouds were moving from the northwest, which was a good sign: a new air mass was finally taking over the weather. After a brief sprinkle the sun returned.

The AT/LT climbed over a hill and ran down to Roaring Branch, which did in fact roar as it rushed out of a beaver pond, overflowing with the recent rains. I hiked on over Consultation Peak and through ankle-deep puddles and bogs. T-Bird and another hiker were at a campsite across Stamford Stream, and we waved and shouted hello over the din of the fast-moving water.

I reached Congdon Shelter around 7 pm. There was a couple, hiking short-term, and a solo hiker there. The solo guy was in his sleeping bag and never came out. The ground in front of the shelter was a muddy mess; we hopped on stepping stones between the shelter and the picnic table to keep the mud off our feet. I wrote my journal entry by the light of my headlamp at the table as I ate a couscous dinner, then cleaned up and climbed onto one of the upper deck sleeping shelves for the night.

On Thursday morning I had a nice time chatting with the couple, who were from Maine. The mystery man awoke five minutes before I left, but said nothing. As I hit the trail at 8 am the sun was penetrating the morning haze. I stopped to take in the view from Harmony

Homecoming

From Kid Gore Shelter

Hill down to the town of Bennington through the broken clouds passing below me. A young guy named Working on It (or maybe he was working on a trail name) stopped there to meditate. Hot Rod passed by. I caught up with him at the bottom of the steep trail which plunges 600 feet to Route 9 on stone steps. We talked for a while by the footbridge over City Stream.

I continued up the trail and stopped for lunch at Little Pond Outlook, watching three big wind turbines turn on the distant ridge. Editorial comment: I would say my experience at that moment was enhanced, not degraded by this sight, although I admit there are places I'd hate to see encroached upon by wind farms. It's either little impacts like this or all the negative environmental and moral consequences of obtaining and burning fossil fuel.

The bugs were not bad, and the mudholes were beginning to firm up, but there was still plenty of water on the trail. After lunch I realized that I had mistaken my position: there are two similar lookouts and I had traveled a mile less than I earlier thought. This imaginary setback made me feel impossibly weary as I stepped over the roots of large beech trees. I slogged on to Glastenbury Lookout, where the sight of Glastenbury Mountain (3,750 feet) across the shallow valley perked me up. The lookout is a little place on the trail with a view north to the mountain that Pieter Breughel the Elder would have liked to paint. From there the trail wound through thick understory in the

Just Walking

dip between the lookout and the mountain. I made it to the wooded summit by 4:30 pm, bypassing Goddard Shelter.

After climbing up the old fire tower for a hazy view, I hiked for another hour and 45 minutes down to Kid Gore Shelter. On the way there were fresh moose tracks underfoot. Suddenly, a cow moose stood up from where she was having a nap on a patch of ferns, scarcely 30 feet from the trail. This was a small moose as they go, but she was bigger than a horse. I took a picture and then walked on while she stood there calmly watching.

Loser was at the shelter when I arrived, and Chemo soon followed. I'd been reading his journal entries in the shelters for weeks. Loser and Chemo both have a sort of antic wit, and their conversation about the time it would take to finish their thru-hikes developed first into some calculations and then into a full blown table of daily mileages needed to reach Katahdin with various combinations of finish dates and zero days taken.

Loser at the base of Stratton Mountain fire tower

Chemo worked on this for at least an hour and stuck it in the shelter register. According to his table, it's possible to go from Kid Gore Shelter in Vermont to Mount Katahdin in two months of hiking while averaging a little less than 10 miles per day!

Kid Gore shelter has a great view down a valley to the east, and Friday morning began with a spectacular pink sunrise that we viewed through the wide-screen opening of the shelter without leaving our sleeping bags. I rose before 6 am and started hiking around 7 am, up and over the next hill and around to Story Spring Shelter for a break. I pushed on to the road, crossing Black Brook on the way. A section hiker named Sky-T was at the parking area at the road crossing. The weather was beautiful and clear, and an angel had left cans of Pepsi next to the road.

The hike up Stratton Mountain (3,936 feet) was wonderful, both pretty and easy to climb. I had lunch on top with Loser, and we chatted with the Green

Homecoming

Mountain Club caretaker, who told us about the big power outage blanketing the northeast U.S. There's something wonderful about being totally oblivious to an event like this, which had affected a huge expanse of the country. Before leaving, I took some pictures from the lookout tower, which is said to be where Benton McKaye dreamed up the Appalachian Trail in the first place.

The trail wound its way down the mountain through American beech woods and past a stealth campsite I had once used. I turned onto the side trail skirting the north shore of Stratton Pond. The one sanctioned campsite was fully occupied by a large group, so I set up my tarp in the woods near the pond. I was politely evicted by Bill the Caretaker an hour later, so I walked back to the Stratton Pond Shelter feeling a bit ruffled but also sheepish about thoughtlessly contributing to the impact on this overused resource. Sky T and Chemo were at the shelter, which was new and beautiful, and the day ended well.

I slept soundly, awoke at 5:45 am on Saturday, and was on the trail by 6:50 am. The mostly level trail north of Stratton Pond was wet as expected, but it showed some signs of drying. It passed through more stands of beech trees. I reached Routes 11/30 at 11:30 am and hitched a ride into Manchester with a former section hiker. This was the first time on the hike that I had been picked up by someone in an SUV, which usually roar past hitchhikers.

My Platypus reservoir had developed a leak, but neither outfitter in town had a

From Baker Peak

Just Walking

replacement in stock, so I just bought another pair of socks and some bug dope. I also bought cheese, tortillas, and cookies at a local store and had a sumptuous cheeseburger at an overpriced restaurant. It was hot now. I walked in the afternoon sun past some outlet stores to a promising hitchhiking spot and caught a ride back to the trail.

Halfway up Bromley Mountain (3,250 feet) it rained and the temperature dropped 15 degrees. I was soon wet, not so much from the rain (thanks to my umbrella), but from brushing against the foliage growing out onto the trail. There were no views from the socked-in summit. I reached Mad Tom Notch at 5 pm and continued on toward Styles Peak (3,400 feet).

After looking for possible camping spots along the way and finding nothing except a little cubbyhole among the spruce trees on the summit of the mountain, I decided to go on to Peru Peak Shelter, arriving a little after 7 pm.

Cairns on White Rock Mountain

Homecoming

There were five short-term hikers at the shelter, including former section hikers Trashman and Einstein. We talked while cooking and eating dinner at the picnic table. Abby the caretaker came by with her dog to collect fees and chat. There was a nice pink sunset, and it was dark at 8:20 pm.

We denizens of the shelter took our time on Sunday morning chatting over breakfast. I was back on the trail at 7:50 am. Griffith Lake was a pretty spot for a mid-morning snack, but it was too cold and windy to swim. From there I climbed up to my old friend Baker Peak (2,800 feet) in about an hour. I had sat on this white marble outcrop twice before, looking out at Dorset Mountain and the surrounding hills. Today there were clouds hovering below in the valley.

I walked the long decline to Big Branch and its suspension bridge and shelter. The register contained a recent entry from a female hiker I didn't know, who extolled the joys of skinny dipping in Big Branch's swimming holes. Although sunny by now, it was too early and too cold to swim. It was a nice thought, though.

Little Rock Pond was large and beautiful, with a backdrop of fir- and spruce-covered hills. After lunch there, I climbed up to White Rock Mountain, meeting SoBo Goggles and NoBo Mountain Butterfly. The real attraction of the place was not the white rocks, a small grouping of boulders, but the beautiful spruce/fir forest through which the trail runs for over a mile. There was also an environmental artwork of many and varied cairns made from pieces of the quartzite that were lying all around; it reminded me of a similar installation at Sunfish Pond in New Jersey.

Tired now, I walked along the trail looking for the wooden sign marking the side trail to Greenwell Shelter. This is a situation familiar to most hikers: the tank is empty and you're running on vapors but the trail keeps going. I rejoiced when I finally sighted that sign.

At the shelter I met my old acquaintance Martha Graham, whom I had last seen at Front Royal, and we caught up on things while eating an early dinner. I retired to my tarp and went to bed early.

Shortly after 7 am on Monday I headed out behind Martha Graham; we were both going to South Wallingford to pick up mail drops. There was little traffic on Route 140, but a nice guy in a jeep stopped for us. I rode sideways in back, MG in front with him and his dog. By this time I had a shaggy beard and ponytail and Martha Graham sported a crew cut; the woman at the post office quizzed us, mock serous, about our photo ID's, saying "This doesn't look at all like you." All in good fun. MG and I went to Mom's Restaurant for breakfast; I had the "Garbage Omelet," which was excellent. Martha Graham stuck around talking to some other hikers who showed up at the post office, and I headed out alone, getting a ride from a woman in a Volvo who was also a hiker.

Just Walking

Vermont field

I was back on the trail around 10 am; it went up and over Bear Mountain, past Minerva Hinchey Shelter. I took a break in a fragrant meadow above Spring Lake, sitting on a soft, moss-covered hummock. Goldenrod, tiny daisies, and other late summer flowers surrounded me, and in the distance fair weather clouds grew in the moist air. I followed the trail through groves of fir and spruce and stopped at a lookout with a view down to a wide valley.

The trail plunged deep into Clarendon Gorge. Below the suspension bridge some swimmers played in the eddies among the rapids. The climb up from Route 103 was steep and involved scrambling up talus in a rocky crevice in the mountainside, always a nice change of pace. At lunch I stretched out on the bare rock at Clarendon Lookout and gave my feet a chance to breathe. From there I walked further up and over the hill past Clarendon Shelter and finally reached Governor Clement Shelter, where I set up my tarp and relaxed on my foam pad.

Homecoming

Martha Graham soon arrived with thru-hiker Jenn and two Israeli short-term hikers. The shelter is next to a drivable woods road and there was a semi-permanent camp set up next to the brook, with a pickup truck parked at an alarming angle in a ditch. The woman who lived in this camp came over before dinner to visit. We talked for a while, exchanging tales about the joys of having teenage children. She said she was unable to work because of a bad back and that she and her boyfriend lived on his pay for baling cardboard at a recycling plant. It was her birthday and she wasn't having a good day after having wrecked their truck the night before. It looked hopelessly stuck. She declined our offer to help push it out but thanked us for listening before she went back to her camp.

Jenn, the Israelis, MG, and I talked for a while over dinner. Jenn gave me a delicious slice of fresh zucchini that she had sautéed with garlic and oil, a wonderful contrast to dried food. We were all invited to help celebrate the Israeli woman's birthday, sharing a blueberry pie and wearing the party hats her boyfriend had carried up to the shelter. Stars began to emerge and we went to sleep listening to the sound of the brook.

When I woke up on Monday I realized with a thrill that all my gear was dry! It had been that way for the past week, but I was still getting used to it. The morning's hike was a steady steep trek up Little Killington (the trail bypasses the wooded summit), but I eventually reached big Killington (4,235 feet), and climbed the steep side trail to its rocky top. This was the first 4,000-footer since the Priest in Virginia and the first of many more to come.

It was sunny but cool on the summit, and I used my rain jacket against the wind. The morning haze limited the views to perhaps 30 miles, but they were very nice nonetheless. Martha Graham arrived soon after, and we walked over to the summit lodge for very expensive cold soft drinks. We returned to Cooper

Clarendon Gorge

Just Walking

Sketch and Gazelle and friend

Lodge, a cabin-style shelter at the base of the summit trail, and I collected water from the spring before leaving.

I walked on alone to Sherburne Pass on a stretch of trail that seemed never to end, stopping for lunch sitting on a mossy patch next to the footpath. I talked for a while with a trail maintainer, a 75-year-old tri-athlete. I played leap-frog with MG and Mountain Butterfly. Blaze blazed on by. I finally crossed Route 4 in the pass, went up a path bordered by stinging nettle, and continued behind Deer Leap to Maine Junction. It is another of the big milestones on the trail, the place where the AT departs from the Long Trail and turns east for the Whites, Maine, and, ultimately, Katahdin.

This was a beautiful moment on a beautiful day. Deer Leap loomed ahead but I didn't need to climb it, I was headed for New Hampshire, and all was right with the world. From there it was two more mostly downhill miles to Gifford Woods State Park, where I registered with the female ranger. After a hot shower I was writing in my journal at the campsite's picnic table when Gazelle, Sketch, and Martha Graham happened by. They decided to walk a little farther after using the facilities. A pleasant end to the day, and it was still sunny!

Tuesday brought another dry, clear morning. It was actually a little cold during the night sleeping on raked gravel. (Gravel drains well and is easy to keep clean, so I understand why the park rangers like it, but it is uncomfortable, it's hard on your ground sheet, and the sand in it gets all over your gear.) I had a pleasant time organizing my stuff and eating breakfast at the picnic table. I hit the trail at 7:45 am, dropping off a bag of trail trash on my way out: two ounces less to carry. Sketch and Gazelle were near Kent Pond, where they had camped. They had just made friends with a pot-bellied pig, which probably lived on the adjacent farm.

There was plenty of climbing in store for the day. I hiked up Quimby Mountain from Ottoquechee Gorge, then down to Stony Brook Shelter for a break, talking to a couple of section

160

Homecoming

hikers. This was followed by another 1000-foot climb, then down again and back up to Lakota Lake Lookout, for lunch in the warm sun. I took a side trail up to "The Lookout", a platform atop a semi-abandoned cabin. When I looked inside there was my old trail companion Leaf, spreadeagled on the floor of the bombed out cabin, basking in the heat.

There was no water on this stretch of trail and I was feeling hot, tired, and worried about running dry as the afternoon wore on. I looked at several muddy seeps along the trail but decided they were worse than nothing, so I kept going with the water I had left. The final climb of the day went up the Pinnacle (which must be the third or fourth thing called that on the AT) and then down to Winturi Shelter, where I set up my tarp, ate, and crashed for the night.

Thursday's hike began with a long downhill trek through a hemlock woods. The trail emerged into a meadow above Route 12, where a huge white cloud, brilliantly lit by the morning sun, filled the valley up to the level of the next ridge. The meadow had clumps of flowers – goldenrod, Queen Anne's lace, Joe-Pye weed, as well as milkweed plants with giant seed pods. The effect in the morning sun was psychedelic. I then began the roller coaster for the day – nice trails running up and down hill through hemlock, spruce/fir, beech, or

A cloud fills the valley, Vermont Route 12

Just Walking

red pine for the most part, with several high pastures, and farmhouses at the road crossings. There were some long views from the high fields to Mount Ascutney, Killington, Bromley, and Stratton. Leaf, Buttercup, Oreo, Morph, and Moonshadow were all at Thistle Hill Shelter when I stopped for lunch. The shelter has a unique hexagonal privy with window screens all around that resembles a garden gazebo.

After lunch I double-timed my descent through fields and woods to West Hartford and crossed the old truss bridge over the White River around 3:30 pm. It was still warm and sunny, and I swam in the river while hikers and local folks sat in the sun on the rocky ledge along the shore. This was the best swim (and one of the few) since Sunfish Pond. I swam up the big eddy and out into the rapid, then back downstream into the lower end of the eddy, which carried me upstream to the starting point. After a couple of these laps, I sat drying in the sun talking with Gazelle and Brew. I dressed and walked to the West Hartford country store for a strawberry milkshake.

I had quite a bit of energy left after being refreshed and fed. The mosquitoes were bad though, and my coating of DEET soon sweated off. They were worse at Happy Hill Shelter. "Happy Hill" is the best piece of P.R. since Leif Erickson came up with the name "Greenland" in the hope it would attract settlers to the barren island. I crawled into my net bivy as fast as I could and ate a cold supper so I didn't have to come out. These

The beach at the White River

Homecoming

were the most energetic and aggressive mosquitoes I've ever seen – perhaps their ancestors had escaped from a Dartmouth biology lab. I was looking forward to my last planned visit home as I fell asleep.

I woke up at 5 on Friday morning after a not very good night's rest with roots sticking up into my back and mosquitoes buzzing and trying to reach me through the netting with their long probosces. I made quick work of packing and started hiking toward Hanover at 6 am. The mosquitoes were still fierce on the trail, biting under my glasses, in my ear, anywhere they could reach, and the DEET seemed to wear off in minutes. I high-tailed it through the sparse woods, afraid to slow down. The trail became a road in Norwich and – finally free of mosquitoes – I strolled past historic houses and the town green, across I-91, and over the Connecticut River bridge into Hanover.

After locating the Vermont Transit stop in front of the Hanover Inn I went around the corner to the Dirt Cowboy Café for an excellent breakfast – a large cup of custom-brewed Guatemala Antigua, a huge fresh-squeezed orange juice, and a ham-and-cheese croissant. Mountain Jack came in and told me he was going to flip to Katahdin and finish his thru-hike southbound back to Hanover. I wished him good luck and safe hiking. I took a stroll around town, bought some new synthetic undies at an outfitter's, and settled down to wait for the bus.

I arrived home that afternoon. Sheila and Matt had gone to New York where he was about to begin his first year at Pratt Institute in Brooklyn. Greg and I packed his stuff into the car and drove down on Saturday morning. After helping Matt carry his things to the room, we said goodbye, and Sheila, Greg, and I spent the weekend sightseeing in the city. It was a gorgeous weekend, sunny but not too hot. We walked over the Brooklyn Bridge, and went to a free jazz concert at Tompkins Square in the East Village.

Back home on Monday, I did some laundry, mailed some food ahead to post offices in New Hampshire and Maine, and prepared to hike some more.

Jazz in NYC

7
Tasty Stuff

Tasty Stuff

Every hiker has favorites. A great hike may include inspiring views, beautiful surroundings, challenging terrain, memorable people, points of interest, great meals, dangers averted, etc. Most of my great hikes have been in the White Mountains. Guidebooks rightly extol the long walks above treeline on the Franconia and Presidential ridges and warn hikers to be prepared for the elevation gain, tricky climbs, and dangerous weather in the Whites. Although these mountains rise to heights that are puny compared to the Rockies, Sierras, and Cascades, the trails in the White Mountains are second to none in difficulty. (All right, all right, second to few. We can debate it some other time.)

Consequently, thru-hikers look forward to the Whites as a major attraction on the AT. People who had never seen them talked about their challenges and their reputation for scenic beauty. Those of us who had hiked them before wanted to return and show the newcomers what they'd been missing. I was impatient to re-experience some of my favorite hikes, my enthusiasm tempered by the knowledge that it's never the same twice and that the weather doesn't always cooperate. Perhaps this was a little different than being in the moment on the trails in Virginia, Pennsylvania and Vermont, beautiful though they were. My mind was leaping miles ahead as I approached the Whites, and I was rewarded with spectacular views when I reached them. Almost as in my first days on the AT in Georgia, there was a feeling of wonder that I was actually here doing this.

Approaching the Whites
Hanover NH to Glencliff NH:
[Mile 1,729.3 to Mile 1,772.7]

Tuesday, August 26. I returned to the trail in Hanover. After a nice weekend together, Sheila was very cool to me on parting – these transitions are hard for her.

Arriving on the bus at 4:30 pm, I ate at a local restaurant and set foot on the trail at 6:30 pm for a short hike to Velvet Rocks Shelter. Mosquitoes were present but not too bad, and there were a few brief sprinkles on the way. In the shelter someone had pinned up a drawing of the World Trade Center towers, whose absence was a sad undercurrent in the places in New York City where they used to be so visible. Loser and Roamin' Around came to the shelter around 9 pm.

Fair weather crowd on top of Mount Liberty

167

Just Walking

I slept well and was back on the trail at 7:45 am on Wednesday while my shelter mates were still sleeping. It was a pleasant morning with breezes from the northwest. After climbing up the Velvet Rocks, I took a detour to the spring (the Velvet Underground?), and then walked down to a cattail marsh and up Moose Mountain (2,300 feet). A woman with two dogs was on the south summit, where I took a much-needed rest.

T-Bird and Looser

A while later on the north summit, I ate lunch talking to a SoBo named Roadkill who complained about fatigue; he had hiked Maine and the Whites, so he had a good reason to be tired. From our lunch spot we could see Smarts Mountain and Mount Cube to the north and the surrounding little hills and valleys below.

I replenished my water near the road, and then made the steep 1,200-foot climb to Holt's Ledge (2,100 feet), which kicked my butt. It was quite similar to the climb from Galehead Hut to South Twin Mountain in the Whites but without the glory of a summit above 4000 feet. The view was nice, though.

Three other hikers were at Trapper John Shelter, NoBos Jason and Sarah, and her father, an econometrician from Albany. I put up my tarp and net bivy against the mosquitoes, and wrote in my journal. NoBo Brown Bess arrived around 6 pm.

It was a clear, cold night. Stars were flashing though the tree crowns, but it was warm in my 3-season bag, which was again part of my gear after returning to Hanover. Much of the day was spent climbing Smarts Mountain (3,240 feet), 2,400 feet of elevation gain, most of it steep. I hiked for a while with T-Bird and Loser, and we saw Jason, Sarah and her father on the summit. There were good views from the fire tower, though Mount Mooselauke eclipses most of the Whites from this angle. The trail passed over exposed ledges with black and white swirl patterns in the quartzite.

I crossed Jacobs Brook at a pretty spot and made a short climb to Hexacuba Shelter, which is spacious and comfortable (and hexagonal). It has a 5-sided privy known as "Pentacuba", which presumably serves as a refuge from demons, owing to its geometry.

During the day I had run into AT Addict, with whom I had shared a shelter in southern Virginia; he was finishing up his seventh end-to-end hike of the AT with this section. Tim, a Brit section hiker, was at Hexacuba that evening,

Tasty Stuff

along with Hot Dog and T-Bird. Another clear, cold night followed. I slept near the edge of the shelter floor and could see stars through the trees. Coyotes sang in the middle of the night, an eerie but beautiful sound.

Friday morning was partly cloudy and not too cold. I climbed the hard quartzite ledges of Mount Cube and visited the north summit (2,911 feet) via a side trail. High clouds gathered, creating an overcast white sky. There was good visibility below the clouds, which thickened and lowered to the top of Mount Mooselauke by mid-afternoon. Although there were some mosquitoes, I was tired of slathering myself with DEET and applied it only at the afternoon rest stop; my attitude got me a dozen bites, but it seemed the lesser evil when the bugs weren't swarming around me. After a closer view of Mooselauke from the top of Mount Mist, I hiked down to Oliverian Notch and into the Hikers Welcome hostel at Glencliff village, a short distance down the road from the AT.

On Mount Cube

Just Walking

Having made it to the hostel at 4 pm and stowed my gear in one of their guest tents for the night, I took a shower standing in a puddle of water on the gravel floor of the bath house, then ate some leftover slices of pizza given to me by one of the other hikers, and washed them down with a couple of cans of Dr. Pepper from the hostel fridge. They didn't have a vehicle to shuttle hikers that weekend, so I planned to hitch to Kinsman Notch the next morning, having already hiked Mooselauke during the ATC meeting in July. Loser, T-Bird, Brown Bess, Roamin', and a half dozen others were at the hostel that night

○ **Live Free but Don't Die**
 The White Mountains:
 [Mile 1,772.7 to Mile 1,873.3]

Saturday, August 30. It rained during the evening and into the night, which was

The Whites from Mount Wolf

warm, but the skies were clearing on Saturday. I left the hostel before 8 am and hitched to the village of Warren to buy food for a seven-day traverse of the Whites — the loaded food bag barely fit into my pack. I walked to a restaurant called the Garlic Clove for French toast and their tasty "red flannel hash". While walking back toward Route 118, a woman driving the opposite way stopped to see if I needed directions and ended up taking me all the way to Kinsman Notch, for which I was very grateful. She was a hiker, naturally.

I started up the trail at 9:40 am. It was very steep going from the trailhead to Mount Wolf (approximately 3,500 feet[17]), with many rocky climbs over a series of knobs on the mountain's backbone. I reached Eliza Brook Shelter (2,300 feet) around 2 pm. Trace and 1/3 were there, looking cold. The weather

Steep climb up South Kinsman

---

[17] In contrast to some of the peaks further south on the AT, the summit elevations of the significant peaks in the White Mountains have been measured to the foot using GPS. Peak baggers take these data very seriously in this part of the world. Mount Wolf, however, is not even in the 100 highest of northern New England, so its exact height has not been published.

had turned mostly cloudy and breezy by 11 am, and it was definitely chilly if you stopped for long. A quick lunch and I was ready to tackle South Kinsman (4,358 feet).

The trail up Kinsman from the south is a very rocky 2,000-foot climb that presents many little technical problems and scrambles requiring you to stop and figure out the best route to take up the steep pitches. The trail was very nice initially, following a brook and then crossing a wetland with South Kinsman's cliffs looming overhead. Despite the gray light, the view was very beautiful in an austere way. It looked completely different from all the sections of trail that had come before, even since Hanover. At a crest, there was an interesting prospect looking down to a large wetland south of the mountain, all of it wreathed in shreds of drifting fog. I had been up South Kinsman a number of times but never from this side. It is one of the most rugged trails in the Whites.

It was too cold to stop at the summit, but I enjoyed the view of Cannon, North Kinsman, and Franconia Ridge with their tops cut off by the cloud layer, as well as Mount Carrigain, the Hancocks, and Osceola in the distance, to the east. I descended into the closely hemmed-in spruce/fir corridor that crosses the saddle between the peaks and raced on to North Kinsman (4,293 feet) and then down a somewhat easier trail to Kinsman Pond Shelter. A man with a little boy and a teenage nephew were in the shelter along with a weekend hiker from Exeter. It was colder by dinnertime, and we cooked well within the open-fronted lean-to to avoid the wind.

Kinsman Pond

Just Walking

Mount Lafayette from Lonesome Lake

After a foggy night, the sky was clear on Sunday morning, and the temperature was in the low to mid 40s. This made for a great view of the Kinsmans, everything glowing rosy pink in the morning sun under a royal blue sky, the view doubled in the surface of Kinsman Pond. I walked at an easy pace down to Lonesome Lake Hut where drinking water was available, rinsed out my shirt, and sat in the sun enjoying the classic view of the Franconia Ridge skyline.

After a pleasant rest stretched out on the edge of the lake, I followed the white blazes down Cascade Brook Trail to Franconia Notch. Walking along the West Branch of the Pemigewasset River under the highway bridges, I felt what seemed to be the quintessence of the last weekend of summer – something about the combination of the sunlight, the buzzing insects, the river water a clear jelly green in the pools, and the small ferns and milkweed along the banks.

The AT re-enters the woods and climbs a never-ending staircase of rock steps on the Liberty Spring Trail that must have taken many person-months to put in place. The hiker from Exeter who had been at Kinsman Pond Shelter was an apprentice mason, and he had explained the slow process of setting stone steps. That operation had been repeated hundreds of times on this piece of trail. I rested at intervals going up and finally came to the Liberty Spring campsite 2,500 feet above the Notch. I rigged my tarp to provide a windscreen on one of the wooden tent platforms that are strung out along the steep mountainside. This camp was one of the most pleasant of the entire hike.

Home Sweet Home

The caretaker suggested taking advantage of the unusually good viewing conditions, so after setting up camp I hiked up another 650 feet to the summit of Mount Liberty (4,459 feet). It was great advice – on the summit it was sunny and warm with not much wind, and the view, reported to be 120 miles that morning, was spectacular. I begged a sip of water from a boy hiking with his dad from Mount Garfield to Lincoln Woods (an ambitious hike), took photos of a German couple with their camera, and soaked up the view. Mount Washington was crystal clear and Mount Mansfield and the northern peaks of Vermont were easily visible. It was beautiful up there; it was also like the beach, with many kids, sleeping dogs, etc., but I didn't mind the crowd, which made it seem more festive. That night I left the tarp folded back as a wind screen and slept in the open next to it.

Around 6:30 am on Monday, what seemed like raindrops were hitting my face when I awoke, but it was either a very brief passing shower or condensation dripping from the trees. Back on the trail at 8:30 am, the sky was mostly

Just Walking

covered by high clouds that filtered the sun and allowed a sunny break once in a while. The AT climbs up to the Franconia Ridge, passes through spruce woods and beds of ferns atop the ridge, and then heads up a steep pitch with a couple of rocky scrambles to Little Haystack (4,780 feet), where I ran into Hot Rod.

We walked together toward Mount Lafayette (5,260 feet), over perhaps the most beautiful above-treeline ridge walk on the AT, climbing over several knobs and Mount Lincoln (5,089 feet) before we summited Lafayette. The wind was cold but bearable if you kept moving or stood behind something; (I was wearing a windshirt and shorts). The cloud-filtered light actually brought out the subtle colors of fall alpine plants, lichens, and granite.

We met Leaf and walked down from Lafayette together, occasionally climbing down a ledge drop. I split off and hiked up the short side trail to the summit of

Hot Rod coming up Little Haystack

Mount Garfield (4,500 feet), where I ate lunch in the lee of some boulders while savoring the view. The AT continues down Garfield, behind Galehead Mountain, and up to the hut (3,780 feet), which was visible from several places along the way. The afternoon at Galehead was spent talking with Kismet, Spock, Floating Widget, and Leaf.

Spock designs and builds very fast, light fiberglass-over-cedar-strip canoes, and as we chatted after dinner he described the process very well and in detail. He and Kismet were NoBos doing a southbound flip flop from Katahdin; (by now you understand how to parse this sentence). We also talked about tarps versus tents. Spock reassured me that my tarp would be comfortable in Maine even when the temperatures dipped into the thirties if it was rigged properly to manage the flow of air. A three-season tent on the other hand, might become damp inside on cold nights from the condensation of your breath.

Tasty Stuff

Alpine landscape on Mount Guyot

The Galehead croo[18] had prepared a great dinner, something you expect at the White Mountain huts. Among the guests at the long table were a couple of doctors (one was a former croo member at Lakes of the Clouds hut), a helicopter pilot and his son, and a retired gent from a town near Atlanta who was working to combat urban sprawl in his town, but none of the thru-hikers.

It felt strange to be a paying guest while my hiker friends waited outside for their turn to eat (in return for doing some chores). I had made hut reservations back in April but hadn't anticipated this – it was like being a first class passenger on a cruise ship while your buddies are in steerage. Around bedtime the work-for-stay thru-hikers were allowed to set up their sleeping bags under the mess hall tables while the paying guests retired to the bunkrooms.

Tuesday, the second day of September, was cool and gray. Visibility was good

---

[18] This idiosyncratic spelling of "crew" is a tradition of the huts.

Just Walking

beneath the cloud deck, which was at approximately 4,800 feet, judging from the surrounding peaks. It was breezy and in the high 40s when I left Galehead hut at 9:15 am, having been well fed. The climb up South Twin (4,902 feet) was easier than I remembered it from past years. During the day hike up this trail that I had led in July at the ATC meeting, we were going very slowly to keep the group together, and there was very little weight on my back, but this time, even with a full backpack, it wasn't that difficult. Unlike July, though, I didn't hang out on the summit, which was cold and windy.

I trekked on at a brisk pace toward the alpine area on the Bondcliff Trail where the Twinway turns to the east. At Mount Guyot's rocky "beach" I talked to four SoBos, including Bean Pie, Land Squid, and Deuce Bigelow the Trail Gigolo, whose name was somehow familiar. Bean Pie recognized my trail name and remembered seeing a note for me and other NoBos from Mountain Momma,

Atop Webster Cliffs

who was staying at Pinkham Lodge for a few days. Unfortunately, Pinkham was several days away, and we never connected.

Walking on, I tagged the summit of Mount Zealand (4,260 feet), and took a long rest break sitting by the side of the trail with Widget and the guys from Georgia who were at the hut the previous night. We talked about city planning and transit-oriented development, something they had worked on with the well-known neo-urbanist planner Andres Duany in their town, Covington, Georgia, which was the location for the movie "My Cousin Vinny."

It was getting warmer, and I shed my rain pants and windshirt at a lunch stop atop Zeacliff (3,740 feet), which offers an astounding panorama. I continued on to Zealand Hut where I chatted with a couple of southbound section hikers before moving on around 2:15 pm. Below the hut, the AT turns south to follow the Ethan Pond Trail, a former railroad grade which is easy after the Twinway. The views back to Zeacliff, 1,300 feet above, are kind of cool when you remember looking down on the place you're now standing, from way up there a little while before. It's another instance of the wonder of getting from here to there, just by walking!

After the Ethan Pond trail turned the corner at Whitewall Mountain, the hike became a bit of a slog, but the sun came out around 4 pm and I reached Crawford Notch at 5:15 pm. I was headed to Dry River campground, a couple of miles from the trail, so I stuck out my thumb. It is difficult to hitchhike in Crawford Notch because most of the cars are driven by tourists, and they rarely stop for hikers, but on this occasion I was picked up by an Italian couple in a rented sedan with their baby in a child seat in the back. They had to rearrange the usual backseat vacation clutter to fit me in and were very friendly and interested in details of my hike and my lightweight gear. At the campground a friendly ranger let me stay for free and gave me detergent and shampoo as well as change for the laundry and shower. These facilities were brand new and very nice.

The trail to Mount Monroe

Just Walking

On Wednesday the skies were partly cloudy. I ate, packed up, and was standing by the side of the road at 8 am with my thumb out. Two guys on their way to an AMC meeting at the new Highland Center further up the notch took me to the AT crossing. It was a steady climb up to Webster Cliffs (3,100 feet), where two men from Long Island were taking a break. They gave me half an orange and some cookies. You really appreciate small delicacies like this when you're hiking. From much of the clifftop trail there are views down into the notch across to the Willey Range on the opposite side.

The trail up Mount Webster (3,910 feet) and Mount Jackson (4,052 feet) was easy compared to the Webster Cliff Trail. At one point I could see Mitzpah Hut perched on the side of Mount Pierce. Reaching the hut around noon I left my food bag untouched and enjoyed a lunch of soup, leftover bread and pancakes, and chocolate chip cookies. It was a reward for burning all those calories on the way up. The hut croo told me that a bed would be available at Lakes of the Clouds Hut even a day earlier than my reservation. A helicopter arrived and lowered a cargo net full of supplies – I stuck my head out the door to see it and came close to being squashed.

The trail took me up to Mount Pierce where the AT joins Crawford Path, said to be the oldest continuously used hiking path in the United States. There was a series of views ahead to Mount Eisenhower, the connecting ridge to Mount Monroe's double peak, and Mount Washington, with its head in the clouds. Just below Pierce's summit (4,312 feet) a peregrine falcon circled several times with swooping motions almost like a giant swallow. I pointed it out to two women who were hiking south and it reappeared, making another pass for them.

Inside Lakes of the Clouds Hut

The walk up the Eisenhower ridge and past Monroe was outstanding. The trail is completely exposed and runs from 4,200 to 5,000 feet. It was windy, 35-40 mph with stronger gusts, and the weather was deteriorating, so the element of danger added some spice. In fact, this was one of the most beautiful hiking days I've ever experienced. The light was wonderful as clouds billowed by, often almost close enough to reach out and touch. I needed my hiking sticks to maintain balance in the gusts but found that the wind also

Mount Washington in the early morning

could help boost me up big steps in the rocks. Two older hikers who looked very competent told me that the wind was gusting up to 60-70 mph in the notch on Mount Monroe. They wished me a good hike and were obviously digging the conditions too. I stayed on the AT rather than go over Monroe and reached Lakes of the Clouds Hut (5,012 feet) around 3 pm.

It was a good afternoon and evening at the hut talking with folks who weren't thru-hikers, as well as Jimmy, Elf, Regan and Soultrain, who were.

Thursday started out rainy and then foggy, in the 50s, so it wasn't hard to decide to take a zero day at the hut and wait for the weather to improve as forecasted. I passed the day hanging around, reading, writing a birthday letter to my son Greg, and talking to other guests and with croo member Andy, who had recently lived a mile from me in Newton, Massachusetts.

I kept warm most of the day sitting on a bench with the lower half of my body in my sleeping bag, reading and drinking tea. Jimmy, Elf, Regan, and Soultrain carried backboard loads of trash up to the summit of Washington to give the croo a break. T-Bird and Hot Rod arrived. Around 4 pm someone yelled that the clouds were lifting, and everyone ran out and watched the summit of Mount Washington appear.

Lakes Hut had a much different attitude toward work-for-stay hikers than Gale-

Just Walking

head. They ate dinner at a second seating, but at Lakes it was at a big table in the kitchen with the croo, and it had the feel of a party. Also, there were plenty of bunks, and they put all the thru-hikers in the bunkroom where I was sleeping, so I felt less estranged from my trail friends. We went to sleep listening to T-Bird and Soultrain singing.

The promised clearing didn't occur on Friday, but the wind freshened without becoming too strong. I set off for Mount Washington (6,288 feet) a little past 8 am. It was an easy 1,300-foot climb, and gaps in the clouds provided neat views down to the valleys below the Presidential Ridge and back to Lakes Hut and the tarns it was named for. Washington's summit is nothing special — parking lots and tourists abound, so there was no point hanging around for long.

The wind picked up on the back side of the mountain. I was wearing a wind-

On the Gulfside Trail

shirt and rain pants and was comfortable, even warm, in the sheltered spots. I stopped to talk about thru-hiking with three women in Edmands Col. For some reason I like open cols even more than summits, and Edmands Col (4,938 feet) is one of my favorite places in the Whites. It has a spring and is sparsely covered with alpine vegetation; the grasses and sedges[19] turn rich shades of reddish brown and gold in the fall.

More views opened up as I made my way up to the wonderfully (and accurately) named Thunderstorm Junction (5,490 feet). The AT, now on the Gulfside Trail, skirts the north side of Mount

---

[19] As the resident naturalist at Lakes of the Clouds had explained, three similar plants can be distinguished by the formula "Sedges have edges, and rushes are round, and grasses are hollow right down to the ground."

Adams, where between 1892 and 1910 Rayner Edmands set huge slabs of rock, selected from the talus slope to form a sort of level Roman road that still exists and provides a nice relief from hopping from one jagged chunk of rock to another.

Arriving at Madison Spring Hut (4,825 feet) around 12:30 pm, I read the register while dining on breakfast leftovers and a bowl of excellent barley soup. Madison Spring has a high-energy, cool-hand croo, which, incredibly, included thru-hiker Karma, whom I had met in Pennsylvania. He signed me in and just smiled when I told him he looked familiar – it took me a couple of hours to realize who he was. (It seems Karma did home remodeling in his civilian life and had helped the croo re-install a toilet; they had adopted him the previous week.) The weather worsened and hikers came in throughout the afternoon, wet and cold from the light steady rain and wind.

Dawn from Madison Spring Hut

Just Walking

It was a full house for the weekend, plus a bumper crop of thru-hikers, including Loser, Roamin' Around, Elf, Jimmy, Hot Rod, Blink Blink, Kung Fu, Scubaman, and others. There was a very good nature program after dinner. Jimmy, Elf, and I talked for a long while with the croo naturalist. They are very experienced bird watchers.

I woke up on Saturday to the sight of a lovely pink sunrise through the window opposite my bunk. After breakfast, Loser helped the croo naturalist deliver the weather forecast by singing and playing "It Ain't Goin' to Rain No More," a crowd pleaser. Before leaving, I removed a Powerbar wrapper from the urinal, presumably left by a disgruntled guest; I hoped it was not a thru-hiker.

The morning was fine and clear. The top of Mount Madison (5,366 feet) was beautiful and not too cold.

> Sun warms summit rocks,
> Raises clouds from below me,
> Glints on spider silk.

The trail dropped down, down, down to Jackson Road and Pinkham Notch (2,032 feet). I sat on the porch of the AMC visitors' center with Blink Blink, Scubaman, and Kung Fu for a while and then hitched into Gorham to buy supplies. Morph and Moonshadow were walking down the street there. Back at the Pinkham Visitor Center, I sat with Loser, Roamin', and Cheesecake in the hiker room on the lower level waiting for dinner. I slept in a shared room in Pinkham's Joe Dodge Lodge.

In the wee hours of Sunday morning I awoke with a toothache. This pain had been coming and going for three or four days, but it was definitely getting worse. The best alternative seemed to be to go

Washinton and Adams from Madison

home and see my own dentist in Boston; there is a bus that stops at Pinkham, so access is easy, which wouldn't be the case a few days later if I hiked on.

It was a smart move to see the dentist: the tooth was abscessed and would have become a medical emergency. As it turned out, I needed a root canal, which the dentist wanted to leave open for a week for "good drainage" (you get the idea).

I was concerned about my itinerary, because the trail on Katahdin is usually closed for the winter on October 15. Rather than lose a whole week, I drove back up to the Whites very early the following Friday to hike Wildcat and the Carters. After eating a large breakfast in Gorham and picking up my mail drop, I drove to Pinkham, parked, and was on the trail at 9:15 am. As I walked the flat section next to Lost Pond, eerie fog banks slid by. The trail ascended the steep Wildcat Ridge, where I was not actually in the clouds but could look out at the side of one hovering in the notch. At about 3,000 feet the trail rose above the clouds and there was a panorama of the Presidential summits, all in the clear.

Wildcat is a tough climb – lots of jagged rock, some tricky ledges to creep up, and it keeps on coming and coming. I lost count of which of the five Wildcat summits I was at, but eventually made it to the last one (Wildcat A Peak, 4,422 feet) around 12:30 pm. I rested and talked to Triple 7, a northbound flip-flopper, as we enjoyed the view straight down into Carter Notch.

The descent to Carter Notch was an easier trail than the one up from Pinkham. I crossed the 19-Mile Brook trail at the low point (3,300 feet) and continued up Carter Dome (4,832 feet) without a side trip to the hut. The climb up the Dome was long and steep but less nasty than Wildcat had been. In fact, the trail up South Kinsman a few days earlier was the only one that had come close to Wildcat. After a rest on top of Carter Dome, I went down to the col and up to nearby Mount Hight (4,675 feet), then continued down to the 3,890-foot level in Zeta Pass, a cool shady place with a neat name. Not many people were on the trail – a woman on Carter Dome and a couple on Hight, all dayhikers.

It was around 3:30 pm and I was getting tired. I made South Carter (4,430 feet) by 4 pm and Middle Carter (4,610 feet) at 5 pm. The long, steep descent from North Carter (4,470 feet) was tricky, and I was too tired to have fun on the scrambles. There were great views across to the Presidentials and down to the Wild River from several lookouts along the Carter Ridge, one of the pretty trails in the Whites. It was very peaceful and quiet on Middle and North Carter. I had hiked this trail a few days after September 11, 2001, and will always remember the feeling of peace that day in a setting completely removed from the insanity that grips the modern world, and completely unchanged by the ghastly events that changed so much else.

Just Walking

Around 6 pm I reached Imp Campsite, whose shelter was dark and damp looking, so I pitched my tarp on one of the tent platforms. It was getting dark at 7:15 pm, and it had been a long 13-mile day on challenging terrain.

I got up in the cold on Saturday morning and headed out, going down initially and then steadily up to Mount Moriah (4,049 feet). It was crystal clear up high, but there were fog banks in the valleys below. The trail followed ridges with many views to the south and west. I scrambled up a crease in the steep rock face to the summit, which offers a good view of the Mahoosuc Range, the next stage in the hike.

The trail north from Moriah is a long, jarring downhill slog most of the way to Route 2 (elevation 760 feet). At the Rattle River Shelter the register contained recent entries from several of my trail friends. At the highway a Gorham High School teacher was kind enough to take me to the Route 16 junction, and from there a mother/son hiking duo brought me back to my car at Pinkham. I drove back home to have my dental work finished and then return to the trail for the last of the fourteen states.

The Mahoosucs from Mount Moriah

8
The Way Life Should Be

The Way Life Should Be

Maine has a special place in the AT itinerary. It's that far-away land over the rainbow that you think about all the way from Georgia. It also has the reputation – well deserved – of being one of the most beautiful, and hardest, sections of the Appalachian Trail, a 281-mile stretch capped with the daunting 100-mile Wilderness. It had a special allure for me, because I love the state of Maine, but I had never hiked any of the AT there. In fact, my mental map said that Maine begins with the Mahoosucs, although half of this mountain range is really in New Hampshire.

One of the great things about Maine for northbounders is that by the time you reach it, most of the challenges and uncertainties of the thru-hike are past, and although you are feeling the fatigue of months of hiking, you're pretty sure you can make it. ("Pretty sure" allows for the fact that some hikers have become disabled by injuries just a few days from Katahdin, there's always the possibility of early snow that will close the mountain, and you might get stomped by a bull moose in his fall rut.)

The familiar rhythm of each day, each step, each 2-by-6 white blaze, the flow of endorphins, and the Zen experience of just walking extends on into Maine. The principal change from the Whites and all the miles that came before is the unique and beautiful scenery and smell of the trail as you enter the last of the fourteen states traversed by the AT. You're ready. Enjoy the ride.

The Hardest Mile
The Mahoosucs to Andover, ME:
[Mile 1,873.3 to Mile 1,914.7]

Monday, September 15. After concluding matters with my dentist, I went directly to Boston's South Station and rode the bus to Gorham, the home of Hiker's Paradise Motel and Hostel, run by a Polish mountaineer and hiker named Bruno Janicki.

As forecasted, it was raining lightly on Tuesday morning. After entertaining me with his sardonic conversation at breakfast, Bruno shuttled me to the parking lot where the AT crosses Route 2 and heads into the Mahoosuc Range. I had never hiked in the Mahoosucs, but a few years before had spent a weekend hiking on the Kilkenny Ridge, a few miles to the west. At the time I was in good hiking shape, but I was beat at the end of that weekend, and my knees hurt. The profile of the AT through the Mahoosucs is similar but even more extreme, a long series of steep ups and steep downs. These mountains are not especially high but they had certainly looked rugged from the top of Mt. Moriah. "So, here we go," I thought as I stepped off.

The first climb of the day over Mount Hayes (2,555 feet) was easy but wet. The rain was often no more than a drizzle, but there was water everywhere on the trail, flowing down the steep sections like little brooks and standing in puddles between the roots of trees. My feet soon got squishy wet, and I actually poured water out of my boots at lunchtime.

Just Walking

Clouds rise from the Androscoggan Valley

These boots were the Garmonts I had bought when I came home from Pennsylvania, but they were well worn by now, and besides, no boots are really waterproof if you walk through puddles for a few hundred miles.

Page Pond could have been painted in shades of gray. I briefly lost the trail at the shore, turned left, reached a dead end, and then found the real trail which skirted the pond to the right.

As may be apparent by now, at the end of a long day a hiker watches hopefully for that lovely trail sign announcing a shelter, which offers blessed rest and repose in a dry, comfortable place like Gentian Pond Shelter, my destination for the day. I parked my hiking sticks against the side of the shelter and hopefully peeked in. It was full of thru-hikers – 16 in a shelter that sleeps 14. There were people I hadn't seen for months: Reason, Mr. Pumpy, Very Small Animal, and Last Minute. Wet gear was hanging everywhere and dripping onto the floor in front of the double-decked sleeping platform. There was truly no more room; cold, wet hikers were compressed shoulder to shoulder on the two sleeping platforms.

I sat in one of the patches of dry floor leaning against the wall and pondered what to do next. The rain had stopped, and the clouds started to lift around 3:30 pm, opening up a view of the hills across the Androscoggin valley to the south. People scurried around trying to dry their tents. I sat cross-legged on my foam square to make and eat an early dinner.

A couple of people decided to move on, so I inherited a slot to sleep in. It was in the loft under the eaves. The sloping roof came almost to the level of the sleeping platform, so I couldn't sit up straight in the triangular prism that was my place for the night; I had to wriggle

The Way Life Should Be

Board bridges cross the bog on Mount Carlo

into it feet first. However, it was dry and horizontal and it felt much better than being wet and cold and sitting on the floor.

In contrast to Tuesday, Wednesday turned out to be a gorgeous day. The sky was clear at 6:15 am. I lay there a while, wanting to get up and pee, but I couldn't leave my slot without waking the woman sleeping next to me.[20] When I could wait no longer I literally wormed my way out. A front header to the floor five feet below was not a good idea, so I hung onto a rafter to get my feet under me and dropped down. I took my backpack off a nail, removed my food bag from one of the hangers,[21] and packed and left without waking anyone.

What followed were two of the best days of the hike. The trail climbed up Mount

---
[20] It turned out to be Triple-T, whom I saw along the way in Maine and summited with.
[21] In places where bears are not a major nuisance, there is still a good chance that rodents will get at your food at night if you leave it unprotected. Accordingly, most shelters have a few food bag hangers – a short length of parachute cord suspended from the roof with a short stick tied crossways at the end to hang the bag from and an inverted tuna can halfway down the cord to discourage mice.

Just Walking

Success (3,565 feet), descended with alarming steepness over jagged slabs of rock to a col, and then went up to Mount Carlo (also 3,565 feet). Both mountains had rocky tops with 360-degree views. There was a very beautiful boggy area (not an oxymoron) just below Mount Carlo's summit, and I stopped to absorb its quiet ambience.

Shortly after, the AT crossed the last state border, which was decorated with a blue hand-painted sign announcing "Maine: The Way Life Should Be," a slogan that is familiar to anyone who has driven into Maine on I-95. (Until recently, that is; this existentialist statement has been replaced by a more conventional tourism promotion slogan.)

Two SoBos, first Bulldog and a little later The Colonel, passed me. Both complained about belligerent NoBos at Carlo Col Shelter, one of whom actually called Bulldog out, i.e., challenged him to fisticuffs, that morning because he had yelled at them for keeping everyone up the night before. However, I later heard that The Colonel was up at 4:30 am banging around with his gear. "Why can't we all just get along?"

It was a beautiful climb up Goose Eye Mountain, including a nearly vertical segment. From the bottom of this pitch you can see the trail junction sign at the top and a ladder halfway up, marking the trail's course. There were a couple of challenging scrambles along the way. I detoured left at the top and had lunch on Goose Eye's West Peak (3,870 feet), taking in a view that extended all the way back to Mount Washington. I could pick out all of the Presidentials and the peaks of the Carter Ridge as I munched on a tortilla and cheese.

Looking back to Mount Washington from Goose Eye

Moments like this define the trail experience for me. You are sitting on the ground, your muscles are thanking you for an opportunity to rest, you are eating stuff that stokes the furnace with the calories your body is craving (peanut butter spooned from the jar, cheese, Oreos). There is an almost incredible view extending for miles, all of which you have bought and paid for by putting one foot in front of the other. It is quiet, and the endorphins are coursing through your system. I thanked my lucky stars again for the opportunity to do this.

After lunch the lovely walk continued along the ridge from East Peak (3,790 feet) to North Peak (3,690 feet). I reached Full Goose Shelter a little before 3 pm and pitched the tarp on a tent platform – I wasn't up for another claustrophobic night packed into the shelter like a sardine in a can. Reason and Cruiser arrived at 5:30 pm, followed by Orbit, Indiana Slim, Mr. Pumpy, Very Small Animal, Superman, and two women named Pipes and Phlegm. There were

Morning on Fulling Mill Mountain

also four short-term hikers there, one of them a doctor from Pennsylvania. We chatted at dinner, but it began to turn cool and we all retired early.

I enjoyed a good night's sleep, except for a persistent daddy-longlegs determined to walk across my face. (I try not to kill fellow arthropods like spiders and their kin.)

Thursday's sunrise was blood-red through the trees. An amazing 100% of the hikers were up by 6:30 am – perhaps a sign of adrenaline pumping through our bodies at the thought of hiking through Mahoosuc Notch, universally known as "the toughest mile on the AT."

I started hiking around 7:20 am. There was another pretty bog on top of Fulling Mill Mountain (3,395 feet) and long views back to Goose Eye Mountain and the Presidential range.

Mahoosuc Notch was all it was advertised to be: a jumble of giant boulders, tricky scrambles, slick surfaces, and bad purchase for your hiking sticks. Beginning with the approach trail down to the notch, I teetered on knife-edges and slipped or staggered several times. I fell hard on my butt when a rock suddenly turned slippery on me. I slipped again and took a twisting fall that didn't hurt except for a little skin off my shin, but it would have been quite a different story if the rock I ended up straddling

Just Walking

had been a foot higher. There were several near-falls too. I had to wriggle under boulders twice, and one of these passages required me to take off my pack and push it ahead of me through a small opening. This confirmed my prediction to Last Minute that we would be doing some crawling on our bellies to get through the Notch. I was glad it was a dry day. I emerged from this obstacle course in an hour and a quarter and was relieved to have it behind me.

I climbed 1,600 feet of trail up Mahoosuc Arm (3,765 feet) in the morning sun, resting for a while at a crossing where a brook ran over the bedrock. It was steep but not all that difficult for the hiking machine my body had become. At Galehead Hut Spock said that he had done it southbound and had been led to expect great slippery sheets of slate but was relieved to find it not much of a big deal. No hubris here, just the facts.

At Speck Pond I missed a sharp turn in the trail at the campsite. The caretaker saw me looking around for the trail, and when I asked where the AT went he said, "It's the one with the white blazes" with no hint of irony.

The trail mounted some high-angle exposed rock to Little Speck, and a side trail led to the summit of Old Speck (4,170 feet). On top an observation tower with a near-vertical 20-foot ladder afforded great views forward to Baldpate and back to Mahoosuc Notch and Goose-Eye. I spent an hour there eating lunch and talking with a young couple from Pittsburg and a compact New Hampshire woman wearing a Red Sox cap. All three had climbed each of the 48 4000-footers in New Hampshire and were now working on the ones in Maine. The woman told me about meeting a northbound flip-flopper with a white beard who talked about the wild plants along the trail: it had to be Mountain Jack, and he was headed my way. She also told me the worst was over now that I had completed the Mahoosucs – music to my ears. As I packed up, a peregrine falcon flew over the summit.

Obstacle course in Mahoosuc Notch

The Way Life Should Be

I hiked down, down, down Old Speck on a trail that was easier than I had seen in a long while. A kestrel hovered for a moment at an overlook. The weather remained sunny with some high clouds. The AT crossed the highway in Grafton Notch and went up the side of Baldpate where I reached the eponymous lean-to by 4:30 pm and was joined by Feral and Triple T, two of my shelter-mates at Gentian Pond.

I awoke at 6 am on Friday to a pretty sunrise. I ate a bowl of granola and packed outside the shelter so as not to wake up the others. The trail continued up Baldpate's West Peak (3,662 feet), much of it on the mountain's exposed smooth gray granite. From the summit I watched a curtain of clouds move swiftly across the sky from the south. I walked down into the col, which was mostly open, and up the bare rock dome of East Peak (3,810 feet) as the wind gusted. I called the Pine Ellis B&B from the summit with my cell phone and arranged a pick-up at the next road.

The trail down the mountain was in good shape and had few ledges and obstructions. As I reached the lower half of the mountain, the grade became less steep and I was able to freewheel[22] for the first time in weeks. The prediction that the worst trails were behind me seemed to be true. Birch, beech, and maple leaves were beginning to fall, although the color was not very well developed yet.

Exposed granite on Baldpate

I arrived at Dunn Notch ahead of schedule for my 11:30 am pickup, so I detoured down the side trail to the base of a high waterfall. Returning, I continued on through a grove of hemlocks to the road, where Paul, the owner of Pine Ellis, was waiting for me. He gave me a couple of new apples to eat during the ride back to Andover. Paul waited at the post office while I picked up my mail drop, and then took me back to the B&B. I did the laundry, borrowing a T shirt from the hiker box, and then walked two blocks to the village center in a light drizzle. At one of the stores I bought lunch supplies, wine, and peanuts and gratefully accepted four slices of several-hours-old pizza. Passing the town's other B&B on the way back, I stopped to chat with Mr. Pumpy and a bearded hiker named Kunga. We discussed whether to use Heet fuel injector cleaner (methyl alcohol with

---

[22] Freewheeling is my term for scooting along with your legs bent in a sort of crouch, using your hiking sticks to control your speed. You can cover ground swiftly with a minimum expenditure of energy.

Just Walking

some additives) in my stove, as no other fuel was available. We tentatively concluded it might work; (it did, but left a gummy residue). I walked back to Pine Ellis through a grassy vacant lot behind the fire station and took a nap in my room.

That evening I dined at Addie's restaurant – homemade clam chowder, bright red franks with baked beans, and a slice of truly excellent apple pie, which had been baked by an 85-year-old blind grandma, according to the waitress. I've noticed that the odds of getting excellent pie are very good at most small towns and truck stops in Maine, one reason why it's the way life should be. I shot the breeze with an old gent at the counter who was nursing a cup of coffee and said nothing for a long while until I started the conversation; then he talked with animation, a common trait in Down-Easters I've met. I returned to Pine Ellis and sipped wine while listening to the Red Sox game, which they won.

o Walking in Beauty
Andover to Caratunk ME:
[Mile 1,914.7 to Mile 2,020.0]

Saturday, September 20. I had a good breakfast at the B&B with Pipes and Phlegm, who were both from the Boston area. There was light rain, then a heavy burst during the shuttle back to the trail, and light rain again to start the hike for the day. The rain soon stopped, and the sun broke through for a couple of minutes around mid-day. However, the trail was flowing, and I tried in vain to keep my boots semi-dry by skirting the brooks and puddles and hopping from rock to rock and root to root. Ultimately I gave up, which was just as well because the trail forded two brooks in the afternoon. I encountered P-Nut and Peach Monkey a couple of times, and Indiana Slim was at Hall Mountain Lean-to when I stopped for lunch.

The trail over Wyman Mountain (2,920 feet) was easy, apart from the puddles, but Moody Mountain (2,440 feet) was a steep son-of-a-gun to climb, even with only 1,300 feet of elevation gain. After fording Black Brook, I walked down the road to the spring recommended by B&B owner Paul (whom I saw again when he showed up to pick up a slacker) and camped by the road in a little grove of trees rather than cross back over the brook to the larger campsite on its west bank. Indiana Slim arrived soon after. He was out of cash and low on food, so I gave him two food bars, feeling a little greedy, but not willing to leave myself without a dinner for the last day before resupplying. We sat in the tiny stealth campsite and talked for a while before crawling into our respective shelters for the night. It was dark by 6:45 pm.

At this point in the hike, I began to be aware of some less than admirable traits in myself as I single-mindedly pursued the goal of getting to Katahdin before it closed for the winter. I'm a born worrier, but I worried more than usual about injury and hypothermia. I noticed myself feeling greedy about food and selfishly hurrying to stake out the most comfortable place in the shelter or the best place to pitch my tarp. I was spurring myself along to get in the mileage I felt I needed to cover each day. I was drinking more when I got to town. I often wanted to be alone. Perhaps the root cause of all of this was simply the accumulated fatigue of nearly six months of hiking. It wasn't a constant thing, and it didn't spoil the beauty of Maine, but it certainly was goal-oriented striving. Not exactly Zen mind, but then, no one should expect that to be easy.

The sound of a moose wading in the brook woke me briefly at 4 am on Sunday. Indiana Slim and I rose at 6:30 am, and we left together before 8 am. It was a bit of a grunt climbing the steep trail to Old Blue (3,600 feet) in a light fog with the aid of some wet, mossy handholds. When we emerged above the fog layer, the views were nice, and it was mostly sunny, although clouds were beginning to gather. The walk to Elephant Mountain and Mount Bemis (3,580 feet) was less fun – all roots and mud puddles. Walking down the moderately sloping granite ledges from Mount Bemis to its lean-to was better.

I was feeling tired and a little low, but lunch at Bemis Lean-to rejuvenated me. After a debate with myself, I decided to go on to Sabbath Day Pond Lean-to – eight more miles. It was just after 2 pm when I started this leg of the day's hike. I made much better time after lunch because the trail was easier. The knobs on Mount Bemis looked ahead to some pretty mountains in the distance, and the foliage was changing color at the lower elevations. I crossed Bemis Stream almost dry – just a couple of the steppingstones were under water – and made it to the highway at 4:30 pm.

Clouds passing the summit of Old Blue

Just Walking

On the way I talked to Kunga (which means "much joy" in Nepalese, he said). I also met Mud Elephant (GA-ME '96), and – lo and behold – Mountain Jack, who was well along on the final stretch of his hike. After this pleasant reunion I hauled myself up the hill and past Moxie Pond and Long Pond to Sabbath Day Pond, arriving around 6 pm. Kunga came in about 8 pm, well after dark, which was a good trick considering the rocky terrain above the lean-to.

Kunga was from Cambridge, Massachusetts, so it was not surprising that our views were in alignment. In the morning, we chatted about politics and the evils of Dick Cheney and Karl Rove. It was cool and mostly cloudy. Near the top of the first hill out of camp I heard something crashing around in the woods ahead and then saw a rack of antlers through the trees. My first thought was that it's good to identify the tree you plan to jump behind when you meet a bull moose on the trail, especially during rutting season when they can be dangerous, but the sides of the trail were bordered with spruce trees so closely interwoven that I would have had to drop my pack and worm my way between them on my hands and knees. As it turned out, I heard him trotting away from me on the trail, so the confrontation never took place.

The hiking was easy, and I soon made it to Little Swift River Pond campsite, where I rested, sitting under the pine trees on one of the sawed-off logs they had provided as stools around the fire pit. My legs were still feeling tired from the previous day's 17-miler. I decided to change into my dry pair of socks; they felt good, one of the little pleasures of hiking.

After the break there were some nice sections of trail that were less root-y than usual, and at the top of the day's last pitch there was an excellent view toward Saddleback. I talked to two sisters in

Little Swift River Pond

their 50s, one living in New Hampshire and the other in Damariscotta, Maine. I learned from them that the forecast called for rain on Tuesday.

At Route 4, I scored an eagle into Rangeley with a guy hauling firewood in his truck. I walked around town, scouting for lodging. A sign on Main Street proclaimed that Rangeley is equidistant from the equator and the north pole. Mountain Jack had recommended the Gull Pond Lodge, but when I learned that it was a mile or so out of town I decided to check into the Rangeley Inn, which was expensive but right in front of me.[23] Half an inch of rain was forecasted, so I decided to take a zero day.

After unpacking I ate dinner at the bar in a restaurant down Main Street and had an interesting talk with a gray-bearded local resident who had been discussing the fine points of hunting rifles with the bartender. Contrary to stereotype, he was arguing against hunting on compassionate grounds, an unusual attitude

The AT climbs Saddleback over granite ledges

to find in these parts. It was a pleasant conversation, fueled on his side by a few rum-and-cokes and on mine by wine. Never make assumptions about people.

On Tuesday the rains came as predicted. I ate breakfast at a little restaurant up the street while my clothes were drying in the laundromat, and afterwards spent most of the day in my room, reading a mystery purchased at the local bookstore (the classic *Daughter of Time* by Josephine Tey). I ran into some other hikers on the street, including Mr. Pumpy, Very Small Animal, and Reason, who were headed for the pub across the street from the Inn. As I looked back on my days in the White Mountains a few weeks before, it seemed that time was flying by.

[23] I stayed at the Gull Pond Lodge the following year. It is a great place and well worth the detour.

Just Walking

From the summit of Saddleback

On Wednesday I breakfasted at the same place as the day before, a joint called the "Stones Throw" where lots of Rangeley folks eat; it serves decent food and was full of local color. A woman who had just taken her daughter to school gave me a ride back to the trail; she was a retired soldier who had returned to her home territory after her recent discharge. I started hiking at 8:15 am just as Reason, Cruiser, and others arrived in the Gull Pond shuttle van.

I walked fast to be by myself, not a reflection on the others but of my desire for solitude. My AT experience had boiled down to the act of walking, the rhythm, the exertion, the technique of finding a place to put each step. I was enjoying the scenery, which changes slowly except at major landmarks like summits with wrap-around views or groves of hemlock, or at river crossings. Part of my focus was on my old obsession of getting from here to there: checking the mile markers on my map's trail profile and using my watch and altimeter to estimate my progress. I felt compelled to keep making miles, partly because my dental emergency had put me a week closer to October 15, when the trails to Katahdin close for the winter, but also for its own sake. That's what long distance hikers do. Until reaching camp. Then it's a social affair with the people you've met along the way.

The trail went up, gradually at first past some small ponds, and then more steeply to treeline on Saddleback ridge. The white blazes continued up the bare gray granite ledges to a pretty summit (4,120 feet) with some alpine vegetation and views in all directions. The sky was blue above a layer of scattered clouds that were passing at eye level, and Rangeley Lake was a blue expanse below. The wind was blowing on top, but not too hard, maybe 25-30 mph. In the distance, to the east, was a distinctive double summit: the Horns of the Bigelow Range.

After a rest I walked down into the saddle (get it?) and back up to the Horn (4,040 feet), then down and up again to Saddleback Junior (3,665 feet). I sat on Junior's summit for a while, enjoying the view ahead to Mount Abraham and Sugarloaf. The jumpoff from the summit was a steep downhill scramble that required some careful foot- and hand-work. From there it was a mile-and-a-half down to Poplar Ridge Lean-to, where I stopped for lunch.

The Carrabassett River crossing

Poplar Ridge was where I had planned to spend the night, but it was still only mid-afternoon when I finished lunch, so I decided to keep hiking for a while and find a place to camp in the woods. The trail went down the hill to Orbeton Stream (named after Rock and Roll immortal Roy Orbeton), which I forded in sandals, and steeply up the other side to a flat area following a pretty stream in a natural stone channel. By then it was 4 pm. I looked around for a decent campsite but couldn't find one, so I went on to Lone Mountain. I passed over the mountain without seeing a campsite to my liking and continued down to Spaulding Mountain Lean-to, which I reached at 6:20 pm. That was plenty for one day. I cooked as it got dark, talking to Texas Jack, the only other person there.

It was clear during the night – I could find my way around the campsite by starlight alone and I even thought I glimpsed the elusive Andromeda galaxy; (you have to look slightly to one side to

Just Walking

see it with the light-sensitive rod cells in your retinas).

On Thursday I walked quickly to the junction with the Spaulding Mountain side trail and ran up to tag the summit (4,000 feet). It was a sunny morning. Mount Abraham stood handsome, off to the right a mile or so from the AT, a trip for another day. When I reached the side trail to Sugarloaf, I didn't have enough gas in the tank to summit it and still make it to Stratton village before dark, so I passed it by.

The AT is interesting and scenic as it descends steeply from the foot of Sugarloaf following the edge of a rocky ravine. A couple of short-distance hikers who were coming up stopped for a rest and we engaged in some gear-talk (tent versus tarp, etc.) There was a pretty sun-dappled stream, the Carrabassett River, at the bottom. Its black water was garnished with yellow maple leaves floating lazily downstream toward winter. A single loose plank bridged a fast-moving chute of water between big rocks.

Triple-T and Feral were on their way up Crocker Mountain. Together we crossed a talus slope, which reminded us of Colorado. The trail went steeply up and down between Crocker Mountain's two summits (4,040 feet and 4,228 feet), and then a long way down from the north summit to Route 27, the road into Stratton.

At the parking area next to the road I received a ride into town from a hiker named Load who had driven up from Pittsburg. I had had a little bout of diarrhea earlier during the day and wasn't feeling great, so after I picked up my mail drop I hustled into the village to find a place to crash. A large group of hikers

Clouds drift past Bigelow Ridge, Flagstaff Lake below

The Way Life Should Be

from New Hampshire had taken most of the rooms at the two motels in town. I rented what turned out to be the last vacant room. I offered to share it with Feral and Triple T when they came up empty, but they declined the offer, and I realized I really wanted to be alone. I fell asleep right after returning from the local diner, where the beans and franks weren't as good as in Andover. I woke up after a while and watched the Sox clinch the Wild Card.

There was rain during the night, followed by the typical fog and shredded clouds of a morning in the mountains, with patches of blue sky showing through. I was feeling a lot better, both physically and mentally. The motel owner drove me back to the trail after a long wait. I climbed up to the Bigelow Ridge and then along it to the South Horn. It was mostly sunny and the visibility was excellent. The AT continues down past Horns Pond, up to West Peak (4,145 feet), down to a col and back up to Avery Peak (4,090 feet). The trails had pretty

Flagstaff Lake

good footing, and the views were beautiful. A raft of white cloud puffs drifted past at eye-level below a blue sky. It was all reflected in the surface of Flagstaff Lake. The maple trees at the foot of the mountain had covered the landscape below with a blanket of reddish-orange. The steep face of Little Bigelow curved away in the distance.

Two women my age were heading up to Avery Peak as I descended; one gave me some grapes. I ran into CC and Chicken Legs, thru-hikers whom I had first met in New Jersey on Kittatiny Mountain. I continued down to Safford Notch and climbed back up to the ridge of Little Bigelow, where the trail went up and down and on and on for a long way. By the summit of Little Bigelow (3,010 feet) I badly needed a rest. CC and Chicken Legs were there, and CC gave me a cheese sandwich, which tasted indescribably good.

It was getting cloudier. Avery Peak had been in the clear earlier but was cloud-topped now as we looked back to it. I imagined it as Mount Olympus, home of the gods, (although the mountain in Greece looks nothing like it). We all reached Little Bigelow Lean-to at 5:10 pm after a strenuous day.

After a warm night it was foggy on Saturday morning. The AT skirts the sandy edge of Flagstaff Lake, where four kingfishers flew off chattering into the fog. The trail went over a couple of low hills, varying from smooth and fast to root-y, rocky, and annoying, but I covered 17 miles in seven hours, so it was mostly fast track. On the way the trail crossed a road with a big "2000" painted on it, another milestone but less captivating than the mosaic "1000" on the trail into Harpers Ferry. Was that in the same lifetime?

I reached Pierce Pond Lean-to at 3:30 pm. The lean-to looks out on the lovely pond, which is only 30 feet away. It was too cold to swim but I sat for a long while on a big rock on the shore and watched the anglers trolling up and down. Only small engines are allowed on the pond, but they're still noisy in the ambient quietude.

The clouds lifted for a little while before sunset, providing a dramatic view, and later the stars came out before the clouds returned. CC, Chicken Legs, and two southbound section hikers, a man and a woman who had just hooked up on the trail, arrived around dinnertime. When we climbed into our bags in the small shelter it was very cozy and rather warm, probably in the low 50s.

On Sunday the trail followed a pretty brook with many cascades. It sprinkled for a while. I reached the Kennebec River, another major milestone, around 9 am and waited for the canoe ferry provided by the Maine AT Club to arrive and carry me safely across the wide river.[24] After the crossing I walked to Caratunk House, which is just off the trail. I met Jay, who remembered me from Tinker Cliffs in Virginia. He was with his mother Jane, a woman about my age, who was hiking for a couple days with him.

After I threw my gear on a bunk and changed clothes, our host Paul drove me to Northern Outdoors (a river guide center) where I had lunch, drank beer, watched the Patriots lose to the Giants, and ate dinner, washed down with more beer. A bunch of thru-hikers staying at Northern Outdoors included Doc and Llama, Phlegm, Pipes (and her mother Wendy, who was from Topsfield Massachusetts), Sleepy Floyd, Backdraft, Torch and Superman, Fuman and Chu. Reason, Cruiser, Very Small Animal and others were at Caratunk House when I returned.

○ Between the Acts
Caratunk to Monson ME:

Monday, September 29. We all had a great breakfast, sitting around a big round table with a Lazy Susan in the middle. Our host Paul served us eggs, pancakes, potatoes, breakfast meats, and good coffee. Afterward I picked up my mail drop at the little post office, had my photo taken for Paul's wall display, and returned to the trail just before 9 am. It was mostly cloudy, but there were no showers. I made good time on some fast trail and climbed Pleasant Pond Mountain (2,470 feet) after a rest at a lean-to. I caught up to Superman on the way down

---
[24] One has to ford many streams in Maine, but the Kennebec is wide, apt to rise without warning when water is released from the dam upstream, and therefore dangerous; hence the ferry.

The Way Life Should Be

to Moxie Lake. We waded and rock-hopped Baker Brook and stopped for lunch at Bald Mountain Brook Lean-to at 3:30 pm.

Superman and I climbed up Moxie Bald (2,629 feet) together; from the top you can see Whitecap and the other mountains to the northeast, but the day was cloudy and we couldn't identify Katahdin. I was glad Moxie Bald is made of granite, not the slippery slate that was becoming the dominant rock underfoot. At the summit we met Widget and Gray Matter slacking south. Superman and I arrived at Moxie Bald Lean-to just after 6 pm. Light rain started around 7 pm.

It had cleared by Tuesday morning and wasn't too cold. Superman and I began hiking around 7:50 am. There were some wet sections, but it was mostly good trail. We forded Marble Brook and the West Branch of the Piscataquis River where the black water was a little more than knee-deep but the current was easy. After crossing, the trail followed the river, and I walked along looking at the rapids thinking, "That would be a nice Class 2 paddle." However, by Horseshoe Canyon the river was a roaring Class 4. This was an outstandingly pretty piece of trail, carpeted with yellow pine needles on top of fallen magenta leaves. Black water, blue sky.

I met Very Small Animal, Mala, Jay, and Jane at the road crossing a few miles west of Monson; they were being shuttled by Keith Shaw, Jr., whose family runs a famous boarding house for hikers. Superman and I had walked together for some sections during the day and separately on others. My left hip was a little sore, but it was just one of those pains that comes and goes, which I'd been having since Georgia. I felt lucky

Sunset from Moxie Bald

Just Walking

and a little surprised that no injuries had lingered and gotten worse. I was tired, though.

I walked on past the direct road into Monson to end the day's hike at Route 15, where I hitched a ride into town. I went to Shaw's – a famous institution in the last town before the 100-Mile Wilderness. It deserved its reputation for hospitality and good fellowship among hikers. I bought lunch stuff and beer, took a shower, and settled into the place. After dinner some of us sipped beers and watched the Cubs-Atlanta game. Together we tried to explain the rules of baseball to Very Small Animal, who had lived in France most of her life. Quiz: what are the seven ways to get to first base?

○ The Hundred Miles
  Monson ME to Abol Bridge:
  [Mile 2,056.7 to Mile 2,156.1]

Wednesday, October 1. Today we had a memorable breakfast cooked by Keith

Fording place at the West Branch of the Piscataquis

Shaw, Sr. From our table in the kitchen we could see the chef at work. I opted for the "Two-Around," which means two of everything, resulting in a heaped-up plate of eggs, potatoes, pancakes, bacon, ham, and sausage, washed down with good coffee. After breakfast and the usual fussing-around with gear, Keith Jr. shuttled the whole gang to the trail in his pickup truck; the group included Greenman and his partner Sunkist who had stayed up the street. Mountain Dew, who doesn't like the cold, was dressed to summit Katahdin in January, but I have to admit it got chilly back there. I disembarked at the Route 15 trail crossing, while the others went on to the next road, planning to slack back for another night in Monson.

It was a gray, cloudy, and cool morning. A pair of loons floated on the first pond the trail passes. Is there any other waterfowl that looks and sounds so pretty? There was a series of minor ups and

Little Wilson Falls

The Way Life Should Be

downs and a long traverse atop the slate ridge. In the early afternoon the slacker crew greeted me as we walked in opposite directions on Big Wilson Tote Road about nine miles from Route 15. I waded Big Wilson Stream, climbed up the hill, and crossed the Canadian Pacific Railroad tracks; I had heard the lonely whistle of a passing train a mile from the crossing. I stopped at Wilson Valley Lean-to for lunch and chatted with a volunteer trail maintainer. Beyond the top of the ridge was a mile-long slabbing traverse, which was slow and tiring, with lots of little ups and downs.

At Long Pond Stream a pinned-up note in a plastic bag suggested a fallen tree a quarter mile downstream from the trail as a better alternative to wading the stream, which looked dangerous. There was a series of drops where the black water was deep above the drop, very fast moving over the lip, and deeper still below — mid-thigh except where it thinned out over rocks, and there it was moving too fast to keep your feet under

Fallen leaves on the trail

you. I once was a whitewater boater, and the first thing we taught beginners was never to wade in fast water above your knees: beside the obvious problem of getting washed downstream, there is a real risk that you'll put your leg between submerged rocks and be bent over backwards by the current, trapped, and drowned; there are little diagrams explaining this hazard in most books about whitewater boating. This crossing was a textbook example, never mind that hikers cross these things all the time. Just call me squeamish.

So I walked down the road and found the fallen tree, which was maybe two feet wide at the near end and a foot wide at the far end. It rested on a boulder on each side, about four feet above a fast, deep chute of water. Crossing it wasn't hard if you didn't look down, but you needed to in order to see where to put each step. I took a deep breath and stepped off, made it across, and then bushwhacked back to the trail.

Just Walking

The AT follows Long Pond Stream up past Slogundy Falls; there weren't any crossing points that would have been much better. The stream is pretty here, cascading through a slate gorge. I reached the Long Pond Stream Lean-to at 5:30 pm and made mac-and-cheese as it got dark.

I was alone in the lean-to Wednesday night. It was cold Thursday morning – mid-30s to low 40s. The climb up Barren Mountain (2,660 feet) was not too difficult, and there were some views at the top beneath a cloud layer at the level of the higher surrounding peaks. The clouds thickened into a mat, and it was mostly cloudy through the middle of the day, with some clearing in the late afternoon. It was pretty much a rollercoaster day, going over the four summits of the Chairback range (around 2,000 feet). I met two southbound guys plus NoBo Mover, who had jumped up here to finish this section before the trails on Katahdin closed for the year.

By the lunch stop at Chairback Gap, I was growing tired and a little worried about hypothermia. Everything turned out fine, as usual. There were nice views from the ridges of upended slate on Chairback, but Katahdin still was not visible. It's much easier to walk on slate when it is tipped up so you're walking on the edges of the bedding planes instead of their smooth faces. That's what I was thinking when I slipped and fell hard on my butt. I took a shot on my tailbone, which was OK, but bruised the heel of my left hand breaking the fall.

After a long traverse of the ridge, I descended in improving weather to the West Branch of the Pleasant River, a 30-yard-wide, mid-shin-deep crossing. I waded in my sandals, and the only problem was a pair of really cold tootsies. Several women who were returning from a day hike in the Gulf Hagas were on the other bank of the river. (It's not really a wilderness if you can drive in via logging roads to take a day hike.) There was a decent stealth camping area a hundred yards from the crossing, so I pitched the tarp and cooked in the middle of the trail. It started to rain lightly about dark.

The rain picked up just after I went to bed and continued for several hours. I slept warm and dry, and as I lay there I thought back to my conversation with Spock at Galehead Hut about whether a tarp was adequate for cold rainy weather in Maine. It is.

On Friday I emerged to find a clear sky and cold temperatures. The trail was very nice up through the Hermitage and past the Gulf Hagas loop, following the brook up to Newhall Lean-to. I stopped for a rest. As I sat on the edge of the shelter floor munching a Bearito Bar, water dripped from the roof. Sure enough, there was a residue of snow up there melting in the morning sun.

There was more where that came from, The rain during the night had fallen as snow at higher elevations. Little patches began to appear on the fern beds, and

Snow on Whitecap Mountain

there were parallel piles of snow in a campsite where it had slid off someone's tent. There was an inch of it on top of Gulf Hagas peak (elevation 2,700 feet), mostly on the plants. The trees were frosted on the next peak, and I could see snow on top of the distant mountains.

This is where I had my first look, a spectacular one, at Katahdin, snowcapped against a blue sky. Each successive peak in the Whitecap range was a little higher, and the snow on the summits was a little deeper. I had donned raingear back at the lean-to to keep warm, but was having nagging worries about hypothermia should something slow me down or stop me up there, like a bad fall on ice. A number of hikers had been over the mountain before me, probably the people who had been at the campsite, and they had stomped the snow down pretty well, compressing it into a slippery layer on the rocks.

The views were beautiful from the top of Whitecap (3,650 feet), which had three or four inches of snow, making the summit a picturesque winter scene. From an overlook you can see the entire area between you and Katahdin. I was truly near the end of the trail. A guy named Dr. Bob and his father Wooley arrived, and we chatted for a while.

I followed the steep trail down, being careful now not to slip on packed snow on the rocky descent. I met Leaf at the Logan Brook Lean-to, which is at 2,480 feet, just below the snow line. He and I had left Springer on the same day and had first met in Georgia. Leaf left while

Just Walking

I was eating lunch. I was happy not to have had any problems higher up. The snow was behind me and I made good time down to the East Branch Lean-to, arriving at 4:30 pm. Leaf had gone on, but I decided to stop for the night.

After sleeping alone at the lean-to, I was up and out by 7:45 am on Saturday morning. It was cloudy but not too cold. The East Branch of the Pleasant River was not very wide at the crossing. There were two possible routes, one requiring a couple of steps on stones that were an inch or two under water and a dry route that required a three-foot hop over a little chute. I chose the latter, slipped on the landing, and put my foot down in a foot of water – only the latest of many little missteps along the way.

Not far from the river I met Leaf, Mr. Pumpy, and Chigger at a pretty stealth camp. We debated whether to stop at Whitehouse Landing, a rustic resort, which was about 20 miles away, long for one day and short for two. Brew and Jenn were on the other side of Little Boardman ridge at a lovely camp site near the shore of Mountain View Pond. From there, the trail was easy and fast. I was making good time and decided to try for Whitehouse Landing.

Hustling along at 3 mph was not so hard, given the long, gradual downgrade and the good footing. It began to rain at 1 pm, lightly at first but steadily heavier as I trucked on, past ponds and streams. I passed Antlers campsite, and turned onto the woods road leading to my destination around 5 pm. The trail toward the Landing was very wet. Along the way I took a wrong turn that left me on the beach of Pemadumcook Lake being pelted with horizontal rain. I backtracked and finally reached the end of the blue-

The last 73 miles

blazed side trail, where a LOUD air horn hung from a hook with instructions to blow it only once. After 15 minutes, a boat set out from the opposite side of the inlet. It was piloted by Bill, the owner of the lodge.

Whitehouse Landing is an old hunting camp dating back to the 1930s. It is rustic (no plumbing, gas lights) but warm and comfy. The dinner menu consisted of giant cheeseburgers, cans of Budweiser, and pints of Ben and Jerry's ice cream – in other words, everything a hungry hiker needs. I shared a cabin with Paul and Sharon (thru-hikers who never took trail names) and their border collie Bella, Strider, whom I last saw in Virginia, and Brown Bess, a guy nearly my age from Pennsylvania. Since I had last seen Brown Bess back in New Hampshire, I learned that his trail name signifies a type of black powder musket for which he's an enthusiast.

It was a beautiful clear morning on Sunday, and the forecast was good for

Leaving Whitehouse Landing

the next five days. We hikers assembled in the dining room cheered at this news. We ate a big breakfast of all the usual stuff, and I was on the first boat-load back to the trail. On the opposite shore were Jimmy, Elf, and some others who had blown the horn during breakfast and were waiting for a ride to the lodge. Paul, Sharon, Bella, and I started walking at 9:40 am and made it back to the AT in 25 minutes or so.

The trail north follows the Nahmakanta Stream for a long way, finally coming to the eponymous lake. Paul and I talked for much of the way. The three of us had lunch together on the beach at a quiet cove. Bella amused herself by retrieving a stick she made Paul throw into the lake about 20 times. (This dog had covered about 4,000 miles by the end of the hike.)

I left the lunch spot before they did, and started up Nesuntabunt Mountain (1,520 feet). On the way I met Greenman and Sunkist. Greenman had been a sort of bogeyman along the trail. He cultivated a tough-guy attitude, and I was not the only one who felt intimidated and avoided him and his posse. Now, though, he seemed mild mannered as he asked for a look at my map. One of the brass devil's horns attached to his cap was dangling loose.

From the top of the little mountain there were terrific views of the lake below and of Katahdin in the not-so-

Just Walking

great distance. I was now only 36 miles from trail's end.

Coming down, I found two people attending to an injured friend who was sitting on the trail. They said he had fallen and broken his leg as they were dayhiking together. His wife had walked back to their car, which was parked on the road a half-mile down the hill, and had gone for help. I offered to stay with them, but they declined. They were calm and seemed to know what they were doing, so I walked on. There was no one around when I reached the trail crossing, where their car had been parked. I felt conflicted about leaving. Objectively, the man looked ok, they were keeping him warm, the weather was not too bad, and someone had gone for help. So how hard should I have pressed myself on them? The compulsion to keep moving was strong.

Going on, I walked around Crescent Pond and past Pollywog Gorge. It started to sprinkle. I put on raingear,

Katahdin with its head in the clouds

still thinking about the man with the bad leg. I continued up the trail alongside Rainbow Stream, which had some nice cascades and flumes, to the Rainbow Stream Lean-to. Two guys from Ohio who were hiking the 100-Mile Wilderness southbound were there. It was cold during the night, and I pulled the drawstrings of my sleeping bag hood until there was just a tiny hole to breathe through.

It was still cold on Monday morning — hey, it was Maine in October! I started walking at 8 am and quickly passed the Rainbow Deadwaters to Rainbow Lake, which is over five miles long. The glimpses of the lake were gray and cold-looking, but loons sang from time to time, that beautiful sound. The climb up Rainbow Ledge was easy. There was a view of Whitecap up to the 2,500-foot cloud ceiling and a view in the opposite direction of the bottom half of Katahdin. I ate a quick lunch at Hurd Brook Lean-to with two dayhikers from Pennsylvania; one of them gave me some homemade dried fish that was very tasty. Paul, Sharon, and Bella, who had camped near the preceding lean-to, arrived during my lunch break. When they had passed the injured hiker the previous day, the man's wife and another man had already returned to the scene, so things appeared to have turned out OK, and I stopped obsessing about it.

In less than 90 minutes of walking I came to the "Golden Road" used by giant log trucks headed to Millinocket. Very Small Animal, the Dude, and Ladybug were standing by the road where it crosses the West Branch of the Penobscot River. VSA was feeling ill and had decided to leave the trail for a day or two.

I crossed the bridge, heeding the sign that urges pedestrians to use the designated walkway — a log truck going over the bridge at the same time had less than a foot of clearance on each side. I walked into Abol Pines Campground on the east bank of the river and picked out a pretty campsite surrounded by the rich brown foliage of early fall. A cold wind was blowing across the river, so I rigged the tarp as a windscreen.

I walked a short way up the trail toward Katahdin, which sat there majestic and mystical with its head in the clouds. Back at the camp store to buy dinner, I met Greenman's folks, who had driven from Alabama to meet him. They had brought a real down-home feast that was all laid out on the picnic table next to the store. So, just out of courtesy, I had to scrap my plans for a delicious mac-and-cheese feed and settle for ribs, cornbread, chili, and stewed butterbeans. Sometimes you have to make sacrifices. Greenman and Sunkist hadn't shown up by the time I headed back to camp, but it was a pleasant time chatting with his folks and the other hikers who had gathered there.

I walked back to my campsite around 6 pm as it began to grow dark. I lowered the tarp, the windward side still pegged down to stop the cold breeze, and crawled under it. Lying in my sleeping

Just Walking

bag with all my clothes on, I wrote in my journal, using my headlamp in the twilight. As I warmed up in the bag, I stripped off some layers without getting out and slept most of the night in my capiline bottoms, T-shirt, and wool watch cap.

One of the little problems of backpacking in the fall is that it gets dark early, and the night is relatively long, so you go to bed at 7 pm and wake up at 3 am, but it's cold and remains dark for three more hours. You make yourself go back to sleep a couple of times, and finally you wake up for good at 5 am, with an hour to go until first light. It's a great time of day for meditation or contemplation, but you still wish the sun were up so you wouldn't have to start the day in the dark.

Almost
Abol Bridge to Katahdin Spring Campground: [Mile 2,156.1 to Mile 2,166.0]

Tuesday, October 7. Things started very well (ominous foreshadowing). The sun finally rose, and it was a cold, clear, bright morning. I was on the trail by 8 am after having bought breakfast coffee and rolls at the camp store. I walked up the AT from the road and signed in at the little kiosk by the side of the trail. Katahdin loomed in the distance, its head still in the morning clouds.

It was an easy walk, much of it along the West Branch of the Penobscot River and Nesowadnehunk Stream. From Pine Point, where the trail leaves the Penobscot and follows the tributary stream, I could just see the shimmer of whitewater below Sowdyhunk Falls on the Penobscot, where I had played in my kayak years before. The tributary stream had many pretty rips and chutes running between reddish brown rocks. I crossed a board bridge over a smaller tributary and continued up the trail, stopping to look at Big Niagara Falls. I walked past Daicey, Elbow, and Grassy Ponds, and watched a moose grazing on the shore from 150 yards away. Katahdin was in the clear now and looked formidable and beautiful. I arrived at Katahdin Stream Campground, and was invited to join a picnic being put on by friends and family of Peach Monkey and P-Nut.

It was a "Class IV" day in Baxter State Park jargon, meaning that all trails on the mountain were closed because of icy conditions which had lingered since the snow storm on October 3, the day I hiked over Whitecap. This was really frustrating, because the mountain was visible from the campsite, and it looked clear and very hikable. Double Dare showed up in a van, ready to summit, and Paul and Sharon and other hikers started to arrive, with more just behind them. A ranger drove into the campground, and I asked him about the situation. He told me that, frankly speaking, the mountain

The Way Life Should Be

Along Nesowadnehunk Stream

was 99-percent-sure to be closed again the next day and maybe indefinitely, possibly even for the season, unless the head ranger (who is known as "BP1") decided to open it. This was the same command structure that had closed the mountain during a summer heat wave, so I was not confident the trails would re-open soon.

I'm basically a law-abiding guy, and sneaking up when the trails were closed was not an option for me. So, I had to think about what it would mean if I didn't get to the summit. What I discovered is that although I really wanted to become a certified thru-hiker, I had already accomplished the thru-hike in my own mind and felt satisfied. I'd seen a big slice of the USA, met lots of great people, felt close to nature, and proved to myself that I could do it. I would just become one of the longest section hikers ever to do the trail if I couldn't finish before winter and had to complete the last five miles the following year.

Just Walking

Morning light on the way up Katahdin

After the ranger's forecast I didn't waste a minute picking up my stuff and heading to Millinocket. The campground was small, thru-hikers would continue to arrive, and the place would soon be overcrowded with disgruntled people. After waiting for 15 minutes for a vehicle to come by, a car left the campground. It was driven by a dayhiker who had Sharon, Paul and Bella in the backseat and gear piled up to the windows. He stopped and apologized for not having a couple of empty cubic feet to put me in, but Sharon and Paul saved me by piling up gear all the way to the headliner (OK, a little poetic license here) and fitting me in with my pack across all of our knees. I checked into the Hiker Inn in town, had dinner at the AT Café, and made plans. I would take the bus home to Boston and drive back up to finish, if and when the mountain reopened.

On Wednesday I woke up at 3:30 am, full of nervous energy, another case of sleeping poorly in a bed. I started making a list of things to do when I got home, including writing about the meaning of the whole hike.[25] I ate breakfast at the AT Café at 5 am, a smaller breakfast than normal since I wouldn't be expending more than 2000 calories that day. I walked around with Paul and Sharon who were in a tougher situation than me; they lived in Pennsylvania and didn't have the option of leaving and coming back to finish. I called Sheila at home to tell her to expect me. We got through to the park headquarters after 8 am and confirmed that it was another Class IV day. Then I took a cab to Medway and caught the bus to Bangor and then to Boston.

[25] See Epilogue.

On Thursday I called the park and learned that it was a Class III day, with the Hunt Trail (the AT) open to the summit, and more warm weather forecasted for Friday. I did the laundry, packed, and hit the road in my car at 11:30 am. It's a long drive from Boston (six hours) but less tedious than some of the green tunnel hiking days I had experienced on the trail, and easier! I listened and sang along to *Highway 61 Revisited* on the way up, finally catching some of the lines that had eluded me on the trail when I sang those songs to pass the time.

It was a beautiful afternoon and I could see Katahdin under a huge clear sky as I drove into Millinocket. Tomorrow would be THE DAY. The weather report predicted more partly cloudy warm weather. I stayed at a motel (avoiding the one named after Pamola, the evil spirit that protects the mountain from intruders, according to Native American mythology). Around dinnertime there was a luminous sunset with saturated color everywhere. Later, the Red Sox lost to the Yankees in the second game of a disastrous playoff series, which I'm sure Lumberjack richly enjoyed.

Finally
The last five miles

Friday, October 10. Here we go. As I edit the words written on the loose-leaf pages of my trail journal, which has taken longer than the hike itself, I realize that this is it, the denouement. Yes, a thru-hike is a minute-by-minute, day-by-day experience, trying to be in the present, but I've been conditioned since I was a boy to attain a goal, any goal. And there is no goal more alluring than the summit of Mount Katahdin at the end of a six-month hike. Even the maps make it look special: the mountain is all by itself in a flat area; the trail profile pokes along with little bumps and dips for most of the miles north of Whitecap until it gets to Katahdin, and then it goes straight up.

After a not very good night's sleep at the motel in Millinocket, I ate breakfast at the AT Café at 5 am. It was empty at that hour except for three local businessmen who were obviously regular customers. They sat at different tables reading newspapers but carried on a conversation with each other and the presiding waitress.

I had my car waiting at my disposal for the first time in the whole hike, something we take for granted in ordinary day-to-day life. I drove in the dark to the Baxter State Park gate and waited for it to open.

They limit the number of cars entering each day, and it was foliage season, so I had worried (that word again) about arriving late only to find a long line of cars and missing the cut. Besides, I wanted to get an early start. As it turned out, I was the third car through. I drove up the park road to Katahdin Stream campground as the day began to grow light. I parked and walked to the shelter and met Brown Bess. We were both ready to go. We signed the trail register

Just Walking

and started hiking together just before 7 am. All we had to do now was climb the 4,200 feet from the campground to Katahdin's 5,286-foot summit. We brushed past wet bushes as the trail ascended and caught a glimpse of a tidy little peak called Owl's Head, painted by the richly colored early morning light.

It turned into a beautiful, warm, cloudless day, everything one could have hoped for on the last day of an often rainy thru-hiking season. We were overtaken by Sleepy Floyd, Pipes, Phlegm, Superman, and Torch, and I went on with them when Brown Bess took a break. The whole hike was distilled into that one morning – hike your own hike, go at your own pace, love the people you're with, but remain an independent entity.

Here's an important point. It was as good a morning to finish a thru-hike as one could wish for, but that didn't matter. Trail friends like Moonshadow, who had finished a week earlier, did it in cold, wet, miserable conditions. It didn't matter, because time doesn't matter on the trail. We all had had our share of lovely, gentle days and harsh, trying ones. The last day was no more significant than any other, and they could have happened in any order.

The bouldering section up Hunt Spur was challenging in places, and I was glad to be climbing when it wasn't icy. The AT ascended a seemingly vertical pile of huge light gray speckled hunks of pure granite that one has to climb like a jungle gym, assisted in places by rebar staples set into the rock. We stopped for a break halfway up this stretch, made it up over the Gateway at the top of the spur around 11 am, and stopped again at Thoreau Spring, a trickle of clear water bubbling up out of the ground in the rock-strewn Tablelands. After a short rest we walked across the barren flatland and started up a ridge.

Sleepy Floyd climbing Hunt Spur

I thought about the breakfast at Miss Janet's in Erwin, Tennessee, where we dreamed about the theme music we would like to accompany this last mile of the AT. Stairway to Heaven was the first song to cross my mind. But after that morning, I thought more about it. On many days scattered over the hike I would pass the time by trying to remember elusive melodies – the ones that are on the tip of your tongue but you can't quite get hold of. One melody that really caught in my mind and stayed with me was the aria from the opera Turandot, whose melody is unresolved in the first chorus and then resolves itself big-time with a slight change in the final bars. It has been used in a number of movies, because of both the great melody and its ending with the words "Vincero, Vincero, Vincero!"[26] OK, it may have been trite, stupid triumphalism. Nonetheless I sang it out loud with gusto, the foolishness of it dispelled by the breeze.

Peace

I had just remarked to Pipes that we were on our last mile when we topped the ridge and I realized that I had been looking ahead to the South Peak, not the main summit. For there was Sleepy Floyd, waving from the unmistakable A-frame sign, and suddenly we were all at the end of our 2171-mile hikes.

So what happens at the end of a thru-hike? After a lot of cheering and hugging, the six of us passed around

[26] Translation: "I will conquer." Pavarotti was famous for his rendition.

Just Walking

Made it!

cameras and took photos of each other individually and in a group at the trail's end sign. It was warm with light winds, and we were in no hurry to leave. Dayhikers cheered for us, God bless them; I'll do it for someone else some day. Sleepy Floyd surprised us with cans of Budweiser, with which we toasted each other. Superman put on a T-shirt with the big red "S", and a dayhiker who must have been in cahoots with someone presented him with a knit hat with the Superman logo on it. He and Torch unfurled a large peace flag and held it above the sign while we took pictures and toasted the concept.

Soon, we were joined by another group comprising CC, Chicken Legs, her sister Triple T, and Feral, and shortly after them by Brown Bess. After first cheering as we did and being cheered by us, they cried. This is just another instance of the idea that everyone hikes their own hike. We all crowded together, eleven of us now, and a dayhiker took group photos with all eleven cameras. Some

The Way Life Should Be

of us also had our pictures taken lying back on a flat rock at the edge of the precipice, the suggestion of a former through-hiker who was at the summit.

We hung around from 11:30 am until 1 o'clock and then decided it was time for the final five-mile trek down to Katahdin Springs, which doesn't count toward the thru-hike mileage, as if you could just hang-glide down the mountain. We were all well satisfied with the day. The descent was uneventful after all we had been through since spring, although there were still a few scrambles to solve without breaking our necks, which would have been an anti-climax.

Back at the campground, I looked through the many pages of the register at the ranger station while waiting for the others to finish the return lap. I saw the names and messages of many of the friends I had made on the trail. Some were gloating, others humble, and many congratulated us and the other thru hikers who would finish after them. Pinned up above the register was an envelope with my name on it (!); it contained a photo of me, Mountain Jack and the nice couple from Barcelona who had been at Bascomb Lodge, with a note wishing me well. This was just the last in a series of good omens and little acts of kindness from strangers that I had been blessed to receive over the previous six months.

I shuttled a carload of folks from our summit group down to Millinocket, while others rode with some dayhikers. We exchanged addresses and said final goodbyes in a parking lot. I drove away

Mixed emotions

Just Walking

from Millinocket before dinner, ready to return to my family and the rest of my life.

Postscript
No More Miles

A couple of days after returning, I went to downtown Boston to see my friend Skip with whom I'd had dinner in Front Royal. He had left our old firm and set up a new one with the two other partners I was close to. The people working in the new office had given me an enthusiastic sendoff, and they reacted with happy surprise when I walked in with my trail beard and pony tail.

My friend Gordon, who had sent me an email that I read in Pearisburg, had worked with all of us years before, and he rendezvoused with me at South Station before we walked over to see our friends. As we were talking at one of the tables over coffee, a guy with an unmistakable red beard walked by.

It was Sleepy Floyd.

Millipede on top of the World

Epilogue

Epilogue

What Does It All Mean?

It takes around five solid months of hiking to complete an end-to-end hike of the Appalachian Trail, six months with some breaks. That's a lot of time, and effort, and cost, and lost earnings, and lost time with your family. So, it must be important in some way. It must have some greater meaning. What *is* it that makes it all worth doing?

Walking

Hiking is just walking, with a rocky scramble thrown in here and there. Walking is one of the most basic things a human can do. It's almost automatic, like breathing. Deep inside our brains, there are hard-wired mechanisms that create the rhythm of walking and maintain our balance when we walk. As our feet move, left-right-left-right, tiny electrical impulses fire on alternate sides of our brains.

I believe this rhythm is connected to other parts of our minds at a subconscious or unconscious level. For example, many of us have songs playing our heads for most of the time we are walking, songs that follow the rhythm of our feet and our breathing. If you choose, this rhythm can also be connected to a walking mantra or meditation.

Walking is in itself a pleasant activity, calming us and at the same time stimulating our thoughts and senses. This is true whether you do it on the Appalachian Trail or on the Brooklyn Bridge.

Going Somewhere

Humans evolved on the savannah lands of Africa. Long ago in our prehistory, many hundreds of thousands of years before there were settlements and agriculture, we were nomadic hunter-gatherers living in small groups. We lived this sort of life for the majority of our history as a species, *homo sapiens sapiens*, not to mention the even longer span of the ancestor species from which we evolved.[27] We could see pretty much where we were going when it was time to move to a new area that hadn't been picked over yet. Walking long distances to go somewhere new must have been a scary but also a joyful experience, possibly accompanied by singing or chanting to the rhythm of our feet.

One day, about a month after my AT hike had ended, I walked a half-mile or so to the post office through pleasant, tree-lined suburban streets. I began to think about how nice it would be to go out and take a hike in the woods again instead of walking on pavement. Then I thought about the pleasure of making the hike go somewhere, connecting two different places or landmarks, for instance the successive peaks in a mountain range. Soon I was imagining an end-to-end hike on the Long Trail. It's a lovely sort of compulsion.

The AT is one of the hikes that takes you somewhere on a large scale, about one-twelfth of the earth's circumference. You

---

[27] Note to creationists – we need to talk, seriously.

Just Walking

can imagine your progress on a map of the eastern United States, which most of us have in mind with varying degrees of detail. By hiking the trail over a long distance, you make this conceptual map real by connecting it to actual places, ones that you experience first-hand. Travel at this scale is a thrilling thing to do, and more so on foot or bicycle than the telescoped experience of driving the interstate highways or riding a train or flying at 30,000 feet.

As I've said, the basic experience of an AT long distance hiker is *just walking*, but when thoughts come into it, they're often about getting somewhere, reaching a daily objective, and ultimately making progress toward the mind-boggling goal of walking all the way from Georgia to Maine. You watch the milestones, calculate how many more miles remain to the day's destination, and experience the pure enjoyment of *getting there*.

○ *Connecting to Your Surroundings*

We often think of urban life bombarding us with sensory data that overload and sometimes threaten us. Of course, there are some beautiful urban settings in the world that make us want to connect with our surroundings, and I love walking in these places. But more often than not, we adopt an attitude of warding off the urban experience, hardening and desensitizing ourselves to it. Simply being in a congested area with a high noise level and automobiles passing close by probably raises our stress levels.

Walking in the woods, or on a trail above treeline, on the other hand, makes us feel more connected with our surroundings. Unless there are threatening environmental factors (approaching thunderstorm, hypothermia, etc.), walking for hours in a natural environment reduces stress. Absence of stress makes us even more open to the environment we are walking through.

Hikers sleep on a bare wood shelter floor or on the ground, cushioned by a thin layer of foam or an inflated pad. We eat in the open air. We collect our water from springs or streams as we pass them. The cycling of food and water – from the environment through our bodies and back into the environment – becomes more apparent. We experience the contours of the land by hauling ourselves over them. We are brushed by vegetation along the way, we lean against trees and sit on fallen logs or rocks or mossy hummocks. At the end of the day we stop, eat, and lie down on the ground or shelter floor again to sleep.

In a day's hike, we see, hear,[28] and smell many kinds of woody and herbaceous plants, fungi, and lichens. We see and hear birds and animals, some of them large, like deer, bears, or moose.

Our exposure to our immediate surroundings is mediated only by thin layers of fabric. We feel the wind, sun, rain, and snow. Changes in temperature

---

[28] Just stand still in the middle of the woods and notice all the sounds trees make.

Epilogue

and humidity are apparent to our skin. Our attitudes as hikers make us open to these connections with the immediate environment. We disregard most of the discomfort of exposure, and as a result, we connect to our surroundings.

On the trail, you hear the quiet and see the dark. At home, things are different. Unless you live well out in the country away from roads and streetlights, there is always ambient noise and light, but you learn to ignore it. When the dishwasher stops running, you hear the hum of the refrigerator. When they are both quiet you hear passing traffic and the hard drive on your computer. Try it.

The Appalachian Trail is not wilderness, not for most of its length anyway. But there are mile after mile of trail far enough from roads to be quiet and dark. You sit by the trail, taking a rest. What do you hear? Insects. Birds, some of them far away. Wind in the trees. And when even these sounds are absent for a while, you can hear your breath, the rustle of your clothes, and the actual singing of your own nervous system deep inside your head.

This is what Jack Kerouac experienced that night when he slept in a desert arroyo three miles outside El Paso:

"There just isn't any kind of night's sleep in the world that can compare with the night's sleep you get in the desert winter night, providing you're good and warm in a duck-down bag. The silence is so intense that you can hear your own blood roar in your ears but louder than that by far is the mysterious roar which I always identify with the roaring of the diamond of wisdom, the mysterious roar of silence itself, which is a great Shhhh reminding you of something you've seemed to have forgotten in the stress of your days since birth."[29]

Nearly all settled places these days have street lights, mostly the sodium vapor luminaires that emit a ghastly orange light at high intensity. Neighbors have flood lights outside their houses that are on all night or triggered by motion detectors. Parking lots have high mast lighting. Stores and public buildings have flood lighting. It's all supposed to make us feel safe. The result is that in every metropolitan area, the night sky is polluted with light that blots out all but the brightest stars and planets. It's better in the country but even small towns have so many lights you need to drive for miles to get away from them.

The trail is dark at night in most places. Dark is sort of a paradox because you can see more, not less. If you don't blind yourself with a headlamp, you can see by the light of the stars alone, and if the moon is out, you can see well enough to hike by its light. And the quiet and dark are beautiful.

Where Am I?

One of the most remarkable parts of a long-distance hike is that you experience it simultaneously at several different

[29] Jack Kerouac, *The Dharma Bums*, page 119.

Just Walking

scales, and the contrast between them makes you more centered, aware, and connected to what is around you. On smooth trails, you can almost forget the steps your feet make and feel only the rhythm of movement, but in many places on the AT you need to watch where you step in relation to rocks, roots, puddles and bumps. In some places there are steep ledges and boulders to climb up or down, and your attention becomes almost microscopic, searching for cracks or tiny bumps that will give purchase to the edge of your boot and keep you from slipping. Sometimes you need to consciously plan each step or sequence of steps, and you watch the trail pass under you, foot by foot. In other places your attention flies above the trail. You watch rocks and roots that you could slip or trip on approach and then disappear below your cone of vision. Some mechanism in the brain allows your feet to land in the spaces between the obstructions after they are no longer in view. While this is going on at the most detailed level of perception, you are also aware of landforms and features at a scale of a few hundred yards or more. The trail may climb or descend steeply over switchbacks to the top of a knob or the bottom of a ravine. At the low points you often have to cross streams. Often you can hear a stream or cascade far in advance of seeing it. Trails are sometimes cut into the side of a hill; these trails follow the contours of the land or gradually rise or descend, curving around the knee of the hill or making a cusp as the contour line pulls into the slope at a ravine or brook. The trail may cross a saddle between two hills. This is called a "gap" in the South. AT hikers experience hundreds of these coves and gaps and summits.

Using a contour map or trail profile, the hiker can relate the visible landforms to much larger mountains and valleys and ridges stretching miles from the starting point of the day's hike to its end point. Sometimes, you can actually see the terrain over long distances. The view from McAfee Knob to Tinker Cliffs, the one along the Franconia Ridge in the White Mountains, or the views from peak to peak in the Bigelows are examples of this. There are many places with long views on the AT, and they are all special. When you can't actually see the major milestones, smaller landmarks along the way, like low points in the woods between two mountains, show you where you are on the map.

The largest scale of all encompasses the entire trail from Springer to Katahdin. We thru-hikers keep track of our progress and cheer as we cross state lines and major rivers like the Delaware or the Kennebec.

Long distance hikers also perceive time at several scales. Many of us learn to estimate how long it will take to reach a milestone a few miles away and guess where we are by looking at our watches. We are aware of the passing days but not always aware of what day of the week it is, because there is no more work week

Epilogue

and weekend to consider. Church-going hikers usually know when it's Sunday, though.

Weather patterns change over a period of days, and hikers experience this rhythm in the arrival and passing of weather fronts. We watch the moon cycle through its phases several times in the course of a thru-hike. At the largest time scale, a thru-hiker experiences the change in seasons from spring to summer to fall. As we hike, the life cycles of trees and flowers unroll from the first green shoots to the fullness of summer foliage to the dying colors of fall. The weather changes from cold to hot, snow to rain and back again, and the length of the day provides a sun calendar.

○ *Physical Changes*

Long distance hikers, especially we thru-hikers, work our bodies for hours every day. A 150-pound hiker may burn more than four thousand calories a day, and most of us lose at least 10 pounds while eating huge quantities of food. Our blood chemistry must change while we are doing this. For example, our HDL levels ("good cholesterol") go up despite ingesting a lot of calories from fat, and our stress hormones go way down. Certain muscles get stronger to perform the task of climbing steep trails with 20 to 40 pounds of pack weight. We may get over-use injuries, and if we're lucky the body heals itself faster than it is worn down. Long distance hikers end up with very good aerobic fitness and strong legs, as long as injuries don't knock us off the trail.

○ *Mental Changes*

When you hike for a long distance toward an endpoint, it is a goal-directed endeavor that requires a kind of mental toughness and the ability to set aside discomfort, but even more than that, you must simply want to keep going. On my hike, it was cloudy and often rainy from early May until late June. This was followed by six lovely weeks of sunny weather, and then it started to rain at the beginning of August and continued to rain every day for two weeks – from the Hudson River to the Vermont border. So when you start thru-hiking and get past the physical adjustment to walking every day for eight hours, more or less, there are two possible trajectories. Either you want to keep doing it, or you don't. If you do it for five months or so (with time off now and then for rest and relaxation), you finish. If not, you don't. It's not really a matter of whether you are tough enough to do it: if you can hike for a month, chances are you're tough enough to hike for six months. It's a question of motivation.

○ *Fellowship*

I have no doubt that virtually every long distance hiker finds the fellowship with other hikers one of the most gratifying aspects of his or her hike. I did. If you are thru-hiking, you are part of a special

Just Walking

group of people, and this is true whether or not you finish. (In my mind, this group also includes section hikers who are trying over a period of years to hike the whole trail and long distance hikers who don't give a rat's ass about reaching a goal but are into the trail experience.)

Other thru-hikers are my brothers and sisters. I became closer to some than to others. There were a few I didn't like at all and tried to avoid. But there's very little conflict on the trail. An unkind word is not often heard, and most thru-hikers will make room in a shelter for a latecomer on a rainy night without being asked, even though it is often uncomfortable to be packed in like damp sardines.

Thru-hiking men outnumber women by 2-to-1 or more, but in my experience it is very rare for a male hiker to hit on a woman on the trail. I believe this is not so much attributable to hikers having better character than non-hikers, although that may be true in part. Rather, I think it has to do with not wanting to jeopardize a special relationship in a small community of hikers who see each other every day.

Despite being so often focused on the elementary functions of eating, sleeping, and elimination, hikers tend to be modest. In Georgia I saw a female hiker come into a shelter drenched and cold from the pouring rain with no choice but to change clothes; everyone just got busy with what they were doing so she could change without being hassled. When you're sitting on the unenclosed crapper[30] behind Gren Anderson shelter in New Jersey, it's no big deal to see a head peek around the shelter to see if the seat is vacant.

Hikers rarely ask each other for loans of food or money, but if it is needed it is given, often without being asked for. There is a lot of humor and wit exchanged on the trail or recorded in the shelter registers. Songs are sung. Special friendships are formed, and some thru-hikers even fall in love. We're sharing a unique experience.

○ *Getting Away?*

The ATC provides a questionnaire along with the application for a certificate of completion. One question concerns motivation, and the multiple choices include "To heal from a loss or painful experience" and, "To escape pressures/unpleasant situations". It is a popular idea that middle-aged men like myself (age 55 when I started) go on thru-hikes to escape from a mid-life crisis. In my own situation, my father had died two years before and I wasn't happy in my job, but I see my hike not as an escape but as a way to seize the time and do something positive that I may not be physically able to do when I am older. The majority of thru-hikers are in their 20s. Some of them, too, may be getting away from bad or painful situations, but I think most of them are seizing the

---

[30] "Privy" would be a misnomer.

time as well, before the commitments of children and careers make it impossible to get away for four to six months.

I am one of the hikers who is married and has kids. I went home three times during my hike to see them. My two sons, 16 and 19 when I finished, both encouraged me to go for it, and I don't think I would have started without their support. My wife was not happy about my going away, but I felt it was something I had to do. It turned out that my absence was harder on her than I had thought, and I offered to come home from Virginia, a month into my hike. We talked on the phone and she encouraged me to stay with it. Since my return, we've worked to reaffirm our commitment and repair the damage. She believes that my hike was in part about wanting to get away from our relationship, at least for a while. I've thought about this as hard as I can (I can hear the women saying "typical male") but I really don't think getting away from her was part of my motivation.

I believe that most hikers, whatever their age, are taking an opportunity to live a segment of their lives in the here-and-now instead of every day being part of a years-long process that culminates in grown kids or professional success. For me, a thru-hike is less about getting away and more about getting to.

○ It's Not About Winning

Shunryu Suzuki Roshi wrote the following about Zen practice[31]:

"There are several poor ways of practice that you should understand. Usually when you practice zazen, you become very idealistic, and you set up an ideal or goal which you strive to attain and fulfill. ... So long as your practice is based on a gaining idea [i.e., a goal], and you practice zazen in an idealistic way, you will actually have no time actually to attain your ideal. ... But even worse than this idealistic attitude is to practice zazen in competition with someone else. This is a poor, shabby kind of practice.

Our Soto way [of Zen] puts an emphasis on shikan taza, or "just sitting." Actually we do not have any particular name for our practice; when we practice zazen we just practice it, and whether we find joy in our practice or not, we just do it. Even though we are sleepy, and we are tired of practicing zazen, of repeating the same thing day after day; even so, we continue our practice. Whether or not someone encourages our practice, we just do it."

Like Zen, a thru-hike is best when it's just about walking, one day at a time, one mile at a time. People who don't know the joy of hiking sometimes suppose it is all a great contest: create a very difficult goal and meet the challenge. Hiking in Maine my concern to finish on time and attain my goal began to emerge more and more and to drown out the rhythm of just walking. Yet, when I was at the base of Katahdin and found the trails to the summit closed, I realized that reaching the end of the trail wasn't all that important, even though I would have said at any point in the

---

[31] Shunryu Suzuki, *Zen Mind, Beginner's Mind*, Weatherhill, 1970, pp 71-72.

Just Walking

hike that it was my goal. Likewise, my trail friend Journey had to jump ahead to meet some off-trail commitments and thus didn't hike all 2,171 miles; but in my mind there is no difference whatever between her hike and mine.

This is the aspect of thru-hiking that is most Zen-like: it is best when you aren't trying to win a prize but just do it for its own sake, minute by minute. It is easier to do in hiking than it is in Zen because of the rhythm of walking and the sights and sounds along the trail. But the principle is the same. It's not an act of the will. It's waking up each day you're on the trail with the desire to do it again. And if you don't feel like it some days, you do it anyway, just to keep doing it.

And yet, most of us long distance hikers feel that pull of achieving something difficult when we're doing it, and we feel proud of our accomplishment when we're finished. We even take pride when someone compliments us on being a fast hiker – which means faster than other hikers, right? But the hours spent on the trail would be rather meaningless if it were mostly about reaching the goal, winning the prize or getting there first.

So there is an interesting process going on in the head of a thru-hiker: trying not to lose connection with the hiking experience by thinking miles ahead to a goal, but also succumbing to the goal-oriented thinking from time to time.

The Spiritual Nature of the Hike

Being connected with the natural environment gives the hiker a special relationship with what Christians might call The Creation. Christian hikers often talk about the beauty of nature reflecting God's Plan.

Others of us don't disagree with that but at the same time don't see it quite the same way. Several aspects of long distance hiking combine to allow us briefly, from time to time, to look through the veil and glimpse what really is. The veil is made of the thoughts that are passing through our minds all the time. In the work-a-day world, we do not even notice this chatter, but on a ridge in Pennsylvania that goes on for miles, we become aware of something around us, a reality that is there to see, hear, and smell. Something that lies beyond the umpteenth mental replay of Johnny Cash's Ring of Fire or whatever song is playing inside your head.[32]

The factors that let us pierce the veil are the steady rhythm of walking and breathing, the drop in our stress levels, and the connection with our surroundings. When we can set aside the striving for milestones and other goals and pay attention to the here and now for a little while, hiking becomes a form of meditation, a way of coming closer to sensing the tao that runs through both the hiker and her surroundings. The tao is a Chinese idea sometimes translated as "the Way." The AT experience is a pretty good metaphor for it.

---
[32] See page 105

Epilogue

You come closest to experiencing the tao when you pay attention to the rhythm of your feet and your breath, when you can briefly stop the music running through your head, when you set aside the chain of thoughts and just listen to the small sounds of the environment around you: birds, buzzing insects, trickling water, the wind in the trees. The physical environment is almost but not entirely quiet, and your mind too becomes quieter and more connected to what is all around you.

While hiking, I would sometimes chant "Aum Mani Padme Hum" under my breath. This is an elemental Buddhist prayer on behalf of souls that are in the karmic shit, so to speak. It also makes an excellent mantra in 4/4 cadence for gutting it up steep trails. I believe the Sherpas and porters in the Himalayas use it this way – you might as well help out some lost souls while you have some time on your hands, and it takes your mind off that pain in your side.

Or, I would silently recite Thich Nhat Hahn's walking meditation:

> I have arrived.
> I am home.
> In the here.
> In the now.
> I am solid.
> I am real.
> In the ultimate
> I dwell.

In either case, the words follow the rhythm of walking. (It is difficult or impossible to do this if the trail is too steep to breathe without gasping for air or too rough and irregular to permit a rhythm to develop. Of the two, Aum Mani Padme Hum works best on the steep sections.) Sometimes, instead of words, I would just focus on breathing in and out – hahm, sah, inhale, exhale.

After 10 or 15 minutes of this, I could – almost – catch a glimpse of what was around me, behind the veil of thoughts.

Five or six months of meditation like this is not enough to effect a permanent change in the way one perceives existence. Buddhist and monks, for example, spend years learning to do it (or maybe it's unlearning). But six months without too many other distractions is something. Think of it as a useful workshop.

○ *Jewels*

Two years after my hike, I was walking from the Guyot campsite, about a mile south of the AT in the White Mountains, over Mount Bond and Bondcliff, two 4,000-footers that, unfortunately, most thru-hikers don't get to see. It was early morning, the sky was blue, and the sun elicited the subtle colors and forms of these summits. I recognized the feeling, so frequent on a thru-hike, of being surprised by a treasure that is there for anyone to see who bothers to take a walk. "That is nice!" I said aloud without meaning to.

Just Walking

Bondcliff's summit is an example of the above-treeline environment – angled rock, incredibly hardy alpine plants making their living in harsh conditions. This type of environment is found on the whole Franconia Ridge, the Presidential Ridge, and Mount Mooselauke in the Whites, on Killington in Vermont, and on Saddleback, Avery Peak, and Katahdin in Maine. They are among the treasures found by hikers.

There are also the rhododendron tunnels, the hemlock groves, the waterfalls, the pastures illuminated by early morning sunlight, the views down valleys from above, the big river crossings, the wildflowers, the mushrooms, the smell of honeysuckle, the amazing wild animals and birds, the miracle of fresh water flowing out of the ground, towering cloudscapes, still ponds, historic town centers, friendly strangers, and the hard-to-define beauty of remote coves and hollows where not much is really happening to write home about. These are the things that make you say "That is nice!" out loud, even when you're by yourself.

I mentioned hiking to the mantra, Aum Mani Padme Hum. *Aum* symbolizes both the imperfection that we all embody and the perfection of Buddha, Jesus, Mohammed, and the others who transcended. *Mani* means "jewel" and signifies compassion and love, the means toward enlightenment. *Padme* is the lotus, representing a special kind of wisdom possessed by Buddhist monks and Zen masters. The lotus grows out of the mud but remains unsullied. *Hum* signifies the indivisibility of love and compassion from the enlightened state, the means and end rolled into one.

To me, this is all symbolized by those treasures that suddenly appear along the trail, the jewels that surprise and delight us as we hike our own hikes. The jewels in the lotus of wisdom, may we all attain it. *Aum mani padme hum.*

Ecology, Mindfulness, and Time

So is there a moral to a story about hiking the Appalachian Trail?

I believe there is. Most hikers are familiar with the Leave No Trace principles, and we try to follow them when we are on the trail. But after months of low-energy lifestyle we return home, resume our "normal" lives, and most of us start to burn fuel in large quantities when we use electricity, heat our homes, and drive our cars. Our impact on the earth expands from literally the size of a tent to the enormous carbon footprint that is driving global climate change beyond a catastrophic threshold. We are *Leaving a Very Big Trace* indeed. The effect will be to alter the ecosystems, worldwide, that we are so careful to protect when we hike in them. Goodbye alpine vegetation on the Presidential Ridge. Goodbye Amazon rain forest and half of all living species.

But what can we do about that? Well, we can lead by example and talk to other people. That's where we face the big

Epilogue

disconnect, even among people who value a healthy world ecosystem and understand that human-caused climate change is very real. "How can we possibly reduce our carbon emissions by 80 percent? It would completely change our way of life!"

This is where the Appalachian Trail experience is relevant. Long distance hikers don't bring much with them, it's sometimes a little too warm or too cold, and it takes time to get places. A long time, actually, but that's part of the experience. And most thru-hikers find that they are happy while doing it.

The key to hiker happiness is the mindfulness that comes from just walking. You spend most of every day in the moment, and as a result your stress level is very low. Everyday life presents more obstacles and conflicts than hiking does, but mindfulness is still possible. It requires spending some time every day walking, meditating, doing yoga, riding a bicycle, etc., and using this time to (literally) return to your senses and be in the moment. Mindfulness can be practiced while cooking, eating, doing the chores, commuting, working, or just sitting around home. You have to remember that it is an option, a sort of refuge that you can visit when you wish. And you must decide to actually spend some of your time in this state of mind instead of on competing activities like checking your email, playing video games, or listening to talk radio. Doing so will make you happier and healthier too.

Modern life is constantly speeding up, and time becomes increasingly precious. That's why we need to drive everywhere, and use more and more of the day working (so we can buy more stuff to enjoy in the few remaining hours of the day). Being mindful and slowing down go hand in hand. If you can do one, you're probably doing the other.

Back to global warming, ecological catastrophe, and misery for billions of mostly poverty-stricken people around the world. Changing our modern lifestyle to mitigate these disasters isn't difficult if we can cultivate mindfulness and spend our time on things that really matter.

That's the moral of the story taught by a thru-hike on the Appalachian Trail: slow down, be mindful, and you really can enjoy life – and help save the world to boot.

My Email to Last Minute

Several of the 2003 thru-hikers exchange email from time to time. In March 2004, Last Minute sent a long email reflecting on his experiences of the previous year and his feeling of closeness to the trail community that formed among us.

I sent the following reply:

Beautiful message, Last Minute. Thanks for sending it.

I'm having flashbacks myself, which I am attending to by looking at this year's journals on trailjournals.com. The funny thing about it is that I often find myself thinking about some random moment on the trail when nothing special was happening. It was really moments like that, either alone on the trail or with friends in a shelter or campsite, that made my hike what it was. Last fall I tried to write a little essay on what the whole experience meant to me, but I felt it was missing something.

Now I'm beginning to think that an AT hike is truly a Zen experience. I've been doing some practice at the Cambridge Zen Center this winter. The first thing that struck me was that the people at the Zen Center looked just like thru-hikers (only cleaner). Then someone explained to me that the basic idea of Zen is to just do what you're doing: when you're sitting, just sit; when you're walking just walk; when you're eating, just eat.

And that's exactly what the hike was like. I remember thinking about this and discussing it with other hikers on the trail: when I got to a shelter it was very satisfying to just sit for a long spell on that wood floor and look out at the woods and do nothing.

I don't know about you, but I can't wait for the snow in the mountains to be gone so I can get a little taste of it again.

Last Minute, one of those fond memories is sitting by Rte 20 in Massachusetts munching the Big Mac you were kind enough to bring back from Lee. I hope life is good for you. Peace.

Gear List

		Weight (g)	Weight (lb)
Subtotal base pack weight			21.2
food (days)	4		10.0
water (liter)	2	2,000	4.4
Subtotal pack weight			35.6
sticks	2	642	1.4
boots	2	1,500	3.3
Trail Weight			**40.3**

Item	Number	Weight (g)	Weight (lb)
backpack		1,130	2.5
sleeping bag		1,330	2.9
bag liner		195	0.4
tarp		540	1.2
net cave		400	0.9
ground sheet		101	0.2
pad		297	0.7
pot		165	0.4
stove		68	0.1
fuel			0.7
spoon		12	0.0
cup		22	0.0
knife		24	0.1
bowl (light)		25	0.1
briefs		100	0.2
T shirt	2	1,130	2.5
shorts		158	0.3
pants		280	0.6
socks	3	291	0.6
liner socks	2	56	0.1
capilene bottom		169	0.4
R1 fleece		327	0.7
fleece sweater		285	0.6
rain pants		160	0.4
wool hat		56	0.1
gloves		104	0.2
Tilley hat		162	0.4
bandanas	2	50	0.1
hanky	1	15	0.03
gaiters		128	0.3
umbrella		260	0.6
Small Items Bag		**474**	**1.0**
spare glasses		68	0.1
sunglasses		95	0.2
camera		185	0.4
first aid kit		318	0.7
toilet items		136	0.3
stuff sacks	4	156	0.3
water res. & filter		178	0.4
spare bottle		42	0.1
books & maps		701	1.5
cell phone		110	0.2
(items worn)		810	1.8
Subtotal base pack weight			**21.2**

Contents of Small Items Bag	Weight (g)
Small Items Bag total	**474**
headlamp	74
spare batteries	36
compass	25
whistle	7
moleskin	16
toe pads	3
long cord	34
magnifier	24
spare camera battery	19
lighter	13
money/cards	37
medications	48
supplements	included
ibuprofen	included
bug dope	72
sunscreen	36
pen	4
after bite	21
bug net	20
vaseline	60
first aid kit	**318**
fire starter	29
ace bandages	
straps	
iodine tabs	
bandaids	
Toilet Items	**136**
toothbrush	15
tooth powder	12
soap	80
towel	11
toilet paper	18
Books and maps	**701**
journal pages	25
reading book	311
AT data book	110
AT maps	158
hiker's companion	97

Itinerary

Overall Mile	Daily Miles	Destination		Date	Overall Mile	Daily Miles	Destination		Date
		Gainesville	GA	13-Apr	332.5	20.7	No Business Knob	NC	12-May
		Amicalola Falls SP	GA	14-Apr	338.8	6.3	Erwin	TN	13-May
2.5	11.3	Stover Creek	GA	14-Apr	355.2	16.4	Cherry Gap	NC	14-May
14.7	12.3	Gooch Mtn	GA	15-Apr	370.3	15.1	Roan High Knob	NC	15-May
26.6	11.9	Woods Hole	GA	16-Apr	384.9	14.6	Apple House	NC	16-May
36.9	10.3	Whitley Gap	GA	17-Apr	385.4		Elk Park	NC	17-May
48.5	11.6	Blue Mtn	GA	18-Apr	401.1	18.9	Moreland Gap	NC	17-May
56.2	7.7	Tray Mtn	GA	19-Apr	417.4	16.3	Wautauga Lake	NC	18-May
63.3		pass Deep Gap	GA	20-Apr	439.0	21.6	Double Springs	NC	19-May
66.8	10.6	Blueberry Patch	GA	20-Apr	457.3	18.3	Damascus	VA	20-May
78.4	11.6	Muskrat Creek	NC	21-Apr			Damascus	VA	21-May
90.9	12.5	Carter Gap	NC	22-Apr	473.1	15.8	Lost Mtn	VA	22-May
103.1	12.2	Rock Gap	NC	23-Apr	490.4	17.3	Wise	VA	23-May
115.0	11.9	Wine Spring C	NC	24-Apr	508.0	17.6	Raccoon Branch	VA	24-May
122.6	7.6	Cold Spring	NC	25-Apr	528.1	20.1	Chatfield	VA	25-May
134.1	11.5	NOC	NC	26-Apr	532.6	4.5	Groseclose	VA	26-May
141.0	6.9	Sassafras Gap	NC	27-Apr	546.5	13.9	Knot Maul	VA	27-May
156.2	15.2	Cable Gap	NC	28-Apr	565.5	19.0	Jenkins	VA	28-May
163.1	8.9	Fontana	NC	29-Apr	589.1	23.6	Jenny Knob	VA	29-May
174.1	11.0	Mollies Ridge	NC	30-Apr	603.3	14.2	Wapiti	VA	30-May
185.8	11.7	Derrick Knob	NC	1-May	619.5	16.2	Pearisburg	VA	31-May
199.3	14.0	Mt Collins	NC	2-May	619.5		Pearisburg	VA	1-Jun
		Newfound gap	NC	3-May	639.1	19.6	Pine Swamp Br.	VA	2-Jun
214.2	15.4	Peck's Corner	NC	3-May	651.8	12.7	War Spur	VA	3-Jun
227.1	12.9	Cosby Knob	NC	4-May	670.0	18.2	Niday	VA	4-Jun
244.7	17.6	Groundhog Creek	NC	5-May	685.9	15.9	4 Pines	VA	5-Jun
257.8	13.1	Walnut Mtn	NC	6-May	711.4	25.5	Daleville	VA	6-Jun
270.9	13.1	Hot Springs	NC	7-May	711.4		Daleville	VA	7-Jun
		Hot Springs	NC	8-May	722.6	11.2	Wilson Creek	VA	8-Jun
281.9	11.0	Spring Mtn	NC	9-May	743.2	20.6	Bryant Ridge	VA	9-Jun
297.2	15.3	Jerry Cabin	NC	10-May	760.4	17.2	Marble Spring	VA	10-Jun
311.8	14.6	Hogback Ridge	NC	11-May	778.6	18.2	Punchbowl	VA	11-Jun

Just Walking

Overall Mile	Daily Miles	Destination		Date	Overall Mile	Daily Miles	Destination		Date
793.0	15.0	Cow Camp Gap	VA	12-Jun	1,232.5	17.4	Bake Oven Knob	PA	16-Jul
810.1	17.1	Priest	VA	13-Jun	1,256.0	23.5	Leroy Smith	PA	17-Jul
823.7	13.6	Maupin Field	VA	14-Jun	1,269.8	13.8	Kirkridge	PA	18-Jul
844.8	21.1	Waynesboro	VA	15-Jun	1,276.4		Delaware Water Gap	PA	19-Jul
844.8		Waynesboro	VA	16-Jun	1,286.7	17.2	MOC Camp Rd	NJ	19-Jul
861.6	16.8	Flip Flop stealth C	VA	16-Jun	1,307.6	21.3	Gren Anderson	NJ	20-Jul
886.2	24.6	Hightop	VA	17-Jun	1,326.2	18.6	Secret Shelter	NJ	21-Jul
906.6	20.4	Big Meadows C	VA	18-Jun	1,339.5	13.3	Vernon	NJ	22-Jul
		Big Meadows	VA	19-Jun	1,356.8	17.3	Wildcat	NY	23-Jul
925.4	18.8	Pass Mtn	VA	20-Jun	1,376.4	19.6	Wm Brian	NY	24-Jul
938.5	13.1	Gravel Springs	VA	21-Jun	1,384.5	8.1	Bear Mtn	NY	25-Jul
951.9	13.4	Front Royal	VA	22-Jun			ATC Hike	NH	29-Jul
967.0	15.1	Dick's Dome	VA	23-Jun			ATC Hike	NH	30-Jul
985.9	18.9	Bears Den Rocks	VA	24-Jun		3.0	Hemlock Springs	NY	31-Jul
1,005.8	19.9	Harpers Ferry	WV	25-Jun	1,403.5	17.0	Fahnestock SP C	NY	1-Aug
		Harpers Ferry	WV	26-Jun	1,419.5	17.0	Morgan Stewart	NY	2-Aug
1,023.7	17.9	Dahlgren camp	MD	27-Jun	1,430.2	10.7	Pawling	NY	3-Aug
1,042.1	18.4	Devil's Racecourse	MD	28-Jun	1,118.6	18.3	Mt Algo	CT	4-Aug
1,067.5	25.4	Quarry Gap	PA	29-Jun	1,462.4	13.9	Caesar Brook C	CT	5-Aug
1,081.2	13.7	Tom's Run	PA	30-Jun	1,478.1	16.2	Limestone Spring	CT	6-Aug
1,104.0	22.8	Yellow Breeches C	PA	1-Jul	1,495.7	18.1	Glen Brook	MA	7-Aug
1,104.3		Boiling Springs	PA	2-Jul	1,500.0	4.3	S. Egremont	MA	8-Aug
1,118.6	14.6	Darlington	PA	2-Jul	1,517.3	22.0	Mt Wilcox	MA	9-Aug
1,130.0		Duncannon	PA	3-Jul	1,540.1	22.8	October Mtn	MA	10-Aug
1,141.3	22.7	Peters Mtn	PA	4-Jul	1,551.9	12.3	Dalton	MA	11-Aug
1,158.8	17.5	Rausch Gap	PA	5-Jul	1,561.2		Cheshire	MA	12-Aug
1,176.2	17.4	501 Shelter	PA	6-Jul	1,568.9	17.0	Bascom Lodge	MA	12-Aug
1,199.9	23.7	Port Clinton	PA	7-Jul	1,589.3	17.2	Congdon	VT	13-Aug
		to Boston		8-Jul	1,608.0	18.7	Kid Gore	VT	14-Aug
		to Port Clinton	PA	14-Jul	1,623.2	15.2	Stratton Pond	VT	15-Aug
1,215.1	15.4	Eckville	PA	15-Jul					

Itinerary

Overall Mile	Daily Miles	Destination		Date
1,643.5	20.3	Peru Peak	VT	16-Aug
1,658.0	14.7	Greenwall	VT	17-Aug
1,672.6	14.8	Gov Clement	VT	18-Aug
1,686.5	13.9	Gifford Woods C	VT	19-Aug
1,703.1	16.6	Wintturi	VT	20-Aug
1,723.5	20.4	Happy Hill	VT	21-Aug
1,729.3	5.8	Hanover	NH	22-Aug
		to NYC	NY	23-Aug
1,730.8	1.5	Velvet Rocks	NH	26-Aug
1,746.0	16.9	Trapper John	NH	27-Aug
1,758.0	12.2	Hexcuba	NH	28-Aug
1,772.7	14.7	Glencliff	NH	29-Aug
1,782.2	9.5	Mooselauke slack	NH	29-Aug
1,793.7	11.5	Kinsman Pond	NH	30-Aug
1,801.1	7.4	Liberty Spring	NH	31-Aug
1,811.5	10.4	Galehead	NH	1-Sep
1,826.2	14.7	Dry River	NH	2-Sep
1,837.4	11.2	Lakes of the Clouds	NH	3-Sep
1,837.4		Lakes of the Clouds	NH	4-Sep
1,844.4	7.0	Madison Hut	NH	5-Sep
1,852.2	7.8	Pinckham Notch	NH	6-Sep
		to Boston		7-Sep
1,865.3	13.1	Imp campsite	NH	12-Sep
1,873.3	8.0	Gorham	NH	13-Sep
		to Boston		14-Sep
		to Gorham		15-Sep
1,885.1	11.8	Gentian Pond	NH	16-Sep
1,894.7	9.6	Full Goose	ME	17-Sep
1,906.7	12.0	Baldpate	ME	18-Sep
1,914.7	8.0	Andover	ME	19-Sep
1,924.8	14.6	South Arm Rd C	ME	20-Sep
1,941.8	17.0	Sabbathday Pond	ME	21-Sep
1,951.2	9.4	Rangely	ME	22-Sep
		Rangely	ME	23-Sep
1,969.9	18.7	Spaulding Mtn	ME	24-Sep
1,983.4	13.5	Stratton	ME	25-Sep
1,998.7	15.3	Little Bigelow	ME	26-Sep
2,016.0	17.3	Pierce Pond	ME	27-Sep
2,020.0	4.0	Caratunk	ME	28-Sep
2,038.8	18.8	Moxie Bald	ME	29-Sep
2,056.7	17.9	Shaw's	ME	30-Sep
2,071.8	15.1	Long Pond Stream	ME	1-Oct
2,087.1	15.3	W Br Pleasant R C	ME	2-Oct
2,103.4	16.3	East Branch	ME	3-Oct
2,125.2	23.0	White House Land.	ME	4-Oct
2,141.1	15.9	Rainbow Stream	ME	5-Oct
2,156.1	15.0	Abol Pines	ME	6-Oct
2,166.0	9.9	Katahdin Stream	ME	7-Oct
		to Boston		
		to Millinocket	ME	9-Oct
2,171.2	10.4	Katahdin summit	ME	10-Oct

References

Hiking

Appalachian Trail Thru-Hiker's Companion, Appaklachian Trail Conference (updated annually)

Appalachian Trail Data Book, Appalachian Trail Conservancy, 2003, 2009

Dan "Wingfoot" Bruce, *The Thru-Hiker's Handbook*, Center for Appalachian Trail Studies (updated annually)

David Miller and Rick Towle, *Appalachian Pages*, Jerelyn Press, 2008

Ray Jardine, *Beyond Backpacking: Ray Jardine's Guide to Lightweight Hiking*, Adventurelore Press, 1999

Chris Townsend, *The Advanced Backpacker: A Handbook of Year Round, Long Distance Hiking*, International Marine/Ragged Mountain Press, 2000.

Zen

Philip Kapleau, *The Three Pillars of Zen: Teaching, Practice, and Enlightenment*, Anchor Books, 2000

Alan Watts, *The Way of Zen*, Vintage Books, 1957

Seung Sahn, *Dropping Ashes on the Buddha*, Grove Press, 1976

Shunryu Suzuki, *Zen Mind, Beginner's Mind*, Weatherhill/Shambala, 1970

James Ishmael Ford, *In this Very Moment: a simple guide to Zen Buddhism*, Skinner House Books, 2002.